DW GIBSON

SIMON & SCHUSTER

New York   London   Toronto   Sydney   New Delhi

14 MILES

BUILDING THE BORDER WALL

Simon & Schuster
1230 Avenue of the Americas
New York, NY 10020

First Simon & Schuster hardcover edition July 2020

SIMON & SCHUSTER and colophon are registered
trademarks of Simon & Schuster, Inc.

For information about special discounts for bulk purchases,
please contact Simon & Schuster Special Sales at 1-866-506-1949
or business@simonandschuster.com.

The Simon & Schuster Speakers Bureau can bring authors to your
live event. For more information or to book an event, contact the
Simon & Schuster Speakers Bureau at 1-866-248-3049 or visit
our website at www.simonspeakers.com.

Interior design by Lewelin Polanco

Manufactured in the United States of America

10 9 8 7 6 5 4 3 2 1

Library of Congress Cataloging-in-Publication Data has been applied for.

ISBN 978-1-5011-8341-6
ISBN 978-1-5011-8342-3 (ebook)

For Tasha

"... we can make America what America must become."

—JAMES BALDWIN

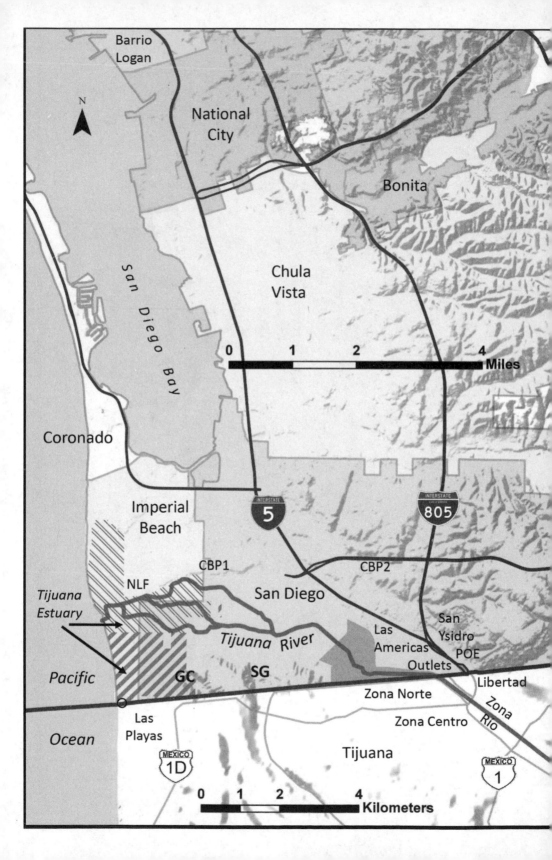

Area Map

░░░░ Tijuana Slough National Wildlife Refuge

▨▨▨ Border Field State Park

O   Friendship Park / Parque de la Amistad

▨▨▨ Tijuana River Flood Control Project

NLF = U.S. Navy Landing Field

<u>Customs and Border Protection (CBP)</u>
  CBP1 = Imperial Beach Station
  CBP2 = Chula Vista Station
  CBP3 = Brown Field Station

POE = Port of Entry

GC Goat Canyon
SG Smuggler's Gulch
CBX Cross-Border Xpress
TIJ Tijuana Airport

End Secondary Fence in 2017

End Primary Fence and Secondary Fence in 2019

Based on data from Esri, USGS, NOAA, Google Earth/Maps, San Diego Association of Governments, and other sources.

Cartography by Kenneth D. Madsen

Detail – Prototype Site

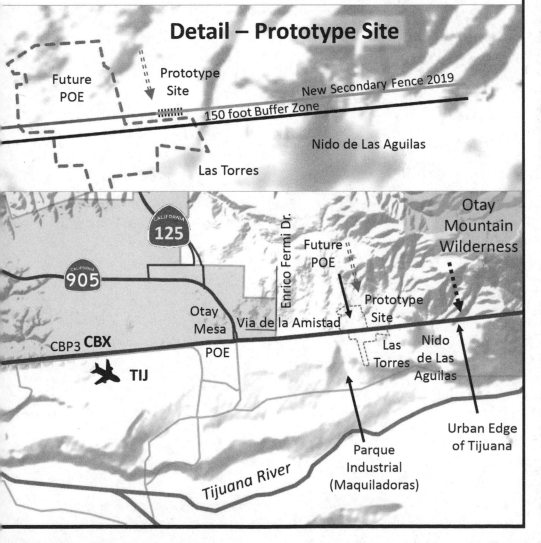

MAY 2017–AUGUST 2019

PROLOGUE

A 4,000-gallon tanker truck comes to a stop on Enrico Fermi Drive. The driver pops out, grabs the free end of a hose attached to a fire hydrant and connects it to his tank. He wrenches open the hydrant and the slack hose goes taut; water squirts out of abrasions in the snaking nylon, collecting in the gutter up against the sidewalk. The concrete all around the small rivulet looks to be melting in the sun. So does the driver, sweat beading on his dark brown skin. The sound of the radio shoots out the open window of the truck; the DJ finishes his traffic report and tacks on a brush fire warning. California is a tinderbox: a sparkler, a tossed cigarette butt—any stray ember is capable of burning the whole thing down.

When the tank reaches capacity, the driver disconnects the hose and gets back into the cab. He rolls up his window and a few moments pass with only the sound of the truck engine, an isolated rumble, all other signs of life hiding in the air-conditioned warehouses and offices of the adjacent industrial parks. Then the pitch of the rumble shifts low; the truck rolls forward and heads straight toward a barricade of hastily clustered road signs on metal tripods—*Slow, Stop, Road Closed, Do Not Enter*. There is a narrow pathway that maneuvers around each sign but clearly no one is encouraged to take it. A man sits to the right of the barricade, under a yellow canopy, slumped over his phone, ostensibly keeping watch. He offers no reaction to the truck driver, who navigates the switchback opening perfectly and rumbles down the forbidden road.

About a hundred feet after the barricade the road dips under an overpass but then it ends abruptly. The *paved* road ends, as does most of the concrete world, yielding to miles of open desert with the Otay Mountain Wilderness in the distance. But there is still something of a dirt road extending into the desert and the driver takes it. It's a slow and bumpy ride; each rocky spot allows spurts of water to escape the tank, haphazardly dousing patches of the cracked earth.

Nearly two miles closer to the mountains, the driver stops at a chain link fence, which is wrapped in green tarpaulin to help conceal the action on the other side. A man in a hard hat and reflective vest motions for the driver to pass through a gate and the truck rolls forward, arriving at the edge of a bustling construction site. For a moment the vehicle is still. Then water begins spraying out the back of the tank and the driver inches forward, deliberate, wetting the earth as evenly as possible. He continues all the way around, taking about ten minutes to encircle the entire construction site, then exits in the same spot where he entered. And just like that, he's on his way back to Enrico Fermi Drive, back to the fire hydrant to pull another 4,000 gallons of water from the ground.

Each water run takes an hour or so and each trip keeps everyone at the job site from being overcome by dust. There are about fifty workers and they do not talk much; instead the soundtrack is overlapping and colliding percussions: drilling, grinding, boom trucks beeping to signal reverse, the groaning joints of excavators, all echoing across the open desert. Occasionally there is some yelling but mostly the men keep their heads down, working with urgency. They are all men on this day—and most others.

Four San Diego Police Department SUVs enter the fenced construction site and seven officers emerge from the vehicles. Leaning up against the SUVs, they track the action from behind sunglasses, arms crossed. Soon a Border Patrol jeep arrives. Then a Border Patrol SUV. Then a Border Patrol ATV. California Highway Patrol stops by for a while too, as does the Sheriff's Department and a sedan marked Protective Services for the Department of Homeland Security. Over the span of an hour they all come, spectating for a few minutes, or the whole hour, before getting back into their vehicles to leave.

The show is one month only and features construction of eight design prototypes for The Wall, which is to extend the length of America's 1,954-mile southern border. The prototypes are going up in a single-file row on a seventeen-acre triangle of federal land at the border with Mexico. Each prototype is 30 feet tall and 30 feet wide, and each is constructed on a separate staging area, approximately 65 feet by 65 feet. *Staging* is the precise word: construction of the prototypes is, if nothing else, theater. The show feels like a beauty pageant with the contestants standing in a line, equal spacing between them, and I ask the man overseeing construction if he's ever seen anything like this before—competing designs, side by side. He shakes his head then lowers it. But he doesn't offer any words to accompany what he has communicated, nor does he offer his name for the record. He has a dusty blue bandanna wrapped around his neck, which he pulls up over his face whenever he feels like a camera is getting too close. The secrecy established by the barricade on Enrico Fermi—not to mention the long, rocky drive across the desert and the covered chain link fencing—it sets the tone for the entire scene.

The closest observer is Aurelia Ávila. She lives in a scrap wood home less than two hundred feet from the prototypes, just south of the border in a section of Tijuana called Las Torres. After two weeks of hammering and drilling, she is inured: "For me, it's normal now," she says in Spanish, her eyes tracing a man rising into the sky on a boom lift.

Aurelia sits on a bucket in front of her house. Her uncle, Gaudencio, stands a few feet away, loading plastic bottles into the back of a pickup. They both wear hats: Gaudencio secures his wide-brimmed straw number with a leather strap under his chin and Aurelia pulls her baseball cap down over her forehead. The family works in the recycling business, subsisting on whatever they're able to collect each day. "Bottles, cartons," Aurelia says, shrugging, unimpressed. "Helping the environment a little bit."

She lives with her daughter, brother, and Gaudencio. They do not have an indoor bathroom or running water, and a tarp hangs over the roof to help when the rain comes—if the rain comes. The house is usually buried behind mounds of plastic buckets, milk crates, and several white tarpaulin bags that are nearly five feet tall when they bulge with sorted bottles.

Gaudencio stops tossing for a moment and rests against the truck. "The heat is nice now," he says, speaking in Spanish. "The weather will change and we're going to want the heat when it starts to get cold." He's in his sixties, well acquainted with the seasonal cycles of the Otay Mesa desert.

A car speeds by, kicking up dust. Gaudencio's unshaven, gray face does not react as the thick cloud closes in on him. His niece does not react either. They are one with the dust. "It's too bad for the people who just showered," Aurelia says, laughing, knowing the feeling. She lives closer to the prototypes than anyone else but still not close enough to benefit from the relief of 4,000-gallon water deliveries. She only gets a hint of the treatment: "With a breeze," she says, "you can smell the wet dirt." She smiles, studying the tops of the prototypes rising over the fencing around the construction site. "They've got five versions of the wall up, three left. I guess, they're deciding which one they're going to use."

She points at the newest model; its royal blue top half, made of steel, glistens in the sun. "The color is pretty," she says. The blue really does stand out because the other designs are all concrete and gray with few details to distinguish them from each other. Some do have cosmetic features— different textures and designs on the surface of the concrete—but those details are only added to the north-facing side of the models. From Las Torres, each concrete panel is unadorned. Aurelia is hoping for the blue steel design but if she gets stuck with a bunch of gray concrete outside her front door she'll use it as a blank canvas. "We'll paint some little hearts," she says. "Maybe we'll draw a few pictures so at least it looks pretty."

Aurelia was born in Ventura, California, about four hours up the 405, nearer the coastal breezes. "My dad is from Michoacán," she says, "and my mom is from Jalisco. They met in the U.S., and they gave birth to me there. My dad got deported, and he came here. He tried a few times to cross back into the U.S. The third time, he decided to give up and stay here. He ended up calling my mom and asking if she wanted to stay in the U.S. or come here. She decided to come here with me."

Aurelia arrived in Mexico as a toddler; she is twenty-one now and has not yet been able to return to the U.S. because she doesn't have all the documents to prove her citizenship.

"My dad says that when he got here in '96 it was just a barbed wire fence."

"The workers would cross over," adds Gaudencio. "After work, they'd come back at night."

"There wasn't this big wall." Aurelia refers to *this* big wall because between her front door and the prototypes there is already a barrier separating Mexico and the U.S. It's about nine feet tall, constructed out of sheets of corrugated metal. And if you make a left out of Aurelia's house and walk about fifty yards, there is a *second* fence. It's ten feet taller than the primary fence and 150 feet to the north. The second fence runs about thirteen miles to the west, shape-shifting in design and materials as it winds its way into the Pacific Ocean, where closely aligned steel bollards yield to the breakers of Imperial Beach and Playas de Tijuana. If one of the prototypes is selected, if the next act begins with construction of The Wall, it will be the third barrier built between Las Torres and the U.S.

"What I don't understand," says Aurelia, "is why here? They could have made it a little over there." She points to the east, farther into the desert toward the mountains.

In front of her home, there are a couple of spots along the primary fence with large mounds of dirt and stacked tires, giving just enough elevation to peek—and, in some cases, climb—over the fence. Border Patrol has declared the prototype site in front of Aurelia's home a "high-traffic" area because it is the spot where the secondary 18-foot fence ends.

"Yesterday I was looking over," recalls Aurelia, "and Border Patrol asked me in Spanish why I was throwing rocks. I wasn't throwing rocks; I was just looking to see what they're building. I said to myself, 'Hey wait, they speak Spanish? You're Mexican!' I said, 'Come over here! Why are you over there?'" She laughs and so does Gaudencio. "Most of them are Mexican or Hispanic. They deny their roots."

"The ones who are really from the United States," says Gaudencio, "the ones who don't speak Spanish, they say, 'Mex-i-ca-no,'" he stretches it out like a gringo as best he can, and laughs at the sound of it. "They can't say it properly," he says.

"I think it's a bad idea, another wall," Aurelia says, perhaps unaware of the major reduction she has just made: from her perch, The Wall—The Big, Fat, Beautiful Wall—is understood to be just *another wall.* "It's enraging. Why make a huge wall if people will find a way to get there if they want to? It's a waste of money. The majority of Americans I know are against it."

Aurelia's seven-year-old daughter, Melanie, emerges from the back of the house, running alongside a couple of mutts leaping after the stick in her hand. Two more mutts come around from the other side of the house and they all merge as one clan in the middle of the dirt road, spinning in tight, dizzying circles. Eventually Melanie and the dogs crash in the shadow of the pickup truck. The dogs are at home next to the girl; she and her mother are the local pushovers when it comes to strays: "Puppies start showing up," Aurelia says, rolling her eyes. "People throw them out. They're puppies!"

"They leave them abandoned," says Gaudencio with tender love in his eyes, in his voice. But then suddenly he turns on the animal in front of him: "Good for tacos," he says.

Aurelia joins in: "Like the Chinese, no?"

They both laugh and Gaudencio takes it further: "People won't know what they're eating, but they'd say, 'the food is tasty.'" He continues through his laughter: "Salsa, cilantro. You wouldn't know it's dog." One of the mutts pokes Gaudencio with his snout, as if sensing the cutting joke, and the old man leans down to nuzzle him.

Aurelia watches them for a moment then her eyes turn north. "I only have my Social Security card," she says. "But I can't get my passport with that. What I need is my birth certificate. Some people have told me that with my Social Security card, I can go to the line and ask," she says, pointing to the west, in the direction of the Otay Mesa pedestrian border crossing, just four miles away. "I'd like to help my family. Melanie was born here. I've been told I can get her registered there and get her documentation fixed. I would also have to get my last name fixed on documents. It should be Ávila, with a 'v,' but doctors there wrote it as 'Adila,' with a 'd.' It needs to be *Ávila*."

One erroneous "d" and two barriers, perhaps a third, are blocking Aurelia's path to the city where she was born and the opportunity to correct her name for the record. She looks up at the dust streaking across the sky, signaling the return of the water truck and relief for the men who work under the big blue proscenium with the sun as their unyielding spotlight.

PART 1

ANTICIPATION

CHAPTER 1

LIFE FOR THE 3.3 MILLION people who live in San Diego County is, in large part, defined by one's travel patterns. A complex of freeways and interchanges carve up the landscape: I have experienced several two-mile journeys that involved three freeways. There's the 5, the 54, the 805—these numbers contribute to each person's identity, establishing patterns that relay something about income bracket and lifestyle; they facilitate relationships and intensify alienation. This persists in the eastern part of the county, where crosswalks give way to cattle gates but locals still orient using highway numbers—Old 80, Route 94.

Even those who use public transportation can't avoid this dynamic: buses use the slow lanes and many of San Diego's signature red trolleys run parallel to the freeways—the sound of sweet, soft bells is enough to terrify any driver within earshot who realizes a trolley is about to temporarily block an intersection or freeway on ramp.

I grew up in the region and don't remember hearing adults reference north or south, east or west. Giving directions always sounded more like "out toward the 15" or "head over to the 73." When I was eight I had no idea how to use a compass but could tell you which freeways led to the beach, the mall, church—any integral part of my life.

Now I'm reacquainting myself with the roads after two decades away, and I'm letting The Wall determine my travel patterns. I've been searching for a way to figure out what a border really looks like in an increasingly interconnected world. I am hopeful the prototypes will help me get to the bottom of this. And not just the construction itself, the crews and the 50,000-pound concrete panels, but the people living and working and crossing the border in the same county where construction is happening, the same county where, every day, 70,000 vehicles and 20,000 pedestrians use the San Ysidro border crossing, the busiest in the Western Hemisphere.[1] I want to know how the reality of the region comports, or doesn't, with all the ideas and expectations we form when viewing the border as a clean line on a map.

So far I have discovered that clean lines generally mark the most complicated places. None more so than the 8 Freeway. Everyone in San Diego County is familiar with it, either by commute or reputation. It runs from ocean to desert, parallel to the line dividing Mexico and the U.S., and it may be fifteen miles to the north but I have become convinced it is the real border. Not because the residents of the South Bay are any less American than the locals in Del Mar or Encinitas, to the north of the freeway, but they are not generally incorporated into the county or the state or the country in the same way. The roads in Nestor do not look like the roads in Torrey Pines, neither do the public schools or job markets or emergency services. And there is a broader disconnect between those who live north of the 8 and those who are south. For many people north of the freeway, going south means tacos at El Gordo or surfing the slews at Imperial Beach, special trips to special places outside the quotidian. Otherwise, the band of land between the 8 and the international line has, historically, functioned more like a U.S.-controlled buffer zone between the two countries.

Congress allocated $20 million for the prototypes to go up south of the 8 Freeway, but the federal government hasn't finished perusing all the bids for the job. The process was supposed to move faster: it is August of 2017 and the Department of Homeland Security originally scheduled contracts to be awarded two months ago—by June 14, with construction to start "eight days later." Those dates passed without so much as a cement mixer showing up. The revised timeline is increasingly unrealistic: completion by next month.

There is no barricade on Enrico Fermi yet, no fencing around the construction site. The rocky drive across the desert is ill advised in my budget rental but still I risk it regularly, parking near the spot where the secondary fence comes to a sudden end and the empty staging area begins. I sip coffee and wait for action. When I get tired of the quiet and the stillness I work on a list of all the things I've ever seen or read about borders and walls—every song and image, every history lesson, story and myth. Two memories from childhood:

—*Mister Rogers' Neighborhood, vintage episode, King Friday builds a wall to fortify his castle.*

—*Memorizing Robert Frost's "Mending Wall" in the sixth grade: "Something there is that doesn't love a wall."*

Every now and then there is action at the construction site but it's generally subtle, meetings between Border Patrol representatives and the local companies contracted to provide everything from porta potties to chain link fencing.

Then one morning, finally, I see a small crew: three men with hammers and a pickup truck full of lumber. They do not wear uniforms, only yellow neon T-shirts and faded jeans; something seems entirely unofficial about them, particularly in anticipation of a major federal government undertaking. The spot where they work is about a hundred feet to the north of the staging area so something *is* a little off. They start by getting posts in the ground and use the rest of the lumber to build two basic frames, at least 15 feet tall.

When they stop for a break I walk over to ask what they're up to. I ask in Spanish because they've been bantering in Spanish. They don't respond, either ignoring me or unable—perhaps unwilling—to interpret my mangled Spanish, I can't tell. I shrink away and turn to look at the Border Patrol agent staked out on the ATV under the shade of a scrub oak about a hundred yards to the north. He is unmoving, slumped over his handlebars. The three men seem to be doing work that is at once rogue and sanctioned.

A couple of days later I return to see what's become of the frames and now they're both billboards with identical advertisements:

TRUCKNET
San Diego's Only Full Service Truck Stop
YARDS AVAILABLE
FOR LEASE

Truck Net is owned by Roque De La Fuente, as is the land where the new billboards stand.

If Aurelia has the closest seat to the prototypes on the Mexican side then it is definitely Roque De La Fuente on the U.S. side. The staging area is trapped between the primary border fence made of corrugated metal and Roque's 2,000-acre spread of mostly undeveloped desert land. He has the government essentially surrounded at the border and they are well-acquainted neighbors (see various lawsuit briefs[2]). Roque positioned the billboards perfectly, to be captured as backdrop for the prototypes, anticipating the moment the cameras arrive. Roque knows theater when he sees it.

His global portfolio of commercial properties fluctuates regularly with new acquisitions, new sales, but in California alone Roque currently owns property in twenty-five different cities. He is often on the move, ubiquitous but nowhere to be found. I have been struggling to meet him in person. He is generous with his time on the phone; sometimes we talk for more than an hour, but he remains noncommittal regarding his location on any given day. He is always dashing off to Mexico City or Chile or *talking* about dashing off to these places—it isn't easy to discern which. Once, we spoke for an hour and a half and the whole time I thought he might have been in Uruguay but toward the end of the conversation I realized he was in San Diego, downtown getting a pedicure and manicure days before his daughter's wedding. (It was "give the girl the extra ten"—softly, in the background—that gave him away.) After offering to meet him in various places at various times, I asked what would increase my chances of making it happen. "Luck," he answered. He easily gives an hour spontaneously but has very real difficulty committing to a specific place at a specific time. He keeps the irregular travel patterns of a person who answers to nobody.

Sometimes I randomly stop in at the offices of National Enterprises Inc., the real estate company Roque founded. I'm looking for that luck he spoke of but haven't caught it yet, though I have had a few minor break-throughs: on one visit a friendly receptionist phoned Roque to tell him I was looking for him; he sent his regards from Santiago and told the re-ceptionist to give me a tour of the place, which, more or less, doubles as a Roque De La Fuente Museum. There is the cover of the *Los Angeles Times* with a picture of Roque walking across the Otay Mesa pedestrian border crossing, the first to do so when it opened in 1985. There is a framed picture of a jumbo billboard, *Roque2016.com!*, which is still up in the desert near Tecate, long after his unsuccessful run for president. The conference room is adorned with proclamations and resolutions from the State of California and the County of San Diego, all involving Roque, and newspaper clippings, mostly featuring Roque. Also multiple credenzas showcase a couple dozen awards, the majority made of engraved glass, cut into one abstract shape or another. Most of them celebrate hitting certain financing benchmarks: $75 million with this bank, $15 million with that bank. There is enough artwork in the lobby to give it the feel of a gallery, and it continues into the hallways leading to offices. A few paintings—including an oil portrait of Roque's younger self—but mostly sculptures, standing and hung on the walls, all revealing an acute aesthetic: intensely bronze and very tough guy.

The walls of the lobby are covered with pictures of Roque standing next to notables, or perhaps I should say *fellow* notables: Ronald Reagan, George W. Bush, George H. W. Bush, Bill Clinton, Gray Davis—Roque treats political parties like he does geography: very noncommittal. Before running for president as an Independent in 2016, he had entered the primary for a Florida Senate seat as a Democrat. More recently he tried to get on the 2017 ballot for mayor of New York City as a Republican but got blocked by a co-op board that wouldn't let him buy an apartment to establish residency. (Lawsuit pending.[3]) Currently he is mulling a 2018 run for Dianne Feinstein's Senate seat in California as a Republican.

Roque was born in San Diego in 1954. "But my parents lived in Tijuana," he told me on one of our phone calls. "At that time, Tijuana did not have good hospitals, so if you had a little bit of wherewithal, you just cross the border and buy your meat or your grocery or you went to the dentist or doctor."

Roque's fortune traces back to a sunbaked lot where his father, Roque Sr., sold used cars in the Otay section of Tijuana. That business grew enough for Roque Sr. to start taking German lessons and, eventually, travel to Wolfsburg to convince Volkswagen to give him a dealership in Kearny Mesa, a growing suburban area north of San Diego. That dealership opened in 1968 and over the next thirteen years Jr. and Sr. added twenty-seven more in Southern California, stretching out east to El Centro in neighboring Imperial County. Somewhere along the way, in pursuit of cheap land for still more dealerships, the family got distracted by real estate.

On one of my office visits a colleague of the two men described the pivot like this: "Mr. De La Fuente Sr. realized, wow, in the car business, you have to be there at the start of the day and at the end of the day—seven days a week—to make sure people show up for work and don't steal from you and you make a nice living. But in real estate, you can sleep in until ten o'clock and show up at a meeting and buy a property right for $1 and sell it for $2. The key is buy it right."

The $1-to-$2 example is central to the De La Fuente orbit, the bright light around which their business model gravitated during its formation. By the time he was twenty, Roque was watching and learning: "The first property my father bought, he bought for $1.00 a square foot. He then sold it for $2.00. Then he bought it for $1.50 then sold it for $3.00, then he bought it for $2.00 and sold it for $4.00. My father enjoyed the growth in the Kearny Mesa area. It was phenomenal. The last property my father bought in Kearny Mesa, he paid $11.00 and sold it for $20.00. At that moment he said, 'I doubt I can buy it for $20.00 and sell it for $40.00.' So, he decided to take that cash and buy property in Otay Mesa." Anything less than doubling your money was, apparently, unacceptable.

As the family branched out with acquisitions, Roque was the first to discover Otay Mesa, and he did so from 5,000 feet in the air. "I got a pilot's license," he said. "At that time in 1974, the practice ground was Otay. One of the things that fascinated me was, you go to Europe, all the border towns happen to be thriving on both sides. And here was Tijuana built up to the border, all the way to the border, from the Pacific Ocean all the way to the mountains but that wasn't the case on the U.S. side in Otay.

"Otay Mesa is flat. *Mesa* means *table*, flat, and historically, people build on flat lands before they go to the canyons or to the mountains. Why was it that Otay Mesa got passed over? If you take a look at Dallas–Fort Worth, basically Dallas was built and Fort Worth was built and in the middle it becomes one huge metropolis, no different than Los Angeles and Long Beach. Why was it that this area, Otay Mesa, was left untouched with so much growth all around?

"It's very simple: San Diego did not want to become a border town. The board of supervisors did not allow that area to develop. They basically said, 'We don't care that you own the property, we're not going to allow you to develop it.' I'm talking fifty years ago. They sold it for agricultural uses, tomatoes and lettuce, but if anybody wanted to put a factory there, it was not allowed. Housing was not allowed there. They did not want to become a border town. Luckily for me, we saw an opportunity. That area should have been developed in the '40s, '50s, and '60s. But it waited for us." Roque smiles, like he really does believe the land, the money therein, was just waiting for him.

In the late 1970s, Roque and his father started buying up Otay Mesa at 10 cents a square foot. "We bought the biggest piece of land in '82 from bankruptcy court. It was a matter of timing and luck. Not only timing and luck, it's taking advantage of the opportunity because a lot of people can have the timing and the luck but they're afraid."

It is nearly impossible to drive around Otay Mesa without happening upon De La Fuente Lane or De La Fuente Circle or some other incarnation of De La Fuente. The family name is integral to the Otay Mesa landscape.

As his interest and time drifted more toward political activity, Roque started relying on a man named David Wick to run NEI for him. David has been with Roque since NEI's founding in 1992, and now he has a 5 percent stake in the company. "He's the hardest-working person I know," Roque once told me. "He *earned* 5 percent of the company, and he *runs* 100 percent of the company." NEI, which has 186 employees, is not publicly traded and does not have investors. Roque Sr. passed away in 2010; David and Roque own the company in its entirety.

Eventually my drop-ins at the offices earn a sit-down with David. We meet in the conference room, surrounded by images of Roque. David is amiable but serious; he might always veer toward a smile but the pugilistic negotiator never goes away. It is easy to see why Roque trusted him with so much—the two men have a similar tone and energy when they speak. Their mix of exceptional affability and ruthless deal-making requires some reckoning, and I think David is aware of this. "Some people call us grave-dancers," he says. "Other people call us bottom-feeders. I guess the best way to describe us is opportunists, constantly looking at the future and how to evolve the business plan and keep the bell curve going as long as possible. Every relationship, every business is a bell curve. Sooner or later, it comes to an end."

When David and Roque started working together, the end was near for savings and loans, or thrift banks, across the country. By the time Roque formed NEI, the Resolution Trust Corporation, a government-run asset management office, had closed 747 thrift banks that had been making bad loans.[4] And that was after another government agency had already closed 296.[5] Over a thousand financial institutions were shuttered and the country was awash in over $400 billion in bad loans.[6] The government had to find buyers for all of it. David and Roque were ready. "The bad loans we were buying," says David, "we were buying these loans for pennies on the dollar. And later, when we would go to sell these properties, typically, the dialogue would be: 'David, we know your company bought this home for 10 cents on the dollar. Why do I have to pay you 100 cents?' So I say, 'I took the risk, I had the money, I had the smarts to do it.' 'No, you're a grave-dancer. You're taking advantage.' 'Well, that's what you say. I'm saying I'm being reasonable. Why don't you pay me 80 cents and we'll call it a day?' 'Yes, but you bought it for 10 cents.' Human nature dwells on things like that."

When I mention the advertisements next to the prototype site David beams with pride. "That's our property, Truck Net—we have the largest truck stop in San Diego County. I can't wait to see photographers trying to get angles without that," he laughs. "It's really great I have to say; it was very enterprising."

NEI, which has owned as much as 4,500 acres in Otay Mesa, is the largest property owner in the area. Historically, Otay fell under county management but in 1985 most of the land was annexed to the city of San Diego—about 9,000 acres, leaving only about 2,200 unincorporated. The De La Fuentes played a big part in that transition. "Roque Sr. saw it as a way to develop Otay Mesa easier and quicker," notes David. "From the city's perspective, you have this huge tax base potential without the burden of the residents to have all the amenities that are necessary, the police and fire and so on. So it has become a city of industry."

Otay Mesa does not actually touch the rest of San Diego on a map. In fact there are two sections of the city that are altogether geographically separate: Otay Mesa and San Ysidro, both of which run along the border, both of which have a terrestrial port of entry—the only two in the county. Otay Mesa and San Ysidro are *seven miles south* of the city. In order to incorporate them, San Diego had to get inventive, using a shared body of water, the South Bay, as the connecting geographic feature. By finding a way to incorporate San Ysidro and Otay Mesa, the city has had a bigger say in the development of the liminal zone.

Since 1985, about a third of the incorporated Otay land has been de- veloped, much of it once belonged—or still belongs—to Roque and David. The industrial landscape is hard to navigate from a passenger vehicle; big rigs define the Otay Mesa experience. There are warehouses and office parks for logistics companies, trucking facilities with vast lots storing ship- ping containers, scrap yards, auto shops, body shops, and tire shops with hubcaps stacked fifteen shelves high. Chain link fences topped with razor wire are everywhere—Mexican flags and U.S. flags. Eighteen-wheelers are coming out of every facility, turning at every intersection, busting down all the wide lanes, on their way to clog up the Otay Mesa border crossing, which is primarily a commercial port. With 2,000 big rigs passing through every day[7] it is an aorta for North American capitalism, the place where products flow north to fill strip malls and showrooms.

"We have a tenant," says David, "it's a logistics company. They own their trailers and trucks. They have a factory in Tijuana, and they have a warehouse in Otay. They typically do what we call the 'donkey run.' They go across the border with raw material and they come back north with a finished product."

Burreros, drayage operators, make the donkey runs. Their short-distance hauls exist because of NAFTA, the North American Free Trade Agreement. Provisions in the agreement make it harder for foreign truck drivers to move goods more than twenty-five miles past any U.S. border.[8] The idea is to protect American truck drivers, even if they work a hundred hours a week without health benefits or a living wage, as many of them do. After dropping off finished products in Otay Mesa, the burreros return to Tijuana with a trailer full of raw goods. If it's a good day, a burrero will make three runs, defined by eight or nine or ten mind-numbing hours spent waiting in traffic at the port of entry.

"Take Toyota Tacomas," says David. "Parts will come into the port at Long Beach, get trucked down to our yard in Otay. The truck that brought it from the port typically will switch out the tractor with a local truck that will bring the trailer into Mexico to the Tacoma factory just past the border. The Tacoma will be assembled there in Mexico, picked up as a finished product and brought across the border back to our drop yard. Then an American driver will connect to the trailer with the finished product and bring it to dealerships."

The factories along the border in Mexico are called maquiladoras and, like the trucking stipulations, they're codified by NAFTA. The maquiladoras allow multinational companies to assemble products in Mexico, paying lower wages than they can pay in the U.S.—and they get to skip duties and taxes.[9] But there are a few catches: the raw materials can only enter a designated Free Trade Zone near the border in Mexico and all of the finished products must be sold in the U.S. The goods pass freely but the people who make them do not.

With maquiladoras thriving along the border, Tijuana has been growing for decades, absorbing migrant workers from all over the country and region. The Tijuana that Roque saw from overhead in 1974, with 341,000 inhabitants, was nothing compared to the metropolis of two million in 2017. But the asymmetry he observed persists: the maquiladoras of Tijuana and the foothills behind them, crowded with listing houses and drying laundry, pulse in a way that still contrasts with the industrialization and emptiness of Otay Mesa. On the north side of the border, eighteen-wheelers pull into drop yards, completing donkey runs between 5,000-square-foot factories and the markets they serve. A line separates two countries but does not faze the travel patterns of capitalism.

It is into this landscape where work is set to begin on eight prototypes of The Wall. The sheriff contacted David and Roque about the possibility of major protests near the construction site. "We signed documents with the Sheriff's Department," says David, "to give them the right to arrest anyone on our properties."

Noted.

"I did get some calls from some protesters. They basically said, 'Would you mind if we came on your property?' I said, 'That's probably not a good idea. There is no upside, only a downside.' In my mind I thought, we'll have a mess like at Standing Rock in North Dakota. Now, if you want to pay rent, we can put up bleachers, have some hot dogs and hamburgers, and have a good time—that would be different." He laughs at the idea but also ponders it.

"Why is Trump doing this on the border, anyway?" he asks. "Those prototypes could have been built at Camp Pendleton. They could have been built at Area 51 in Nevada, but instead he is in the face of Mexico saying, 'This is what we're going to do.' If you're the sheriff, you're thinking you're going to have all hell break loose. You saw what happened in North Dakota. Things could get ugly."

CHAPTER 2

CUSTOMS AND BORDER PROTECTION JUST issued a memo on September 6, 2017, echoing David Wick's concern about the possibility of violence near the prototypes. The memo was distributed to local law enforcement and warned of protests resembling the encamped demonstrations earlier in the year at Standing Rock, where construction of a pipeline threatened the upper Missouri River—drinking water for the Sioux who live there. The language of the CBP memo is nervous, warning that protests "may arise with little or no warning." The possibilities of people blocking construction and cartels infiltrating the scene are both mentioned but the memo offers no plans for responding to any such incidents.[1] The city of San Diego and the Sheriff's Department are amassing more than $1.8 million in local resources to secure the area.[2]

The land where the prototypes will be constructed was originally home to Kumeyaay tribes. The Spanish took it in 1798, Mexico took it from the Spanish in 1821, and the U.S. took it at the end of the Mexican-American War in 1848. The Kumeyaay still have land east of the prototypes—and San Diego County has more reservations than any other county in the country[3]—but the 193 square miles of present-day Kumeyaay reservations is a small fraction of their traditional land. There are ancient village sites that are now buried under the rising water of the Pacific Ocean. Kumeyaay settlements date back 12,000 years in the region and cover 10,800 square miles—nearly all of present-day San Diego County and down into Baja as far south as Ensenada.[4] The border between Mexico and the U.S. partitions the Kumeyaay's historic land into two equal halves, nearly mirror images of each other.

"I guess we would be kind of like the American Kurds," says Stan Rodriguez, a Kumeyaay from the Santa Ysabel Reservation. "If you look at the Kurds, the Kurds right now are in Turkey, Iraq, Iran, and Syria. They have their own language, their own culture, but who was it that partitioned their land? It was the British that did that. Iran is Persian, Iraq is Arabic. Turkey, they have their own language. In between all that are the Kurds, trying to keep their autonomy and keep their sense of identity—because it's important.

"Let me put it into this perspective: the Spanish era was just a speed bump, twenty years, the Mexican era was another twenty years, and the American era has been 150 and some change. Our people have been here for *thousands and thousands* of years."

In 1852, a couple of years after the Mexican-American War, the Treaty of Santa Ysabel provided the Kumeyaay in the U.S. with 1,000 square miles for reservations, a long rectangle of land running fifty miles north from the nascent Mexico-U.S. border. The treaty was negotiated with tribal elders and finalized but never ratified by the U.S. government.

There was a lot going on in the country at the time. As seems to be the case throughout our history, we were coming off one war (Mexican) while building up to another (Civil). And California had just been admitted to the union after a drawn-out fight over whether slavery would be legal in the territory, which was already populated by Mexicans and the Kumeyaay. A steady stream of migrants was arriving in Northern California, ready to wade into streams and muddy mines for better lives, if not over-the-top wealth. Most of the original 49ers were fanning out across the state—some with fortunes, others still looking: California was already positioned, myth-ologically speaking, as the Golden State, the place where Manifest Destiny climaxes. Land grabs were taking place throughout San Diego County, one wave of gentrification after another, and each time the Kumeyaay were pushed farther from the coast, deeper into the deserts and mountains.

In the 1870s, *two decades* after negotiating the Treaty of San Ysabel, the federal government recognized that it had not been ratified and de-cided to formalize the Kumeyaay land seizure by executive order—a series of them over the next three decades, establishing the present-day reserva-tions. "People basically *had* to stay on the reservations," Stan says. "The only time you could leave was if you were working for a rancher and they gave you a note, a permit."

Stan is sitting with a cup of coffee at the Kumeyaay Community Col-lege in El Cajon, a city bisected by the 8 Freeway. He's a fixture at the school, an elder who serves as a border member for the institution. His dark hair is pulled back in a tight ponytail and he wears faded jeans with a bright red flannel shirt. "You know, when I was a kid," he says, "in school they would talk about the missions and say that the California Indians were peace-loving, docile people that loved the missions. But the San Diego mission was the first to go," he says. "Six hundred Kumeyaay attacked it, burned it down—1775, November 5th, midnight.

"Other tribes in the area had a much more centralized government. It was much easier for the Spanish to get converts. If you could convert the leader of the village, then all the other people would come. But the Spanish had a really hard time conquering Kumeyaay. In fact, they *didn't*—except for a little strip along the coast."

Stan tells me how his ancestors burned Santa Catarina to the ground in Baja California, east of Ensenada; how they attacked two other missions along the Colorado River—and then there was the attack at La Misión, between Ensenada and Tijuana. "Remember the John Ford movies?" he asks. "The Cowboy and Indian movies where they say, 'We have to protect ourselves from these godless red devils! They're keeping poor, decent Christian white folks from having a home!'" Stan speeds up through *decent Christian white folks*, putting on a bit of a twang—revenge, perhaps, for everything from Rock Hudson's stoicism in *Winchester '73* to Iron Eyes Cody's famous teardrop. "They forgot to say that they were putting their homes right in our communities and taking our land away. I hear people say, 'I didn't do it. It might have been my grandfather or great-grandfather, but I didn't do it. I believe that there is a wholesale denial that takes place in this society.

"One time when I was in the Navy, I was driving to the base—I was in my uniform—and I got pulled over by four or five Border Patrol trucks. I saw these guys jump out, all young. They must have just gotten out of the academy. I said, 'They probably need somebody to cut their teeth on.' And one guy came up to me, swaggering, and he said, 'What's your nationality?' I said, 'I'm a Native American.' He said, 'What does *that* mean?' I said, 'I'm a Native fucking American, you fucking moron. And how many illegal aliens are wearing a Navy uniform? Do you want to see my Green Card?' I pulled out my military ID and said, 'Now get the fuck out of my way, you motherfuckers! I've got to get to the base.' They pulled out of the way and let me through.

"A couple days later, a neighbor who is Border Patrol invited me over to the house on a Saturday for a barbecue. He said, 'Hey, I'm going to introduce you to some new guys that just started working here.' I walked into the garage and all those guys were sitting there. They looked at me and their heads went down. I said, 'We've already met.'

"Sometimes when new agents come through, we have to reeducate them. Their training teaches them to dehumanize people, that way they can exploit them. Part of the training has to teach somebody to *humanize* people again."

Stan's wife, Martha, joins us. She is the director of the cultural center at the school. She's also the reason Stan learned Spanish. "I'm the American side of the Kumeyaay," he says. "She's the Mexican side."

Martha is from San José de la Zorra in a remote region of the present-day state of Baja—or, as Martha puts it, "way deep up in the mountains." When she was a child, her family had no electricity, no running water—shoes were rare, clothing optional. Everyone gathered food and went hunting. "We would go together," she says, "spend all day in the mountains, cook and eat there, then come back."

Her dad worked on ranches and her mother made baskets. The family spoke Kumeyaay in the house but Martha's mother became one of the first in the community to learn Spanish. It made it easier to sell her baskets. She went down to Ensenada and eventually started crossing over to Kumeyaay land in the U.S. "My mom had aunts who were older but they gave her the responsibility to be the chairwoman in the community because she was learning Spanish. She decided to learn all the bird songs too. The Kumeyaay women have songs, but only for collecting materials, or while making baskets, or lullabies. The bird songs, women don't sing. My mom decided to learn all the songs anyway so she could pass them on to other generations to keep them going."

The things Martha learned from her mother—bird songs, ambition, community leadership—were entirely different from what she was getting at school. In the twentieth century, both the Mexican and U.S. governments established mandated education programs for Kumeyaay children. In the U.S. there were boarding schools. "They eradicated the language and the culture," says Stan, "to assimilate the people, to integrate people into American society."

In Mexico, it was the escuelas bilingües. "They were supposed to be teaching Western education and Kumeyaay traditions," says Martha. "But they gave us teachers that didn't know anything about Kumeyaay traditions. So how could they teach us?"

At eighteen, Martha started working at a preschool and tried doing there what her mother had done at home. She took three-, four-, and five-year-olds to meet elders, and she taught them Kumeyaay words, as the world around them became increasingly Spanish speaking.

After a few years, Martha won a teaching award from the state, and she traveled throughout Baja training other teachers. It was in Ensenada where she first took note of Stan. "I met him at one of the traditional gatherings, where all the communities come together. He was there to sing. I remember he had a bunch of little kids following him everywhere he went. And I thought: 'Oh, Stan has a lot of kids!'" She laughs, pushing her long black hair back off her shoulders. "But he had been going to one of the communities in Tecate and teaching them all to sing and they all wanted to follow him around, wherever he went."

Martha has a quiet, to-the-point demeanor that pairs well with Stan's excitability. He gets them into most conversations and she gets them out. "One time we were in Guadalajara," she says. "He was running into people from lots of places—Tucson, wherever—and I said, 'Damn, we cannot go one place where they do not know Stan!'"

Martha moved to the U.S. in 2001 and became a legal resident through Stan's military service. They maintain homes on either side of the border: Santa Isabel in Mexico and El Cajon near the Kumeyaay Community College.

Stan and Martha are both fluent in Kumeyaay and teach language courses at the school. There are 4,227 Kumeyaay on both sides of the border and Stan estimates that about forty-one of them still speak the language with some degree of fluency. Stan is working on his PhD, finishing a dissertation about the possible extinction of the language. "On the other side of the border," he says, "people speak Spanish and Kumeyaay. This side, it's English and *sometimes* Kumeyaay. The language has become moribund. We've lost a lot of our culture with the boarding schools and what they did to eradicate the language and assimilate the people into American society."

Stan looks at me for a moment then asks, "How many languages do *you* speak?"

"One and a half," I say.

"What's the half?"

"Un poco de español."

"Mira, en esta cultura, mucha gente piensa que es bueno hablar un idioma. Pero una persona que habla dos idiomas, eso es un problema. *Look, in this culture, a lot of people think it is good to speak one language. But a person who speaks two languages, that is a problem.* Stan has isolated the more revealing part of how Americans generally approach language: it is not just that so many of us insist on English but also on *not* hearing other languages. Learning and using multiple languages can, itself, *be* the problem. To stray from English, *eso es un problema.*

"A little while ago," Stan says, "I was on the cell phone with my aunt, and I was talking in Kumeyaay and there was this woman about sixty years old, a white woman, she comes up to me says, 'Excuse me?' I said, 'Yes?' She pointed at the American flag and said, 'We're in America. You need to talk American.' And I—" Stan stops for a moment to consider a tasteful summary of his response but decides to continue in plain language: "I just went off. I said, 'You fucking piece of shit! I am a Kumeyaay Indian. You are on traditional Kumeyaay territory. I *am* speaking American. How dare you ever come up to me and say that. And English is not from America. English is from the other side of that ocean.' I tore into her. I said, 'Don't you ever come to me like that again. Don't you ever disrespect me in my own land in my own home. You probably have a Bible too, and it talks about going to the Holy Land. Well, this is my Holy Land. These sacred mountains are my people's sacred mountains, so don't you ever say that to anyone again. You hear me?' She said, 'I was just trying to be helpful' and walked away."

The woman who confronted Stan not only had a deep sense of ownership when it came to the language—*American* not English—but she was also bothered by the Kumeyaay, which, presumably, she guessed to be Spanish. She didn't want to hear another language—Kumeyaay, Spanish, whatever it may be: to stray from English, *eso es un problema.*

"The thing about it is that the linguistic knowledge, the cultural knowledge, the mores that come with it—that's a beautiful thing. For you to let go of that, I mean that leaves a void in you. With identity, you can do so much. Identity gives you the strength to be able to overcome adversity and it gives you a sense of who one is in the universe. It's a powerful thing. If you take that away from people it's easier to control and hurt them. Assimilation is a form of colonization. By assimilating, colonization is complete. We have assimilated them into our society, we don't have to worry about them anymore because they're just like us. That's what it all comes back down to: be just like us."

Of the twenty-four tribes that identify as Kumeyaay, six are in Mexico and they need permission from U.S Customs and Border Protection before crossing north. Martha is in charge of formally submitting the requests. "We had to work out a system with Border Patrol," she says, "a way to get Kumeyaay people on the Mexican side of the border over here since so many of them don't have passports or visas."

"In the early 2000s," says Stan, "there was the Immigration Department, the American and Mexican consulates, and the different Kumeyaay bands on both sides of the border, everyone was going to develop a process for Kumeyaay to pass and repass.

"One of the problems was that in order to get a passport, you needed to show proof that you were working, gas and electric bills and things like that. We're talking about people who live up in the mountains who have no running water, no electricity. The Kumeyaay in America were helping the Kumeyaay in Mexico to shuttle them to the Mexican consulate, and, working with the consulate, they got passports."

Even still, there is more work for Martha to do to get approval from the U.S. government for a Kumeyaay crossing. "I have to make a written request at least ten days in advance," she says. "I have to send the request to Border Patrol on official letterhead with the names of the people who want to cross. And you have to have a cultural event to come to.

"One time, my cousin on the Mexican side of the border was dating someone on a reservation on the U.S. side. And his papers expired so he couldn't cross over anymore. So his girlfriend went to live with him while they updated his papers. Then her uncle went into the hospital. I submitted requests for both of them to be able to go see the uncle. And Border Patrol denied the request. They told me it wasn't a cultural event and they could only approve crossings for cultural events.

"I said, 'No, it *is* a cultural thing. In our culture we visit our elders when they are sick and in the hospital.' They denied it anyway. Then suddenly the uncle passed away.

"We filed permits for many people to come to the wake. I put my cousin on the list and he got approved. Apparently a funeral is a cultural thing.

"I told the Border Patrol, 'We need to sit down and have a meeting to talk about what is culture for you guys and what is culture for us.' Border Patrol told me, 'Oh, yes, we'll talk about it.' That was two months ago. It still hasn't happened.

"You cannot go freely to visit someone. You have to fill out paperwork and wait and see if *they* want you to go visit. Why? This is our home, this is our land. Then you showed up here. I'm grateful we have the agreement so we can bring some people over but, at the same time, why do we have to ask Border Patrol for permission to visit with our families? I don't like that. This is our territory. They need to learn about our traditions."

"It's always been difficult for us to pass across," says Stan. "Regardless of the administration. But the more the government tightens the border the more Kumeyaay people are becoming fearful of crossing into Baja. For the Kumeyaay on this side of the border who only speak English, which is most of them, going across the border to Mexico can already be frightening. Some of it is cartel activity, and some of it is just not knowing the people out there. The border has done a lot to isolate different groups.

"But, you see, these boundaries are not static. This land used to be governed by a clan system and each clan had its own area, its own territory. Here's your clan, here's my clan. Let's say you shoot a deer and that deer didn't die. It's still running and it runs out of your clan's territory and onto my clan's territory. Well, you shot that deer on your clan's territory, so we would say 'Keep going! Go get it. You can pass through. Get it and take it back.' Again, these boundaries were never static.

"You know, the U.S. has only been a country for a little more than two hundred years. They think it's going to be around forever. My friend, these boundaries are not static."

But in America nothing says stasis like a 30-foot-high barrier. What could provide the illusion of permanence better than physical manifestations of the lines we use to identify ourselves?

Before we part ways Stan tells me I should go to the fiesta.

"The fiesta?" I ask.

"In the desert, on the Campo Reservation. Ask for Mike—Michael Connolly. He'll tell you all about the shootout."

CHAPTER 3

WHEN I ARRIVE IN THE desert, at the fiesta, I see what can only be described as an extremely quaint county fair: a watermelon-eating contest, tug-of-war, horseshoes, a baseball game. "That's a big thing," says Michael Connolly, "you've *got* to have a baseball game—oh, and pie-eating contests."

Mike has a kind face with plump cheeks but his eyes are dark and deep-set. His graying hair is combed straight back. His full name is Michael Connolly Miskwish and he spent seventeen years on the tribal council for the Kumeyaay in Campo.

"So, why's it called a fiesta?" I ask.

"The fiesta is more like a cover," he says. "'Fiesta' is okay because that's like a Spanish, Mexican thing. Now we look more civilized," he says sarcastically. "We don't have traditional gatherings, we have *fiestas*."

We find a quiet table, far from the din of talent competitions and home runs, and I waste no time: "Stan mentioned a shootout here?"

"It all goes back to 1852," he says, reminding me the U.S. negotiated but did not ratify the Treaty of Santa Ysabel, which gave the Kumeyaay communities roughly 20 percent of present-day San Diego County. "The treaty never got ratified but the Indian people weren't told that," he says. "They were living on what they thought was their reservation and then white settlers came in and kicked them off their land. Even land they improved and built a house on—they'd just get evicted. If they were lucky, they'd get to stay on and work as a ranch hand on the ranch they built.

"In 1905, the Senate removed the seal of secrecy on their action, the fact that they didn't ratify the treaty, and a lot of the Indian people got together and said, 'If our treaty was never ratified, what was the legal mechanism that brought us into the United States?' We never became part of the

United States. And so they took that position and in 1919 formed an organization called the Mission Indian Federation. They set up their own police force and said that since we never became part of the United States, the federal officers have no jurisdiction on their lands. They really challenged the authority of the Bureau of Indian Affairs, which is part of the U.S. government. Back then the BIA was supposed to bring food and clothing to the people but it was all one scam after another. The meat was bad. I remember one of the elders told me that they brought shoes and the soles were made out of compacted paper, so when they got wet, the shoes fell apart.

"So the fiestas started up just around that time, when the Mission Indian Federation was challenging the BIA. There used to be traditional gatherings called mutahyuum[1] but in the early twentieth century, the United States was really fearful of Indian religions causing Indians to go out and kill white people. The Ghost Dance started up in Nevada and it was spreading out all across the country."

"What was it all about?"

"The Ghost Dance was about following the right path so that the buffalo and all the game would be restored and the land would come back and the people would be happy again. It didn't really talk about killing white people, but the belief was that white people would all go back to Europe or something—there are different interpretations on it. But it really spread. It found resonance with a lot of Indian communities that had seen all their ways just completely destroyed. Some of them were living like POWs. And so a lot of the Plains Indians really got caught up in the ghost dance. It was one of the things that triggered the Wounded Knee Massacre, and the federal government didn't want anything like that to spread. They were just scared to death that it was going to cause Indian uprisings. And so they suppressed it with federal laws prohibiting native religions.

"So when we would have tribal gatherings, with bird songs and important ceremonies, we changed the name and called them fiestas. Each reservation would have their own fiesta and they would have a priest come out and bless the fiesta in the name of a saint. And we incorporated certain things to help show how innocent it was. We incorporated Americana—watermelon-eating contests and tug-of-war and a beautiful baby contest and all of these kinds of rural things. That way we could still do our songs and dances, but it wouldn't be seen as a threat to the government.

"So in 1927 the fiesta is going on in Campo and there were both BIA cops and Mission Indian Federation cops there. The BIA didn't like the fiestas but they had an obligation to police these things. And they were really despised by most of the people in the communities. People hated them and they were nervous about it. So in 1927 they invited some county sheriff's deputies to come as backup at the fiesta—even though the sheriff had no jurisdiction on the reservations at that time.

"And there was a confrontation.

"See, we had a lot of smuggling going on. This is during Prohibition. We've been involved in smuggling in our community for a long time. People used to poke a hole in eggs and blow the insides out. And then they'd fill them with alcohol and put wax on them. So you'd go down to Mexico and you'd put your whiskey into an egg and bring back a couple dozen eggs that would be all full of alcohol. There were never huge suppliers or anything, but that kind of thing went on.

"So some people are drinking alcohol at the fiesta—and there were different reports. Some said they were drinking moonshine, other people said they were drinking Sterno, a little can you use to heat food—it's alcohol based, but it's a wood alcohol, so it's really not a good thing to drink. Anyway, the Bureau police went to confront some people. And the Federation police intervened and said they were out of their jurisdiction. It escalated to the point where there was shooting and four people died.

"There weren't any fiestas at Campo for a few years after that, and our culture really started dying out. It was being replaced by Plains Indian culture because there were a lot of Indians moving in from out of state. In the '50s and the '60s, there were programs by the federal government to try to help American Indians with unemployment. There was real bad unemployment in the plains, so the federal government relocated Indians into big metropolitan areas, especially L.A., but also Sacramento, San Francisco, San Diego.

"And when a lot of Indians started coming in from out of state, they said, 'You guys have fiestas? Mexicans do fiestas!—you're not even Indians! You don't do powwows, and you don't know how to fancy dance and you guys don't beat the drum!' And I think people actually got kind of embarrassed about the fiestas and they quit having them altogether back in the '60s.

"When I was young it used to always bother me. I thought, we've lost our culture and everything. And in the '90s, we had this resurgence, people started bringing back the fiestas. Now some people don't like calling them fiestas and they started calling them mutahyuum again, going back to the traditional name.

"I guess 'fiesta' is also a way of encouraging white people to visit the reservations, to buy crafts, the pottery and baskets. And when people see the watermelon-eating contests and all of that, how can you feel apprehensive with a bunch of Indians with a watermelon-eating contest?" he says, smiling. "It just tells you right there you don't have to worry about anything."

CHAPTER 4

ROUGHLY 460 COMPANIES SUBMITTED PROPOSALS to build the proto-types.[1] It is hard to get an exact number—the secrecy of the barrier on En-rico Fermi Drive and the foreman with the bandanna over his face extends to all information released by Border Patrol. It is often opaque or shifting or both. When I asked one public affairs agent how many companies bid on the project his answer was a distinctly unhelpful "more than a hundred."

A few companies that submitted a bid have made their designs public. One proposal describes a wall that is partially funded by those willing to pay for engraved memorials or family trees; another pairs a simple chain link fence with a hundred-foot trench holding nuclear waste. There is a design with a castle-looking top, indicating the edge of some kingdom, and another that features a 25-foot-wide aqueduct, like a moat encasing the kingdom. Plenty are reminiscent of prison exteriors, walling in and walling out at the same time. There are a few protest designs; one sketches a vision of the border as open park with an elevated high-speed monorail running along the international line.

At least twenty-three of the companies that submitted proposals have offices in San Diego County. One of them is Concrete Contractors Inter-state, CCI, which is in the city of Poway, about fifteen miles north of the 8 Freeway. Russ Baumgartner is the president of the company. "I'll be frank with you," he says to me when I visit his office, "I'm not a big proponent of this wall." He shifts a bit, sitting at his desk in faded blue jeans and a nicely pressed short sleeve shirt—a guayabera look with a twist of surfer. "But I am in the business of building. And if they're going to build a wall, then I think it needs to be done right and we feel like we have a system that allows it to be done right."

Russ has been working on his building system for nearly five years. It began when he needed a retaining wall at his house in Rancho Santa Fe, one of the most affluent suburbs in the country,[2] just north of San Diego. Like his father before him, Russ has worked with concrete on a commercial scale for decades, so the retaining wall should have been a cinch. But there was a problem. "I was getting pushback from my wife for tearing up the yard," he says, smiling. "She said, 'As long as I can decorate it.'"

This was 2013 and, at that point, Russ hadn't done any decorative concrete. But he had an idea and sketched a design that allowed the wall to be cast flat—so it could be decorated easily like a countertop or floor—and *then* connected to footing in the ground. It not only worked for his wife but it also got Russ thinking about expanding his business.

"I went to a buddy of mine, who I've done a lot of business with, and I said, 'Rick, look at this and tell me what you think.' Rick looked at my design and said, 'You can't do that.' I said, 'Bullshit! You can too! Look at it closer!' He said, 'Okay, I'll take it and play with it a little bit.' He came back and said, 'Can I be your partner?'"

Russ pauses briefly, to let it sink in again, the satisfaction of having someone else see what he saw. "So we brought the decorative work into the mix with the structural work I'd already been doing for decades."

Russ's wife also works with the company. A picture of their wall at the house, the collaboration that inspired it all, hangs in the office. It features a glass mosaic inlay of mountains and ocean waves, the sun and clouds—all with backlights to make the reds fiery at night, the blues deeper. His wife collaborated with an artist to conceptualize the panoramic. She is form; Russ is function.

Russ's father started CCI in 1958 in Brighton, Colorado, and eventually found clients in Arizona and California. "My dad grew up on a farm, never went to college but he was an innovator. He started with a little 1940 pickup, himself and one other guy, doing curbs and gutters. By the time 1970 rolled around, he was worth well over $10 million."

After college, Russ joined his dad on a job in Orange County, just north of San Diego County, and he never left California. One of the happiest days of his life, he says, was the day he threw away the windshield ice scraper that lived in his trunk.

In 1986, at twenty-six, Russ officially opened a San Diego office for

CCI. As he puts it, the company does "anything concrete": buildings, street work, parking garages, and, of course, walls.

Russ shows me the website facilitating the bidding process for the federal government and mentions an online Q&A session a few weeks ago for registered vendors like him. Russ says there were a lot of questions about security because the government's RFP—request for proposals—stipulated that winning bidders will be responsible for their own security detail. Potential bidders seemed keenly aware that California—with some of the strongest gun safety laws in the country, the land of Dianne Feinstein and the 1994 assault weapons ban—is not a good place to stand one's ground. One vendor asked if their employees would be allowed to use firearms if demonstrators attack them while they are working. Border Patrol said it could not waive state laws but promised to respond to any violent eruptions.

"I struggle with getting involved in this," Russ says. "I know how sensitive it is to some people." I can see Russ's serious eyes browsing past all the fragile words: "I have over fifty people working for me and 80 percent of them are Hispanic. We actually asked our employees how they felt about it. They were for it. My engineer was like, 'Let's build the son of a bitch!' We had a few guys that were concerned, but then they heard our reasoning. We've gone through a lot of serious recessions here as a construction company—and survived, but the last one barely. It was a really tough struggle in '07 and '08. I could not see ourselves sitting on the sidelines during the next recession if they had a project that was suited for us. I just couldn't see it. It wouldn't be fair to us as a company or to the employees. I wasn't going to shut that door."

Requirements and parameters for the bidding process evolved over the summer, with the federal government making several amendments to the initial RFP. "Early on it felt very disorganized," says Russ. "They didn't disclose locations. There were no soil reports. On a 30-foot structure, you better know what you're putting it on. There was not enough information to bid on a wall. A project like this takes years of planning. It was just rush, rush, rush. You could tell the government was in disarray. My gut feeling is that the president said, 'I want it and I want it now!' because that's how it felt.

"Usually the government is very transparent, especially in the bid process—you want to be transparent. And this one just doesn't smell good. I don't know what they'll end up with on this."

As the amendments kept coming, the basic prototype specifications remained in place. Each should be 30 feet tall, 30 feet wide, and extend at least six feet underground to help combat tunneling. They can be made of concrete or a mix of concrete and "other materials." Each needs to withstand expert climbers and diggers, pickaxes, sledgehammers, and torches. More than one spokesman for Border Patrol emphasized three questions: Can it be climbed? Can it be dug under? Can it withstand cutting tools?

Russ says, "One of the things I thought was unnecessary was 30 feet high. At one point they did amend it to say that they still want 30-foot, but they *may* consider 18-foot. There are a lot more problems creating a stable foundation for a 30-foot versus 18-foot, not to mention all of the designs that I've looked at are precast. That means you're trucking in panels, so an 18-foot would be much easier to handle. When I saw 30-foot, my thought was that it would get revised, someone will come to their senses, but they ended up keeping it."

"What was required in the proposal?"

"They asked for a whitepaper with technology ideas, ideas for financing—they were asking for a lot of different areas. We have a five-page whitepaper. The request said the prototype needed to be decorated on one side—'enhanced on one side' was the wording—and it just struck me as being not a good idea. We felt like we could provide enhancement on both sides. That's what we do here. We have ways to decorate what we call the 'down side' or the 'reflection side.' In our whitepaper we expressed that we feel it should be decorated on both sides if you're going to do it.

"One of the things I personally believe is that if you build a fence, you ask your neighbor what they would like to look at."

Russ's point reminds me of "Mending Wall," the Robert Frost poem I memorized in sixth grade, and a few more lines come back to me:

Before I built a wall I'd ask to know
What I was walling in or walling out
And to whom I was like to give offense.

In front of the CCI offices, right next to visitor parking, six distinct samples of decorative walls are lined up—colored glass inlays, texture, cutouts, made-to-order. Russ believes he's got the right design for The Wall but still wrestles with the choice he made to submit the whitepaper.

"I wrote the pros and cons down. One of the things I thought about is that, yes, it's a wall; yes, it's controversial, but it's the federal government and I'm not in a position to pretend like I know enough to decide whether a wall is required or not. We're not politicians. We are builders, and this is the kind of stuff we build.

"I think of the time when I built the missile maintenance facility where they test cruise missiles that carry nuclear warheads. The concrete walls are three feet thick; they're designed for a blast to go off. There was no question that this was a facility that could be considered way more controversial than a wall and nobody said 'boo' when I was out there building that. And I had to struggle with that one too. I was just glad that I was not building the missile. At least I was building something to protect the guys testing it, but still it's part of the whole process of acquiring missiles.

"I feel like it's a little hypocritical of a lot of people with this vitriol that I'm hearing. I'm talking about the state legislature I've heard lately, threatening to debar us for bidding on the wall. They like to base it on the fact that back in the '80s the State of California went after companies that did business with South Africa. Well, to compare this with apartheid I think is a little stupid. I say to myself, 'Jesus, this is getting a little crazy!' "

Bills and ordinances taking aim at companies doing work related to The Wall have been coming out of Sacramento and city halls across California. Construction will take place in the southern border state that is, categorically, the most resistant to the prototypes and the 1,954-mile endgame that they represent. Los Angeles city councilman Gil Cedillo proposed requiring companies seeking or doing business with the city to disclose any work on the prototypes—design, building, supplies. Senate Bill 30, written by state senator Ricardo Lara, seeks to identify companies who do any work related to The Wall and prohibit the state from doing any business with them. Many of these proposals are still being debated. But already the San Diego City Council passed a resolution condemning The Wall and seeking disclosure of all companies involved with construction.

"Like I said, I'm not a huge proponent of this idea, but there are places for fences. There was a place called Smuggler's Gulch. It didn't have a barrier and the immigrants would amass on the Tijuana side of the border and they would rush it, knowing that some of them would get through. You can still see it on YouTube, these pictures of this mass group of people rushing the border, and these border agents—totally outnumbered—are running after them. Well, a wall prevents a lot of that. But is a 30-foot-tall concrete barrier the entire length of the country necessary?

"I struggle with it. It's been ongoing. It even happened today. I ask myself if I made the right decision. I have a niece who was going to disown me. I have two sisters that are partners on the bid, both of them are very liberal. They were concerned about us getting involved, but once we sat down as a team and discussed our approach to provide a system that looks better, you could decorate it on both sides, not to mention it would be using local help—and we're not saying just our side. I think it would be ideal to bring people in from the Mexican side and let them decide what they want to look at and even participate in, and financially benefit from the building of it—so it's not so controversial. I think that's a wish and not necessarily all that realistic, however I'd like to see something move in that direction.

"I'm pro-immigrant. We need immigrants, especially in my business, it's hard to find people who are interested in getting in the trades anymore. Everybody is interested in computers. I've got a lot of people I know in this business who are super-right-wing except when it comes to *their* guys—*their* landscaper or *their* maid. It's hypocritical.

I firmly believe that the world is changing and it's becoming a better, more loving place. I really think it is. But there are holdovers and old habits and old fears that need to die that I think will.

"My wife's an immigrant. She's what's called Dutch-Indo. She was born in Holland and she's got a lot of Indonesian blood in her. When she was a kid, they migrated to Canada. We went through that whole process to get her legal. It was time-consuming and sometimes difficult and sometimes I fucking hated it. I thought I could just marry her and she could become a U.S. citizen, no problem. It doesn't work that way. You've got to go through interviews and all this stuff.

"I remember when I decided I was going to marry her.

"It was when she had gone across the border to renew her visa in Canada, trying to keep everything aboveboard, and she got stuck. They stopped her at the border. She couldn't get back. I was stressing. I was thinking, these feelings have got to mean something: I had fallen in love. She had gone up there on our behalf and now she can't get back. What are we going to do? Well, she had an uncle sneak her in by driving her across.

She ended up getting an attorney and we got the process going after we got married."

Most people are willing to take extreme measures when falling in love, including sneaking across a border illegally. It is a human impulse without political affiliation. And for love, some will even design a new way to build a wall so that it can be decorated. But some relationships are more complicated than others, and one man's domestic remedy is not necessarily a prescription for neighboring nation-states. Still, Russ remains hopeful he can build a beautiful wall.

"I consider myself more of a libertarian than anything. I think there are a lot of people like me out there that don't realize there could be another way. We've had this two-party system and I think it's ripe for someone to get in the middle. There is a huge polarization right now between nationalists and globalists. Personally, I think globalization is not bad. For the world to eventually have completely open borders would be great, but it's not practical right now."

It has always struck me as telling that the most famous line from Frost's "Mending Wall" is likely "good fences make good neighbors." And yet it is on this very idea that the voice of the poem pushes back: "*Why* do they make good neighbors?" Like Russ, the narrator isn't so sure about the consequences of a wall: "Before I built a wall I'd ask to know/What I was walling in or walling out . . ." But these lines do not stick, particularly not in America. We choose to remember *good fences make good neighbors*. It is almost as if this very American poet was trying to get us to reconsider the very American devotion to marking property—and he failed miserably. Never mind what we are walling in or what we are walling out: good fences make good neighbors. Our lines are not only static but fortified too. That is the story we tell. Mine is here, yours is over there, and a wall leaves no ambiguity. The U.S. holds the tradition of marking property as so sacred, as so vital to the creation of wealth and stability and identity, that we even gave it a fancy name: the American Dream. We might entertain the idea of sharing—national parks, for example—but we will always like the act of owning and, perhaps more to the point, *marking* our property even more.

CHAPTER 5

"**I HAVE A DISTRICT WHERE** headless bodies have been found," says Lorena Gonzalez from her office in downtown San Diego. She's the state representative for California's 80th, which also includes the site for the prototypes. "I've never been an open borders person. I mean, if I could live in a utopia, yes—of course—then we could all freely flow and it wouldn't matter. But I didn't enter these political discussions with that ideological bent: oh, we should just have open borders."

The 2017 California legislative session is over and both chambers worked late into the final night, jockeying bills to the floor for votes. The land of Ronald Reagan and Richard Nixon is now leading the Democratic resistance, and the end of this session was particularly noisy after months of various drafts of various bills, all pushing back on enforcement of federal immigration laws or punishing anyone who works on The Wall. There is an unmistakable verve to the discourse, as Russ Baumgartner alluded to; lawmakers have been talking about the circumstances in historic terms, harking back to the State Assembly's 1986 vote to divest public funds from companies doing business with South Africa under apartheid. Comparisons like that weigh on someone like Russ who has a niece who might disown him *and* fifty employees relying on him for a paycheck—his own contradictory emotions tangled in the middle.

Ricardo Lara's Senate Bill 30, which would have prevented the state from doing business with any company or individual working on the prototypes, was ditched because of doubts about its constitutionality. In the final weeks of the session, Senate Bill 54 emerged as the most contentious piece of legislation to inch toward a vote. It prohibits local law enforcement from cooperating with federal immigration officials to identify and detain undocumented migrants. State Senator Kevin de León introduced the bill and he asked Lorena to get it to the floor for a vote in the Assembly. It passed around 1:50 a.m. on the night the session ended.

Lorena was an obvious choice to push SB 54 through. Not only is her district directly affected by federal border and immigration policies but she has also known life south of the 8 Freeway since birth. Her parents immigrated from Mexico; her dad picked strawberries, and "by the grace of God, I was born twelve miles this side of the border," she says. Lorena left for an undergraduate degree at Princeton and a law degree from UCLA, then returned home. "A lot of my constituents in San Ysidro don't know they're in the city of San Diego," she says. "They think of San Ysidro as a stand-alone because it's always been treated that way, as separate. Even our school systems are separate.

"For me, SB 54 was just about people in my district being able to live in a semi-normal way. What we were seeing in our communities was this complete fear of any police. And not just police because then you're scared of firefighters and people who are there to help us. You have to have people who are willing to help you. That's how society has to work. That was being totally degraded because it was not clear that they wouldn't call ICE on you."

Lorena is referring to Immigration and Customs Enforcement officers, since they conduct searches for undocumented immigrants, but the presence of just about any uniformed law enforcement official is enough to cause anxiety for hundreds, if not thousands, in a matter of minutes. A recent Facebook post out of the South Bay city of Chula Vista warned locals of an immigration raid at a Starbucks. The message featured an image of a man in a Border Patrol uniform who, as it turned out, was in line to order coffee. Reliable information is hard to come by for some of Lorena's constituents and fear colors routine activities. Parents hesitate to enroll in direly needed school lunch programs. Dreamers don't apply for scholarships intended for them.

"Because people have known me a long time, they trust me, but don't forget: I'm still the government," Lorena says. "There are still people afraid of us. I have better positioning than a lot of elected officials because I came from organized labor. And organized labor has done such a good job of being—next to the Church—a sanctuary for people, thanks to the work of our hotel workers and our janitors unions. But among those people I talk to—neighbors, constituents—there is fear, real fear. Can I go to church? Can they pick me up when I'm walking to church? And I don't want to say to them, 'They can pick you up *at* church.' There's some notion we have of a sanctuary, and it doesn't really exist.[1] I have to stop myself from freaking people out because we can't change that. My entire district is within a hundred miles of the border so Border Patrol really can do anything—and that's scary."

Her mention of a hundred miles refers to the primary jurisdiction for Border Patrol beyond any U.S. port of entry. All of San Diego County is within one hundred miles of Mexico so Border Patrol is a regular presence alongside the police, Highway Patrol, sheriff—nowhere more acutely than places like San Ysidro and Otay Mesa. In these communities, the police do not need to contact Border Patrol to prompt their arrival. Border Patrol is present, always.

SB 54 changes little for Lorena's constituents—and not just because of geography. Governor Jerry Brown spent weeks negotiating details, insisting that local law enforcement have flexibility within the new law. And so a list of exceptions was included in the bill—a list of "violent crimes" that, if committed by an undocumented migrant in the past fifteen years, would allow local law enforcement to hand over that individual to federal immigration officials. What would constitute a "violent crime" became the central issue during negotiations and, in the end, the designation was given to hundreds of offenses including misdemeanors for vandalism and marijuana possession. SB 54 projects a strong message but implements a feckless policy.

Much more consequential is Assembly Bill 450, or AB 450, which Lorena coauthored. It requires employers to bar federal immigration authorities from entering private work areas without a warrant. It also requires employers to give a seventy-two-hour notice if a planned inspection is scheduled, providing undocumented workers with a few days to catch a cold and call in sick. SB 54 has occupied the headlines while AB 450 has gone mostly unnoticed. "If you've enjoyed the luxuries of modern-day America," says Lorena, "it's hard to convince yourself to go out in 113 degree heat and pick fruit for ten hours straight—without basic protections, by the way. Because the agricultural industry, outside California, doesn't have the basic protections of fair labor standards."[2]

Lorena is much more interested in the effects of *documented* migrant workers. U.S. employers can bypass American workers and choose from a variety of visas to offer foreign workers. There's the H-1B for "specialty occupations," known as the darling of Silicon Valley but, in truth, applied broadly across professional labor, from nursing to accounting. There's the H-2B for seasonal and intermittent work, often blue-collar or manual labor; 62 were issued in 1987 and 83,600 in 2017. In most categories more visas are issued every year—hundreds if not thousands more, and the overall number looks something like 1,423,894 jobs filled through one work visa program or another—a number that gets bigger every year.[3] Some visas are discontinued after a few years or a decade, new ones emerge and some continue for generations, all of it driven by industry lobbying. There's the H-2A, expressly for agricultural workers, who, as Lorena points out, have never had basic protections from the federal government, regardless of citizenship—no right to organize or overtime pay. There's the L-1 and the O-1, the P-1 and the P-3—dozens, each designed to import a specific set of workers who are then tethered to one job, unable to act, in capitalistic terms, as *free agents* in an *open labor market*. Each visa is linked to an employer so the worker can't leave for a better job. Over time, this immobility helps suppress wages in any given industry. And visa recipients tend to be young, or, more to the point, cheaper.

"*That's* stealing American work. And I'm afraid we're going to continue to grow this notion that we bring people in from other countries. Now we're expanding these visa programs into fast food work too. And if you're anywhere south of L.A., hotel maids are Latino and sometimes Filipino. You go somewhere else and there's a white woman cleaning, usually Russian or Eastern European—the newest immigrant brought over on a visa to do our really hard work. And pay them substandard wages. These are the only industries that we know aren't going to be moved offshore. They have to be here. So we're going to bring outside workers in and suppress those wages so people can have a cheap hamburger? And where does that end? We see it everywhere. Overall we're going to end up with hardly any jobs for Americans. And it's an upward pressure."

The visa programs are a problem for the nation-state—"stealing American jobs"—*and* for the worker, the individual surviving the suppressed wages of an immobile, ever-young workforce. But neither the individual nor the nation-state has reckoned with the role of migrant workers in society. The globalized workforce is not a possibility to ponder; it is a reality to confront, and it is the lack of awareness that worries Lorena most. "I don't want to sound dire but it really scares me. We have a president who tweets every day about how great Wall Street is doing. And the regular guy doesn't get that that doesn't do anything for him. Do you own stock? I mean maybe you have a 401(k) but we know at the next downturn, that's going to go to shit.

"Work is so governed by our laws and those laws have to change. Or we have to stop working to prove a point—using the strike or a slowdown—you have to create a pressure for these things to change. And what I'm not sure of, in this day and age, is how we can create that pressure. The idea of people self-sacrificing to change the law for a future generation is totally gone. That's not going to happen. Maybe young people like to protest and will come out on a Saturday afternoon, but a sustained campaign? The workers throughout history who were willing to lay down their lives knew that they were working in industries that their children and their grandchildren were going to work in. All that's gone. And a lot of times, people don't want their children to do the work that they are doing. It's the total opposite of what they want.

"So how do we then get political pressure? We have to change federal organizing laws. Something that is so American is the value of work. When I was in organized labor before politics, I had ICE agents as union members and Border Patrol agents as union members. Good lord, it was an interesting dynamic. But we worked through a lot of things."

CHAPTER 6

"I LIKE LORENA," SAYS CHRIS Harris, a twenty-year veteran of Border Patrol. His tone suggests he's just been accused of not liking Lorena. Then proof: "I have pictures of me out there orating, speaking at rallies with Lorena Gonzalez to raise the minimum wage." It's true. Chris and Lorena go back years. "She's not happy with us these days, but whatever. She's conflated us with the president too much. And that's a problem we have to deal with. We'll figure that out sooner or later."

The *us* that Chris describes is not Border Patrol, the agency, as part of U.S. Customs and Border Protection, as part of the Department of Homeland Security; rather he is talking about more than 19,437 agents who make patrols across nine designated sectors of the southern border.[1] Chris is the elected secretary of Local 1613 and appointed director of legislative and political affairs.

And he bought my coffee, let me just get that out of the way. Journalistic integrity forbids gifts of any significance from interviewees. You will judge whether or not the caffeine has affected my reporting. I can tell you with certainty it was really, really bad coffee—and I will try to not let *that* fact affect my reporting.

It's not about pointing fingers, but it was Denny's that brewed the coffee. And I am truly impressed by how this chain manages to bamboozle the good people of San Diego County. When Chris and I met outside this Denny's in Imperial Beach, we were told that a table would be available in twenty minutes. I had forgotten that in Southern California, Denny's just might maintain a wait list from time to time. I have rarely contemplated eating food at Denny's and absolutely never considered waiting for it. But there is something about a Denny's that fits the region perfectly, something that sates the appetite for familiarity and MSG and plenty of parking—comfort, in short—and I doubt there is a region of the U.S. that better embodies the American pursuit of comfort than the coastal corridor of Southern California. Imperial Beach is the very southern tip of this corridor, right up against the border.

Chris has adapted to this existence but there's still upstate New York in his hunched shoulders and accent. He grew up in Newburgh, an old manufacturing and transportation hub that rusted over in the last decades of the twentieth century, as Chris came of age. He entered law enforcement at eighteen and soon became a police officer in Highland Falls, a twenty-minute commute from his hometown. But that didn't last long. "Obviously, you move around," as he put it. "I normally tell people who are in one area and want to stay there their whole life, God bless you if you're happy. I didn't want to do that. I told my wife, I said, 'I don't want to be eighty years old in a rocking chair on our porch here saying, "I was born here, I went to school here, I worked here, raised my kids here and I'm going to die here."' I said, 'I want to try something different.'"

First he tried life at the Treasury Department in Washington, D.C., working as a U.S. marshal. That kept him occupied during the early 1990s; then came a Border Patrol hiring frenzy in 1996. It was the first Chris had ever heard of the agency, and suddenly it was tempting so many marshals with ranging possibilities: narcotics, urban patrol, deserts, rivers, K-9 units, horses, big toys like ATVs and boats. "They also patrol out in the country," he says, "and I always wanted to do that." So he applied.

"I got a job offer. The package was very honest. It said you might go to a place that's basically a shithole with shitty schools and housing. And at first my offer said the Southwest border. And my wife said, 'I would go with you, but I don't want to take our teenage girls.' I said, 'Don't worry, I'm not going to accept that. I won't go. Then they said San Diego and I said, 'Okay.'"

This morning, before Chris and I met up, the Imperial Beach station commander presented him with a pin and a certificate to commemorate twenty-five years with federal law enforcement.

Chris speaks about his first days as a Border Patrol agent without much romanticism: "I had no seniority, so I was on midnight shift and they were teaching us about hypothermia. I came out during El Niño and it rained for months on end. I thought, these fuckers have been lying to me! Where the hell is the sun?

"I was not thrilled with San Diego at first. Houses in the suburbs are so close together. I found out that it's much more of a 'me' attitude out here—people can go their whole lives without knowing their neighbors. I knew all my neighbors in New York. We had block parties. We had clambakes in the neighborhood. We went Christmas caroling together. And everyone wanted to talk to us about how rude New Yorkers are. Naw, my wife and I didn't care for that, the hypocrisy of New Yorkers being rude. No, you guys are the ones that don't even talk to each other.

"Another disappointment: I figured Southern California would have a strong union. It's funny, *The San Diego Union-Tribune* is so liberal but it's still anti-union. It's like, what the hell? I'm from New York, dude, I'm a union guy. And when I first came out here they wanted me to get involved. But I said no because my wife and I had our kids very, very young and I said, 'They're grown up now, they're out, it's our time.'

"But then my wife died suddenly and—you know what?—I said, 'I'm your guy,' and I became a union rep. I've always been pro-labor. My dad was a teacher. I watched him on strike. My mom was a nurse, thirty-some years in the ICU and I watched her in the picket line."

Chris knows each server who passes our table—and the manager working the phone, which is probably why we bypassed the twenty-minute wait. He's a magnet for interaction and the conversations he starts with the people all around us—it's about how many tables they are managing or when their shift ends; work is always on Chris's mind. "I read a lot of books on Cesar Chavez and some of his writings," he says. "That guy was actually against illegal immigration. He understood that it artificially kept wages down and work conditions down. He would call the Border Patrol. He actually had his own green squad that would jump on illegals."[2]

Chavez *did* oppose illegal immigration. In the fall of 1969, he spoke to the U.S. House Education and Labor Committee about several issues including a seventy-two-hour pass that Border Patrol had recently begun issuing to migrants. Chavez said the pass was a bad idea because it "facilitates the entry of the illegals who can apply at the American consulate, get a 72 hour pass, and then the moment they get into the country disregard the pass, the restrictions on the pass which limit their travel and also the time period."[3] Chavez was also for employment verification programs. He wanted migrant workers to be able to live in the open, with legal status, embraced by the society to which they contributed.

"I'd actually push to raise the minimum wage," says Chris. "With real capitalists—which I don't know if we have anymore—the scales would level out, where wages should be." He raises both hands, putting them on the same, equitable plane. "But corporations and big businesses have their fingers on the scale. That's not good capitalism."

Which raises the question: what *is* good capitalism? But before I can ask, he suggests we go for a ride—he's all riled up on bad coffee and bad capitalism.

We get into Chris's SUV and he pulls onto Hollister Street heading south. In less than three miles the road ends at the border and the Tijuana River Estuary, which empties into the Pacific Ocean. Chris suggests we head east, toward the desert.

Of the 60 miles along the border in San Diego County, 46 have at least one barrier already. Only 14 miles, scattered in different spots to the east, await The Wall. Chris drives along the primary fence, which dates back to the early 1990s and is made of the corrugated metal recycled from old aircraft carrier landing mats.

The secondary fence, about 18 feet tall, made of thick wire mesh with concertina wire at the top, runs parallel to us for the drive. It is 150 feet to the north, establishing a defined buffer zone for agents to patrol between the two barriers.

The access road next to the primary fence is rocky with several blind crests. Chris takes each of them without slowing down, lost in his own thought. "What happened to antitrust laws and breaking up monopolies?" he asks. "Teddy Roosevelt—a Republican—broke up tons of them. Even in the '70s, we broke up AT&T, Ma Bell, but now it seems to be going the other way where four airlines run 80 percent of the flights across this country. We've got just a few big tech giants.

"But don't get me wrong: socialism does not work. And every time I say that I get people telling me 'Venezuela did it wrong.' 'Cuba did it wrong.' No, it doesn't work. But what we're doing now isn't good either.

"You know, I have a friend who is very left of center, a labor organizer, a good guy. He checks every box on the left: freedom of choice—this, that, and the other—except he likes to shoot. He's always asking me, 'Chris, can I go shooting with you? I have an AR platform, my wife has a pink AR platform—we love to shoot but I can't tell my other friends.' How horrible is that? There are a lot of people like that. And they keep their mouth shut.

When we've got people scared to say what they think, that's a bad slope to be on. It happens on the right too. I happen to know that firsthand. You can check off every box on the right and still be pro-choice and they hate you. When did that start happening?"

The certificate Chris received earlier in the day for twenty-five years of service in federal law enforcement rests on the dashboard. He wore a jacket and tie for the ceremony, which he still has on: he's trying to get used to the civilian look. He is not in uniform as much as he used to be; those long nights in the desert have been replaced by days filled with court appearances for union grievances and workers comp hearings. We pass several uniformed agents on our drive; a few times we get out and talk for a while. The agents we talk to who follow union activity recognize Chris right away; the ones who don't pay attention to the union look at his suit and tie with suspicion until they find out who he is.

There are peepholes throughout the metal in the primary fence, in the spots where the sheets have been welded together, and *in* the sheets themselves, where rust has eaten through. Each opening offers a one-eyed view of a clogged road or a busy restaurant or a sleeping dog—a small cutout of Tijuana, or the *Southside,* as Chris refers to it. It is true, in literal terms: Tijuana is on the southern side of the international line. And on the surface, *Southside* communicates basic directional information. But the word usually hits my ear like a cliché: *bad side of the tracks.* The agents who do not want to convey this cliché generally do not say *Southside* but they are outnumbered. Language is an identifying characteristic for any community, from the Kumeyaay to Border Patrol, and *Southside* is a prevailing term among agents.

"I was out one day," says Chris, as we approach Otay Mesa, "I was at a 7-Eleven, 6:30 in the morning, the start of the day shift—I was in uniform. This guy came up and said, 'Can I talk to you?' I knew what was coming because I've heard this story before: 'My bosses just fired me. I want you to go after the company.' It was a company that did lawn care on a large scale, apartment complexes and stuff like that. I knew exactly what he was going to say: he had finally adjusted his status, got his Green Card or something that made his status legal. As soon as his bosses found that out, they fired him because they knew he may ask for better pay and better working conditions. They don't even wait to see if he will. I've seen it over and over again. I told him, 'I'm sorry. I'll look into it. Thank you for doing the right thing and adjusting your status, but remember, the entire time you were illegal, you were okay with them.' I felt bad for him, but there was not much I could do.

"And it's not just Mexicans. You hear 'A day without Mexicans.' That's bullshit and I think that actually does them a disservice. Anyone from a Third World country works hard. Look at Southern California lawn services. There are bound to be illegals. To them, twelve-hour days mowing lawns are nothing compared to the eighteen-hour days in the sweatshop. They're willing to work their asses off. But they also get abused and taken advantage of by these corporations like Tyson Foods[4]—and I use them by name because they got busted several times on a large scale. And companies like Qualcomm,[5] companies that are saying, 'We can't find people to work these engineering jobs.' You can't find them? You have the guys already. Some of these companies are firing them after training their replacements from India because they'll work for two thirds the salary.[6] At the high end and low end, these corporations are taking advantage of this.

"We've all seen the movie version of Charles Dickens's *A Christmas Carol*. We laugh about those silly Victorians, poor Bob Cratchit has to beg Ebenezer Scrooge for half a day off on Christmas. Well, we've regressed past that: We have people working full days on Christmas. I watched Fox News one time and there was some corporate Republican right-wing guy talking about retail staying open for Christmas and he was saying, 'That's the new paradigm and get used to it because we have to be competitive.' I'm like, 'Where are the fucking family values by telling a mother she has to be at work on Christmas Day leaving her kids at home to sell a fucking TV set?' How did we get to that point?

"I was at a table at a Republican event in a casino. There was the mayor of one town and a bunch of Republicans and they were good people. They knew me—I was there as a guest for the union. And George P. Bush, Jeb's son, was the keynote speaker. He was going on about slashing taxes and slashing government at the local and state level and federal level, like what they had done in Texas—slash, slash, slash. Everyone was cheering and clapping, standing ovations, and so I looked around the table and said, 'You guys hate cops, huh?' I wanted to provoke a reaction. 'No, no, we love cops.' 'Really? Because that's not what you're saying. You should understand that when you're talking about slashing at the federal level, you're talking about slashing the DEA, the FBI, Secret Service, Bureau of Prisons,

National Park Service rangers, the military, *us*, the local level, firefighters and cops.' 'Oh, that's not what we mean.' 'But that's what you're saying. You get that, right? You've got to think about what you're saying and what it really means.'"

By now we've made it out to Otay Mesa and, in the distance, I can see the spot where the secondary fence ends. The construction area is closed off, wrapped in a new chain link fence. I was out this way just two days ago and it was still an open space. The new fencing makes it feel like the work might actually begin soon. I want to ask Chris what he knows but just as I point toward the construction site he starts a U-turn. "I've got to head back to Imperial Beach," he says.

"Okay, but what's with the new fencing here?"

"Is that new? Not sure."

"Does that mean they're going to start building the prototypes?"

"Not my department, friend. Check in with Public Affairs."

We get turned back west and Chris hits the gas, as if he can't get away from the construction site fast enough. I turn around for one more look but it's already gone behind a cloud of dust.

CHAPTER 7

I TRY TO GET ROQUE De La Fuente on the phone to see if he knows anything about the new fencing but can't get through to him. I go to see David Wick instead. "It's all along your property," I tell him in the NEI conference room. "Did you guys put that up or was that Border Patrol?"

"Some of it was put up by the Border Patrol," he says, "and some of it was put up by the Sheriff's Department."

"Ah, so you guys didn't put up any of it?"

"No."

"Interesting. That means now there's not really any way to see the action at the prototype site anymore."

I give David a moment to respond. He says nothing so I spell it out: "Would it be okay with you if I tell Border Patrol that you guys are giving me access to the land?"

"What would be the . . . ?" He doesn't quite finish, pausing for a moment, which worries me that he might be thinking about making me buy a ticket and a hot dog. He says he's concerned because I recently asked him to introduce me to an archaeologist, which is true, but I only asked because I'm interested in the layers of history buried beneath the border. David put the two together, the request for an archaeologist *and* access to the land, and got the idea—mistakenly and quite flatteringly—that I might be a closeted Indiana Jones. "You hit on archaeology," he says, "so I'm not sure if you're out there looking for stuff."

I assure him I don't have a treasure map.

David nods, mumbles "sure," and I thank him before heading out to the desert.

CHAPTER 8

BACK IN OTAY MESA THE scene has become more complicated: *another* new chain link fence blocks the spot where the paved road becomes a rocky desert path. There is an open gate but Border Patrol agents sit on either side of it—one in a sedan, the other on an ATV. When I approach them and offer Roque's name they give me nothing but blank stares in return. It occurs to me that I might have said it too timidly, so I say it again, with a bit more authority this time: "Roque De La Fuente." Then, stabbing for emphasis or legitimacy, I add: "National Enterprises."

There are a couple of problems with the situation: I am certainly not dressed like a respectable businessman and agents in the Otay Mesa desert do not generally feel warmth at the mention of Roque's name. But still it works and the agents wave me through, annoyed.

I navigate the uneven dirt road, steering around the bigger rocks, keeping my dust cloud to a minimum as I crawl along. Just short of the prototype site I stop and turn off the car. There are far more agents than usual and I can feel eyes on me from nearly every direction. Generally an hour here might bring an encounter with one patrol, rarely two. But now I spot four agents, each at a different perch.

A couple hundred feet outside the passenger side of my car is the Mexico-U.S. border, marked by the secondary and primary fences. I see the patrols outside the window on my side of the car, to the north under the scrub oak—and through the windshield, to the east, with ATVs snaking up into the Otay Mountain Wilderness. The desert all around me isn't so open anymore. It's not just the new fencing at the construction site and the place where the paved road ends but in other spots too. New sections of fencing are spread out over dozens of acres, blocking every possible access point to the general vicinity of the prototypes; there is so much new chain link fencing it's starting to look something like a maze. And there are still more sections of unused fencing stacked five feet high, indicating the work isn't done.

I roll down the window and pull out my notebook:

—*In "Touch of Evil," Ramon Miguel Vargas (played by Charlton Heston) tells us, "All border towns bring out the worst in a country."*

The stillness is unsettling; I breathe shallowly so that I do not disturb it. I want to go right up to the chain link fence at the construction site and peek past the green tarpaulin but I feel the need to be less conspicuous. I decide to walk up to the fence. Just as I move to open my door, a dust cloud materializes a mile or so up the road, presaging the rickety shocks I hear moments later. Then I see the SUV coming my way, and the agent behind the wheel stops abruptly once our driver-side windows are aligned. As the dust cloud peters out between us, I hear an electronic window slide down and then his voice: "What are you up to today?"

The dust clears but I still can't see him all that well because of his dark sunglasses. "Just exploring," I say. "I'm with Roque De La Fuente."

"Can I see some ID?"

"Sure, sure." I acquiesce without hesitation. I acquiesce because I am an Anglo, heterosexual, cisgender, middle-class, Christian-bred man in 2017. I acquiesce because I am from Irvine, two hours up the 5 Freeway, where my family arrived in 1985 and found a white majority, infinitesimal crime rates, and revered police—all three endured throughout my upbringing, continue to this day, and permeate down the white-collar coast all the way to the 8 Freeway. I acquiesce because I am what John Edgar Wideman would call "Non-Colored." I noticed his use (invention?) of the term in *American Histories*, and when I asked what he meant by it he said, "We usually think of colored Americans as the ones who are different. The way I put it means that there is no hierarchy. The difference is in people's minds."[1] I immediately acquiesce for the agent who asks for my ID because, as a *Non-Colored* who has always passed for "white," I have been spared any fears about cooperating with authority.

It's a good thing too, because this agent oozes authority as he gets out of his SUV. There is much grayness with regard to tolerated wandering in the liminal zone—depending on the character, political beliefs, religious views, family history, likes, dislikes, mood, and gut feeling of each individual agent—and from the way this agent looks at me it's clear he would prefer it if I didn't wander anywhere near the construction site.

He takes my ID and gets back into his vehicle for five minutes or so. When he returns he asks me to confirm my last border crossing, which I do, and he checks what I say against what comes back to him over the two-way radio clipped to his chest. My story checks out and he tells me that "a couple of the guys" have been spotting me a lot lately.

"Do you plan to be in the area on a regular basis?" he asks.

"I do, yes."

"Okay, then we'll note your plates so the other guys know we've already checked you."

"Oh but this isn't my car. It's a rental."

"You rented *this* car? To drive on *this* road?" He takes a step back to look at just how close the bottom of my Ford Fiesta is to the rocky path.

"I don't live in California anymore," I say. "Just visiting regularly."

"For what?"

"I'm trying to figure out what a border actually looks like and how it functions every day. I want to talk to everyone who knows the border best."

He offers nothing—not even a nod.

This is often my approach with agents: tell them what I am doing in as much detail as they will allow. The practice repels the assholes who don't have the patience and helps identify those who might have some thoughts on the matter. I give audience whenever the opportunity presents itself.

But there will be no riffing today, as the agent cuts me off to advise that I keep the visit short. He hands back my ID and tells me there are going to be more patrols, as there is increased concern about trespassing.

"Got it," I say. And then to make sure I got it I say, "You're talking about protests against the prototypes," and I let the statement linger like a question.

"That is a possibility. No one is supposed to have access to this area."

"Even Mr. De La Fuente?"

"The landowners have signed documents giving us permission to arrest anyone who trespasses."

"Oh, no worries, David Wick knows I'm here."

"Just keep it short." He gets back in the SUV and continues toward the other agents who had initially let me in at the gate near the paved road. A helicopter circles overhead. Walking up to the fence at the construction site doesn't seem like such a good idea today. I decide to cross and try the view from Las Torres instead.

CHAPTER 9

IN FRONT OF AURELIA ÁVILA'S house, there is a mound of dirt that provides just enough height to see over the nine-foot-tall primary fence and get a full view of the prototype site. The fence is not actually nine feet, that's more of an average. The fence is eight feet or nine-and-a-half or seven-and-a-half, depending on where the measured spot is in the undulating desert.

Aurelia and Gaudencio are in front of their house, sorting through the recycling haul for the day. I share the mound of dirt against the primary fence with an artist named Jill Marie Holslin. She's been taking pictures of the border for ten years, mostly in California. She is a regular in Las Torres—and the person who originally introduced me to Aurelia's family. Jill has lived in Tijuana for six years and is always up for an excursion anywhere along the border. She is fluent in Spanish, fearless behind the wheel, and feels like a patient older sister, always willing to let me tag along.

The construction site in front of us is empty and still. Some equipment has been brought in, mostly for surveillance and security—portable stadium lights, concrete barriers—but there is no one working, just Aurelia and Gaudencio and the sound of aluminum cans landing on top of each other, and Jill's shutter closing in spurts.

"Have you heard anything about when they're going to start work?" I ask.

"Nope," she says. "Apparently they're going to put up a 'Free Speech Zone' for anyone who wants to come out and protest but it's all the way over there on Enrico Fermi," she says, pointing west. "It's an empty lot that's something like three miles away from here. What's the point?"

"Do you know if anyone's planning anything big?"

"I haven't heard anything yet. Reporters are talking, that's for sure—this is the big media story now. It's like San Diego is finally discovering this location," she says, laughing, "like it never existed before."

Jill puts the cap on her lens and pushes her glasses up the bridge of her nose as she steps off the mound of dirt. She has salt-and-pepper hair and wears a green cargo vest, making the most of all the pockets for her phone, keys, more lenses. She walks over to her car and grabs a large brown envelope with printed copies of photos she recently took of Aurelia and her daughter, Melanie. She gives them to Aurelia who half beams, half blushes when she sees them. The images make Gaudencio flash his proud, nearly toothless smile. We all remark on how hot it is, and Gaudencio reminds us not to wish it away because the cold is coming.

After Jill and I say goodbye we go for lunch. We get a little lost exiting Las Torres—we often do. Jill knows the city well but the travel patterns in Las Torres are tricky. The roads that cut between rows of cinder block, scrap wood, and lean-to homes are not paved and often end abruptly; there are no road signs so the uneven, jagged blocks are not easy to keep track of—Google has no idea what's going on here. In Las Torres a sense of direction is born of intimacy more than any reliable map.

It is a working-class neighborhood, or colonia, one of dozens tucked up in the foothills east of downtown Tijuana. Decades ago—as Roque De La Fuente circled overhead, envisioning just how big his future could get—these neighborhoods were detached from the city, more rural in feel. But Tijuana has since grown, particularly after the implementation of NAFTA, and the colonias are now linked to the city by miles of maquiladoras. Churning out American brands, the manufacturing facilities line some of the best-paved roads in town.

Many of the people who live in the colonias work in the maquiladoras. These are compact neighborhoods, outsiders are definitely noticed, kids walk to school, and in the luncherías and abarrotes people are generally patient about giving directions to a gringo with busted Spanish.

Eventually we find a distinct Las Torres landmark: three tire swings hanging from a giant electricity tower, each painted a bright color—blue, yellow, and green. From there, Jill and I get back to Calle 16 de Septiembre, which is broad, paved, and aimed straight at downtown.

Still, the journey in that direction is challenging. The roads are owned by eighteen-wheelers pulling in and out of the maquiladoras, and closer to downtown the lines demarcating lanes lose their significance.

When Jill moved to Tijuana in 2011, downtown neighborhoods like Zona Centro and Zona Norte were already undergoing transformations. Cartel violence had spiked in 2008, scaring away visitors. Bars, restaurants, and nightclubs that had catered to tourists shut down or reinvented themselves to suit locals looking for a different scene. "When I moved here," says Jill, "grandchildren of TJ business leaders started revitalizing underdeveloped, poorer parts of the city with hipster scenes. A lot of people were just handing out free drinks to their friends and it was like, dude, you should be charging me for this," she says, shaking her head thinking about it. "A lot of places were not viable. There was that wave."

Survivors from that wave remain, and other mezcal-drenched bars have come along since, clustered on Calle Sexta, for instance, where at night, plywood decor vibrates with techno beats and drum kits. Days are scented with stale beer and fresh tortas.

The city's violent crime rates have stayed well below the 2008 peak and so the skyline remains under revision. In 2016 there were dozens of condominium high-rises under construction in Zona Centro alone.[1] Real estate developers with international portfolios have been buying up Tijuana for several years now. "A lot of these condo complexes are sort of like chain hotels," says Jill. "They're building precisely the same building in ten different sites all across Latin America—the same building. They pay no attention to the site where the building is located; they pay no attention to the city. It's just like, 'We've got our Holiday Inn and we're going to plop it down here.' They're tearing it all down and chasing people out."

The luxury housing—luring buyers with swimming pools and surveilled parking spots—occupies a stratosphere separate from the immigrants who have driven so much of Tijuana's growth. While there are plenty of buyers from Latin America and the U.S.—mainly California—who might be looking for an investment or pied-à-terre in Tijuana, so many of the newer communities in the city are made up of working-class migrants from around the world. Some have taken jobs in the maquiladoras; others want to continue on to the U.S. but haven't yet figured out how to do so, or tried already and been deported—deportados is the word in Mexican media and politics. Deportados are, in effect, stateless. They cannot return to their home countries because there is no work or safety. Deportados do not have legal status in Mexico and some have already been removed from the U.S. several times. "The reason people come to the border," says Jill, "is because they don't have any other options. It's violence, it's dispossession, it's primitive accumulation."

We stop for lunch at a place with a few plastic tables and chairs, a soccer match on the television—it feels more living room than restaurant. Jill has been here before and recommends the aguas frescas so we order a couple to go with our chicken plates.

Before moving to Tijuana, Jill lived in San Diego for twenty-three years but eventually got pushed out by an escalating housing shortage across the county. The median home price in the county is $655,000 and only 27 percent of households can afford it.[2] Ninety-four percent of low-income earners in the city of San Diego spend their whole paycheck on rent.[3] The region's population is growing and the shortage of housing—particularly affordable housing—is intensifying.

This increase in the cost of living has been steady across the county since the 2007 housing crisis. Over the last decade of rebound, residents who were priced out of life north of the 8 infiltrated neighborhoods just south of the freeway. Yoga studios and gourmet doughnuts overtook North Park and Hillcrest long ago. The reach of San Diego's gentrification has now extended into Tijuana—and by gentrification I mean displacement. The founding of America was defined, in large part, by displacement; the displacement of the people who were already living in communities across the continent—the Kumeyaay and beyond. And displacement remains a defining part of American behavior in places like Central Brooklyn, Austin's East Side, West Oakland, and dozens of neighborhoods south of the 8 Freeway. Marking property, claiming The Dream, has almost always involved removing someone from it first.

The entanglement between San Diego and Tijuana predates any recent economic graphs. Take the red-light district. It's in the Tijuana neighborhood of Zona Norte where it's referred to locally as la zona de tolerancia. "A friend of mine recently asked me why there isn't a red-light district in San Diego," Jill says. "And I told her, 'San Diego doesn't need a red-light district. It has Zona Norte!'"

There is a message, *written in English*, painted onto the side of a police booth in the neighborhood and it reads: Working to serve you Better!

Jill escaped the cost of living in San Diego but she also ran away from the U.S. "I have gone out of my way to *not* hang out with gringos. I've caught myself at parties saying something like, 'Oh man, now all these douchebag Americans are living here.' Partly I was saying it to make people laugh; partly I was saying it because I felt that way. And I realized that's bizarre. But for me there's something about imagining this place as a refuge and escape from San Diego.

"And people say to me all the time: 'Oh you have to meet my friend. She's from the United States.' It's just so funny because everybody here automatically thinks, oh, you're going to have so much in common with someone else from the United States. But no. Zero in common," she says, laughing. "A lot of it comes out of my politics, anti-imperialist activism for twenty years. But then, of course, I realize that the idea that I can run away from imperialism is kind of silly. But can't I find some kind of refuge?"

Before I can answer her question, which I will probably never be able to answer, she continues: "It's like I have this whole mythology around myself, right? I came here not because I wanted to save money on rent. I came here because I already spoke Spanish. I came here because I wanted to be a professional here and do things I couldn't do in San Diego. I came here because I want to be an artist. So I have this whole mythology around myself, which is, I'm not like anybody else, I'm not like all those other gringos. And it's partly true but it's partly the story I build around myself."

The woman running the dining room comes over to check on us. She speaks in Spanish with a French accent and asks if we want anything else to eat. We've already sucked the last traces of meat from the bones, but it's still hot outside so we order another round of the aguas frescas and stay a while.

Jill tells me that the woman with the French accent is from Haiti and she's been running the place for a few months now. "You have this experience where every five blocks it seems like a new group," says Jill. "Very quickly, you say: 'Oh, now we're in the Ecuadorian part and now we're in the El Salvadorian part. Tijuana, to me, has that kind of texture.'"

Over the past two years, the growth of the Haitian community is unmatched in Tijuana—20,000 arrived in the second half of 2016 alone.[4] Some have been migrating since 2010, when an earthquake in Haiti displaced more than 1.5 million.[5] The majority of those who made it to Tijuana have decided to stay but, for some, the journey continues north.

CHAPTER 10

IN 2016, SIX THOUSAND HAITIANS crossed into San Diego County.[1] I'm meeting one of them who is staying above an old church sanctuary that doubles as a shelter for migrants. Those who know the place call it "the loft." It's in the Normal Heights neighborhood of San Diego, about a mile south of the 8.

The entrance to the back of the old sanctuary leads directly into a small kitchen, which is empty when I show up. But the room is filled with the smell of spices seeping out of the crockpot on the counter. I say "Hello" but there's no answer so I walk past the kitchen, down a long hallway. It leads to a room with two sets of triple bunk beds. Three women sit together, all crowded onto one of the lower beds, conversing in French. Two of the women hold sleeping newborns in their arms. The room is all function: bare walls, fluorescent lights, suitcases all over the floor, all open, all in flux.

"Is Civile here?" I ask.

They all smile but no one says anything.

I try once more, "Civile?"

They all nod and smile and one of them points in the direction of the staircase just outside their room.

"Upstairs—thank you," I say.

They do not speak English and I do not speak French; we try Spanish for a minute but don't get too far past greetings and good wishes, which is a start, so we smile at each other and I step back into the hall and head to the second floor.

Upstairs, Civile Ephedouard is sitting alone in a room with two sets of triple bunk beds, just like downstairs. Five of the beds are bare mattresses being used as shelving for large rolling bags stuffed with donated items—clothes, shoes, baby accoutrement, all of which needs to be sorted. Only one bottom bed has sheets and a pillow.

Civile is sitting at a desk cluttered with donated electronic devices—two phones, a desktop, a tablet—none of which are fully functional. He's tinkering with all of them, trying to get each in working order. His jeans are drying in the window behind him. A smoke detector chirps in the hall, tracking the crawl of time. Civile is waiting. He is waiting to receive an update on his asylum case; he is waiting for a pro bono lawyer to call him back. Civile is waiting for another laptop donation, one that *might* be working; he is waiting for a work permit. Asylum seekers can get permits if their case has not closed after 180 days. Civile's case has been open for 270 days. He crossed into the U.S. after two years of migration. He was forty-two when he left Port-au-Prince; he is forty-four now, and still unsettled.

He grew up speaking Creole and French. Traveling through eight countries on his way to the U.S., he picked up Spanish, English, a little bit of Portuguese. He tells me that the women downstairs are from Congo-Kinshasa. "I have not yet traveled to Africa," he says, scratching at his strong jawline. "But I hope to. Because my roots are in Africa, I have to go there." He reminds me that Haiti was the first republic established by revolutionary ex-slaves.

He was born in the countryside, raised in Port-au-Prince, and went to trade school for electrical work and plumbing. He lost his home and all his belongings after the 2010 earthquake, as did most of his extended family. He managed to get a house rebuilt for his mother, but still unable to find work, he decided to leave for the U.S.

Civile traveled first to the Dominican Republic with one bag of clothes and documents, including his certifications in plumbing and electrical work. He flew to Ecuador where he found a job for four months in Quito. From there, he applied for a work permit in Brazil.

At the time, Brazil was racing to complete construction on all of its 2016 Olympic facilities and the government issued 43,000 work visas to displaced Haitians.[2] For eight months, Civile worked in a laundromat, washing clothes for the other migrants who were building the athlete villages and competition arenas. When the Games arrived and the work ran out, Civile started hopping on northbound buses, from Peru to Colombia, through Panama and Costa Rica, and he eventually wound up at the

Mexico-U.S. border. "I went directly to the door of immigration," he tells me. "When I got to the border I applied for asylum because everybody knows Haiti is a poor country. It is a country where people lead a difficult life because of the missing responsibility of the leaders, missing job. The first thing people need to live is a job. If there is no job you cannot just stay there until you die."

Since 2012, only 14 percent of Haitians who have sought asylum in the U.S. have been granted it; this is an even lower rate than 21 percent for Salvadorans or 22 percent for Hondurans over the same five-year period.[3] The outcome depends so much on individual judges all over the country, and even though some already have rejection rates as high as 90 percent,[4] moving through a couple dozen hearings in a day, the Justice Department is currently drafting a memorandum outlining possible disciplinary action for those who do not meet case completion quotas.[5] Even without the memorandum finalized it's not uncommon for a determinative hearing to last a couple of minutes. And for that brief experience migrants often wait years. In 2017, the number of pending cases has climbed to over half a million and the total is growing.[6]

The U.S. government grants asylum only if it is convinced that a person faces a real and immediate threat of persecution. And the persecution must derive from a few very exact categories—skin color, religion, nationality, political beliefs—but there is one wild card: persecution because of "membership in a particular social group." It is the only broadly worded category that can be utilized by a range of people—to varying degrees of success: a child soldier, a transgender person, someone whose family member has crossed a crime organization, a woman—it is a catchall for any established identity that becomes the target of violence.

Civile is applying for asylum through this social group category but wants to get a lawyer before he talks about the personal circumstances that drove him to the U.S. "The time will come," he tells me. "Not yet."

Asylum seekers are not guaranteed legal representation and the majority go without. Those who are lucky enough to have a lawyer are five times more likely to win a case.[7] "You cannot represent yourself alone in front of the judge," Civile says. "You need a defender."

Civile spent twelve days at the Otay Mesa detention facility after requesting asylum at the San Ysidro Port of Entry. He was then transferred to Adelanto, 150 miles north in San Bernardino County, while his case began sputtering through the court system. After eight weeks he secured his release from detention by fulfilling two requirements: he found a friend from Haiti to sponsor him with a place to live and a bond company to put up the $17,000 required by the court. "They just take the money in your hand," he says, "and release you in this country without any papers, without any documents."

U.S. Immigration did give Civile a tracking device to wear on his ankle—and the bond company gave him a second one. "I don't know if you know much about bond companies," he says. "They will send the bond money if you give them 20 percent. After the 20 percent, I paid $880 for an ankle monitor like this one. And every month I have to pay $420—while I still owe $17,000. The $420 is just for interest." Most months Civile can't make any payment at all and the interest accumulates. Apropos of the American Experience, Civile is beginning his life in this country with overwhelming debt. He scratches at his shaved head and shrugs because it could have been worse: "I have a friend of mine who got a bond for $35,000."

The friend who helped Civile put up the 20 percent required by the bond company was also the one who took him in. The two lived together in Los Angeles but the arrangement was short-lived: the friend was also a recent immigrant, just a bit further along assembling his life, and he had already overextended himself with the bond payment and temporary shelter. But he knew about the loft in San Diego, and he knew Bill Jenkins, the man who had opened it. "My friend said to me, 'Send an email to Bill.' So I sent an email and Bill sent an email to me and said, 'Okay, you will be welcomed.'" After just a few weeks in Los Angeles, Civile got a ride from his friend to San Diego and moved into the loft.

"People say I need to get my working permit to let me work. So I applied two months ago. Immigration send me an email to say they receive my request. But up until now I don't receive anything. I'm still staying here, like this. I am able to do any kind of job but I don't got any money to pay the bond company. If I can't work, I can't pay. Some months there are some people who pay for me but that can't happen every month. And what is important for me is to get some work to do."

He walks the neighborhood looking for people who might need help with landscaping, painting, moving, housework. He's become friendly with a few elderly people who have paid him to tag along on shopping trips and help load groceries or big boxes into cars. The reach of San Diego County buses and trolleys limits where he can look for work, and he must let immigration know if he travels outside the county. He sweeps the courtyard outside the loft and helps look after the place—no income, just purpose. "Sometimes there is an older person from Africa who comes here and they don't speak too much English," he says. "I don't speak English very well but at least I can help the communication pass with him a little bit."

Civile came to San Diego with no contacts, only Bill's invitation. Most of the people he has met either stay at the loft, volunteer, or live in the neighborhood. "Just now I'm creating a family," he says. "I don't only consider people family when we're from the same blood. It could be that I create family with you. It depends," and this word he repeats, sticking it the second time, "it *depends*, on the way that we are living. Family is the persons who know how to live together. We create the possibility together, to live together."

A friend set up a GoFundMe campaign to help raise money for Civile's next bond payment. He pulls up the webpage on his phone and through the shattered glass screen of the donated device I see that the campaign has only secured $80 toward its goal of $420.

"I don't give money the first place in my life. I don't give food the first place in my life. I need them to live but they are not the first thing in my life. The first thing in my life is peace of mind. The first thing in my life is health and freedom. I am outside but I don't have freedom yet. I want to sleep normal. I want to get my own car, my own job, and pay my normal rent. And take care of my family. All the good things in a life. Somebody who has a normal life can't sleep like this," and he motions to his bottom bunk in a room overwhelmed by bulging rolling bags stacked to the ceiling. There is an immediacy to the items in the bags—from khakis to diapers, to extra-wide shoes and generic reading glasses—each donation is a reminder of the practical needs that stack up for a person who shows up with only a backpack of clothes and certifications for plumbing and electrical work.

Before I leave the loft I ask Civile if there is a particularly good time of day to come around again. He smiles for only the second time in two hours and says, "I am always available." On my way down the stairs, the smoke detector chirps once more and I am reminded that it will continue to do so even after I have shut the door behind me.

I step into the grassy courtyard and stare up at the old sanctuary from the outside. Next to it is another wing of the building with signs indicating offices. I walk that way, looking for Bill Jenkins, the man who invited Civile to stay in the loft—we've spoken only briefly on the phone and he told me to drop in to say hello.

A couple of volunteers lead me back to his office and he waves me in from behind his desk. He is a retired Methodist minister and says he still brings out the collar occasionally but today he's casual in a short sleeve, blue-striped pullover. He has a big smile and a shock of white hair. Bill was born and raised in the Mississippi Delta and you can still hear it in his voice. "There was nine of us living in a four-room tenant house without running water or electricity. I know what it's like when someone gives you a hand up. That's all you need is just someone to believe in you."

He moved to San Diego eighteen years ago when his wife got a job with the Department of Defense. The only post that was available to him was at the Christ United Methodist Church in Normal Heights. "Nobody else wanted this church because it was a career ender," he says. "I was told it was a falling knife. In the ministry, if you want to make a move, you always want to make a move up, but this was a church on the way down. Basically, I was brought in here to help this church die."

Bill was able to keep the congregation alive for twelve years. "The last Sunday when I preached," he says, "we had thirty-five people in the sanctuary, which is depressing—that sanctuary is built to hold three hundred. You've seen this movie before."

When the church leadership shut down the parish, Bill talked the bishop out of selling the building; he was convinced he could convert it into a community center instead. "I said, 'As far as a Bible church at eleven o'clock on Sunday morning, that's not sustainable, but I have a vision here of this becoming an urban ministry center. And the bishop said, 'What is an urban ministry center?' I said, 'I don't know, but if we follow the Holy Spirit, we'll find out.'"

In the six years since, the facilities have served as clinic, food pantry, teaching center for everything from English classes to help with résumés— and of course there's the loft. But Bill says it's not always easy for the center to get to the people who need help the most. "A lot of times people won't come to get free services that we offer," he says. "We have two free clinics, we have a food ministry; many migrants will not come to get that because they're afraid now to put their name down because they may not be documented."

The old church is now known as Christ Ministry Center and Bill works to make sure the old sanctuary remains, in one way or another, a sanctuary. "We have fourteen different congregations that share space in this building," he says. "They come from all over the world. Several of them are Hispanic. We're a seven-day-a-week church. I have over a thousand people come through the doors every week. Most mornings when I get here, there are already two hundred people in the building. Never did I have two hundred sitting in the pews.

"The loft was never intended for this but it's basically a big shared apartment—right behind the pulpit. I have eighteen mattresses in there and the city says I can only have six. But I'm not going to say no. I'm not going to have a pregnant woman or a woman with small children on the street. It's just not going to happen.

"We've had folks from all over the world here. We've had folks from the Marshall Islands, we've had people from Ethiopia, Eritreans, Hondurans, Haitians. To my knowledge, we are the only migrant shelter in Southern California. If you go over to Mexico, there are several—and a lot of them are run by the Catholic Church and they do an awesome job. And when migrants cross the border, they ask the question, 'Where is the shelter?' And the answer is 'There are none for migrants. Go to the Methodist church, they'll take you.' And so, we do.

"After the Haitians built the Olympic stadiums in Brazil and the government there kicked them out, we had what I call the 'mass exodus.' About 6,000 Haitians were able to cross the border. Five thousand of them came here, into *this* building, because nobody else would take them. Starting on June 1, 2016, we were averaging thirty-three new arrivals every day, seven days a week for six months.

"Our councilman called and he said he was getting a lot of complaints. I said, 'Fine, come on, shut me down. I've got three hundred people in the building. You take them.' He said, 'Well, we'll work with you.' I said, 'When they stop coming across the border, we'll stop, but as long as they keep coming, we're not going to turn them away.'"

Some stayed for a couple of nights, others stayed for months. At one point, Bill had 307 people sleeping in the building. "We had people in the sanctuary, sleeping on the pews, under the pews, in the hallway upstairs.

You couldn't even walk in the hallway at night because they were laid all the way down the hall.

"If you spent one hour with each person that comes in—to find out who they are, why they're here and what they're needs are, if they want to move on to Florida or Boston or wherever—if you spend one hour with every person, there are twenty-four hours in a day, you wouldn't get any sleep and then there are thirty-three more—we were like that, constantly doing that."

The federal government has indicated in public statements that it will not renew the Temporary Protected Status that was granted to over 60,000 Haitians who arrived in the U.S. in the years after the earthquake.[8] Bill estimates that 90 percent of the 5,000 Haitians he helped have gone on to places like Montreal and Toronto to seek legal status and preempt the possibility of deportation. "A lot of them had become productive citizens," says Bill. "They had jobs, they were paying taxes and becoming a vital part of this community."

Among the migrants who have remained is Harry, age five. "When they said this little boy needed a foster home we couldn't get any Haitians to take him because they were suffering. So my wife said, 'We'll take him.' My mouth dropped open! We were sixty-eight years old and going to become foster parents? Really? That was not in my plan. But the minute he walked in the house, it was like somebody flipped on a light.

"The last thing I did this morning before I left was give him a big hug and a kiss. If we can adopt him, we will. I don't know that we're going to get the chance to, but he's changed our lives. God sent him into our home to heal us. I needed healing." Bill stops himself from crying by bringing out his phone to show me more pictures of Harry. I say *more* pictures because Bill's bookshelves and filing cabinet and desk are already adorned with images of the boy and his dimples.

"I'm preaching this Sunday," he says, staring at Harry. "I don't do it often but every now and then I still get up there. And this Sunday I'm preaching on the fact that from the beginning of Genesis—Adam and Eve were kicked out of the Garden of Eden, they were migrants—all the way to the last story in Revelation, John the Apostle was exiled—*exiled* I emphasize—to the Island of Patmos. From the beginning of the Bible to the end of the Bible, it is a story of human migration."

CHAPTER 11

THE PRESENCE OF LAW ENFORCEMENT is growing around the construction site. It's not just more Border Patrol agents but police officers from the city of San Diego are on the scene more often now, as are sheriff's deputies and California Highway Patrol officers. All the agencies are working together to coordinate responses to any possible protests, sharing the anxiety. Recently I overheard two Border Patrol agents fretting about protesters. They talked in a room just off the lobby at sector headquarters, where I sat waiting for a different agent.

"We still aren't getting any protesters," I could hear one of them say to the other, "which is shocking. I would have expected they'd be out there once the fencing went up."

"They're going to *have* to come, at some point," said the other.

"Yeah."

"I mean, they *want* to come—it's fundamentally against what they believe so they're going to protest."

One agent noted that "protecting Standing Rock" cost $20 million.

"That's not our worry," said the other. "It's a state issue."

Local law enforcement agencies are picking up the tab for security around the construction site. The idea is that managing protests falls under the jurisdiction of local agencies because Border Patrol needs to stay focused on its mandate: protecting the border. But the reality is that protecting the border in San Diego County means being the biggest law enforcement agency around. There are 2,200 Border Patrol agents working in San Diego County, more than the number of officers in any police department, more than the total number of sheriff's deputies, or Highway Patrol officers working in the county.[1] This creates problems for people like

National City chief of police Manuel Rodriguez. "One of the things I've learned in law enforcement is that you can't be an invading army," he says.

Manuel has been a police officer for thirty-two years, first with San Diego and now with National City, an intimate enclave of 58,582 in the middle of the South Bay. Manuel sits behind his desk in a full uniform with a firearm at his side. He might be in an air-conditioned office for the moment but with just ninety-two officers he is always ready to respond to action. His radio rarely stops and he turns it down but never completely tunes it out. "If people perceive you as an invading army," he says, "you are going to lose their support. And if you lose their support, you're not going to be around very long."

The feeling of an invading army is only enhanced by the way Border Patrol agents are dressed. While there are some plainclothes, undercover units, most agents are easy to spot in some variation of an OG-107, which is the basic utility uniform for the U.S. military. The "OG" indicates the olive green, classic army color of the fatigues. Boots and bulletproof vests are the usual accompaniments. But in the San Diego Sector there are several specialized units and a few different looks. The San Diego Sector Border Patrol Tactical Unit, or BORTAC, with elite agents trained for terrorist threats and combat conditions, is usually clad in Kevlar ballistic helmets when they practice parachute landings onto Roque De La Fuente's land. And each time I see them do so I can't escape the feeling that I am witnessing an invasion and, surely, I should notify someone.

The number of Border Patrol agents across the country has increased by more than 400 percent since 1992. They work for the only law enforcement agency empowered to enter private property without a warrant within twenty-five miles of the border.[2] Agents are also authorized to set up temporary checkpoints on public roads and highways: an intersection across from a school, a stoplight down the block from a factory. There are also four fixed highway checkpoints throughout the county—and at least 120 in the U.S., though the number fluctuates with changes in personnel and budgeting.[3] Encounters with agents at these checkpoints can rattle immigrants like the three French-speaking women I met in the loft, people who've fled places like Congo-Kinshasa—or Eritrea or Honduras or El Salvador—violent landscapes marked by checkpoints run by armed agents, only to arrive in a new landscape marked by checkpoints run by armed agents.

"You look around the world, people are fearful of law enforcement in Third World countries," Manuel says, "because they're often not looking at the welfare of the community. So when immigrants come to the United States and they have to deal with people in authority, it becomes challenging for them because they have this internal fear. And for us in law enforcement, it's a constant challenge to try to make sure that we work with immigrant communities, because they're afraid. And city leaders are on edge because constituents are calling them and saying, 'Look, is Border Patrol just driving around hauling people away?' And honestly, we have no reassurance for them other than we know it's not our police officers doing that."

Manuel grew up in National City but was born in Nogales, Mexico. "I'm actually one of the immigrants they always talk about," he says, laughing. "Spanish is my first language which made it really tough in elementary school because I was always in the slow reading group. And, as a kid, you think you're just dumb. When I was in junior high, they had me doing speech therapy because they said the *e-l*, I wasn't pronouncing it correctly. Of course, that's my first name, Manu*el*. But in English, I couldn't say it right. So I remember they used to drive up in this motorhome and they used to call me out of the class. And I used to go and sit there and practice with the therapist. I know the pressures that immigrants face, okay—from every direction—and that's before you even start talking about random checkpoints."

Whenever Border Patrol agents do set up a temporary checkpoint in National City, Manuel calls the sector chief to ask about it. "He'll say, 'Yes, I planned that checkpoint' or maybe he'll say, 'No, we weren't scheduled to have any checkpoint there today.' I think what happens sometimes is three or four of the Border Patrol guys just decided to do a checkpoint on their own and start checking people's immigration status. And I can see how that happens when you have a large agency.

"One time, somebody called me from the City Council and said, 'You know, Chief, we heard Border Patrol's out there.' I said, 'Well, they may be. They have the right to do that. As a police officer and even as the chief of police, there's nothing I can do.' I think people don't understand a federal agency like Border Patrol is controlled by the presidency. So they have to take whatever direction is given to them.

"What Border Patrol does by setting up a checkpoint is legal. *How* they do it, that's a different story. When you look at these things, yeah, they are legal. But when you look at *how* it was done, that is really where the challenge is."

How things are done at the border, the tone of things, has been set from the earliest days: in 1892, when a field party set out to *re*-survey the line between Mexico and the U.S.—the boundaries are not static—the team of sixty included twenty military escorts, a mix of infantry and cavalry.[4]

"We don't sever our relationship with Border Patrol," Manuel says, "because we know they need us. And we need them. One of the things with the passage of Senate Bill 54, it doesn't allow us to work with Border Patrol when they're dealing with people. But if Border Patrol calls us for cover, we're going to respond. Because what I have seen in my experience is, if Border Patrol needs us and we don't respond, things only get worse. When we get there, we're able to calm the situation down. We're able to let them do their work and we're able to deal with the public because the public recognizes us. We kind of bring legitimacy into this. And so we will always respond to calls for cover.

"But one of the things we always put out there as a police department is, 'Look, immigration status is not our concern. We're state officers. We're not federal officers. We don't really enforce federal laws. We enforce state laws. So if you're in the country illegally, we're not going to really mess with you. That's the message we're trying to get to people. We prioritize communicating within our communities—it helps build trust.

"When I first started in San Diego in the '80s, the IndoChinese community was often terrorized because they were afraid of law enforcement. Not because they were here illegally, but just because back in their country law enforcement was looked at as carrying out the policies of the regime. So what would happen is you had these bands of gangs that would do home invasion robberies, rape the girls, do all this stuff and the communities would never report it. They were afraid of the authorities and what the authorities were going to do to them. Well, the issue is that, as people commit these crimes with impunity, they get bolder and bolder and it just continues to grow.

"The more comfortable people are with law enforcement, the safer the city is. And I think that's what sometimes gets lost. The people in immigrant communities make a huge difference because they see things. And they can help you or hinder you."

CHAPTER 12

IT IS A SATURDAY MORNING and I'm looking at a roomful of wide-awake teenagers. They're getting fitted for uniforms. As they hover over boxes of trousers and shirts, samples of each size, a glass case gleams under the fluorescent light of an adjacent hallway, showing off trophies won by predecessors. The teenagers rummaging through the boxes are the latest recruits to Border Patrol's Explorer Program.

They have gathered in a conference room on Britannia Court in Otay Mesa, the building where Border Patrol maintains its Brown Field Station—the closest to the prototype site. April McKee is the agent in charge of all the teenagers. Twenty to thirty come through the program every year. April says three years is an ideal commitment. They give up six to seven hours every Saturday: one or two hours of physical training then the rest of the day is for talking through different scenarios, acting them out—making a traffic stop or approaching a crime scene. Eventually the Explorers will demonstrate their ability to role play these scenarios at competitions and, if they excel, bring back trophies to add to the case in the hall.

There are eight stations in the San Diego Sector and six of them have Explorer programs—the other two are in the most rural stretches of the county without enough kids to participate. "Youth is our greatest asset," says April. "The Explorers program allows us to get at kids so they do not become predisposed to not liking law enforcement." But then she adds another layer of purpose to the work she does—less defense, more offense: "The program allows us to guide the youth of the country."

When I ask her to describe the direction, the place to which she is guiding the Explorers, she says, "We teach that you need all the facts before you make a judgment. We teach trust but verify. And," she adds, "we teach them what it means to be a border agent."

"What does it mean to be a border agent?"

"My job is keeping people out who don't belong here. My job is to protect my country. The public has the privilege of not seeing what I see on a daily basis. And maybe they don't want to see it. I've come across cadavers on patrol—we all have—I've stayed hours with women to make sure they are safe after they were attacked by bandits. I approach my job with compassion and understanding. I've given away my lunch. I'm a firm believer in karma."

The word *bandit* sticks out—and it's not the first time April has used it in our interaction. I realize she's been an agent since 1995 but my mental image of a *bandit* goes back much further—decades, probably centuries. It requires stagecoaches and six-shooters. Using *bandit* instead of *criminal* sounds to me like an antiquated, romanticized kind of danger, woven into Manifest Destiny, westward expansion, staking a claim. But for April, and some of her fellow agents, the word is in regular rotation, the image of a bandit—a *border bandit*, more specifically—persists.[1]

With the stress of her job, April says it's gardening that keeps her steady. And the Explorers keep her steady. She still remembers what made her want to start working with the program nearly twenty years ago: "Seeing these kids, bright-eyed and bushy-tailed, I thought, 'I want to be a part of that.'" And most of all she still remembers the day the first girl joined Explorers. "It gets you *in the feels*," she says, bringing a white-knuckled claw up to her chest like she just might actually dig at her heart.

April introduces me to one of the Explorers named Giselle Haro. She is eighteen and earning an associate's degree at a nearby community college. Giselle has been an Explorer for a couple of years; the others are rummaging through boxes for the right size but she already has a uniform. Still, she beams with the freshness of a new arrival: "I *love* wearing the uniform," she says, flashing a smile. She stumbled onto the website for the program—she doesn't remember exactly how she got there, she only remembers one phrase: "'Protecting our borders.' That caught my attention," she says.

Initially it strikes me as odd that this phrase, *protecting our borders*, would catch the attention of any teenager but then I remember King Friday erecting a border fence around his castle on *Mister Rogers' Neighborhood*: regardless of whether it is nature or nurture or both, the idea of defending the lines that define us is there from the beginning.

Giselle doesn't hesitate when I ask what she's learned as an Explorer: "Responsibility. Taking responsibility for when I make a mistake."

April nods, approvingly. "These kids already know what it's like to be an agent," she says, "what's expected." As I ask Giselle questions, April is inches away, and I can see that Giselle feels the strong presence behind her: her answers remain brief, her shoulders clinched. Over the years I've proven adept at putting others at ease in conversation, mainly because I am so good at proving to be an ass in short order, but here I can't get Giselle to budge open. With April at her side, I wonder if Giselle has been taught evenhandedly about the humanity of Border Patrol agents and the humanity of writers. Or I should say *the media*. I'm sure April told Giselle that I am The Media. I don't feel like The Media. I feel more like a writer, and an ass, but this moment has little to do with my approach to work and—my bet says—so much more to do with how April prepared Giselle before meeting with me, and her surveillance of our conversation. So I thank the young Explorer and apologize for cutting into her time with the others.

Before we part, I ask Giselle what her friends at school think about the program. She shakes her head, letting slip what strikes me as her first unguarded response when she says she doesn't mention it to them. She likes to keep it private. "And besides," she adds, "my closest friends are already in Explorers."

CHAPTER 13

I'M LOOKING FOR MORE OF them, these Explorers, these eager protectors of the border. I find myself back in Manuel Rodriguez's hometown, National City, at the Community Youth Athletic Center. Edgar Sandoval has been the head volunteer boxing coach at CYAC for a year. "A lot of people get saved by sports," he says, "and I use that avenue to try to help people. That's what I try to do. I practically live at the club."

Edgar actually grew up a couple of miles closer to the border, in Chula Vista. "We were a rock throw away," he says. He went to Castle Park High School on Hilltop Avenue in the late 1990s, during a time when, a mile and a half down the road, the Arellano-Félix Organization—AFO cartel—held socials in Castle Park. "That's what they called them, 'socials,'" says Edgar, "that was the ambience."

Edgar was the first generation of his family born in the U.S. His parents came from the same Mexican state, Sonora, but very different backgrounds: "My mother's family, they were considered rich because wealth is in livestock and they had a little store. My dad was definitely worse off. He'd get up early in the morning at five years old selling eggs and shining shoes. He would tell me, 'Man, you don't know what hunger is.' And I *don't* know what hunger is because, as poor as we were here—we didn't have a lot of money—I was never hungry."

For decades Edgar's parents worked fifteen-hour days at low-wage jobs, a lot of food service, and, eventually, they became naturalized citizens.

His dad was a boxer and he determined Edgar would be one too. "He sat my ass down and I watched boxing every Saturday," he says. "I didn't have much of a choice." He joined his first club at nine and started boxing competitively at twelve. "I loved my coach to death. He was a grumpy-ass old Mexican man. He was very blunt, sometimes too blunt, but he trained us for free. He had a backyard boxing club that he built. He did everything on his own and he didn't charge us a dime. He was there with us every single day."

Edgar earned the name Vampire; apparently he kept sucking the life out of his opponents. He has a tattoo on his neck: blood coming out of a bite mark. "Everyone thinks it's bullet holes, but it ain't. It's definitely a conversation starter."

He is thirty-four now and, over the years, he added several tattoos; his body is, more or less, covered. "People will say, 'I thought you were a tattoo artist.' But they look at my nose and know I fight, so that's one thing I can't hide."

After high school he started coaching at a private boxing club. "It was an excellent center for people who can afford $130 a month. But a lot of kids don't have the money to pay that. So I started volunteering at a few different nonprofit clubs. My coach did it, so it was my time to give back. Eventually I found CYCA. It's placed in a perfect area, a very low-income area, and that's very appealing to me.

"A lot of the kids that I deal with are borderline associated with gangs. I try to get to them before it gets too far. I've got a little sixty-five-pounder, his dad's in prison. His introduction to law enforcement was when they ripped his dad out of his house. That's what he knows the police for. He's very timid. I have to be very gentle. I can say something, but I've got to tread lightly because you don't want to break them.

"Then I've got a fourteen-year-old kid who's been in foster homes his entire life. Mom's a user, gave him up for adoption. He's never had a place to call home. He's been arrested, he's pulled knives on people, he's smoking weed, drinking and he comes to me—that's the plate I got served to me. But when I saw him, I'm like, okay: the kid wants to fight. I gotta get that addiction in him, I gotta get him to want to box so bad that he will give up that other stuff. When you're dealing with an addiction, you always have to replace it with an addiction, always. That's the way out. You can't go cold turkey or you're always going to go back to it. You need to do something else and you've got to find it.

"And now I can honestly say this kid is addicted to boxing. He's addicted to the pain. He's a fighter. He's got so much potential. He's built—he just shreds it, that type of genetics. He needs a boot up his ass constantly to keep him in check and he's never had that. He's a fourteen-year-old going on twenty-five. He's probably lived more life than a lot of us. This kid, he's my project, man. He's still got the worst grades I've ever seen in my life, but he just started a new school year and I have access to all his stuff," Edgar says, smiling, "so I know when he's in class and when he's not. And he's so terrified of being taken away from the sport that he's willing to deal with it. 'We're going to call your coach'—that's his foster parents' go-to. And that's a shutdown immediately. I explained to them, 'Listen, that kid is one inch away from ruining it.' We're pack animals. If you go around hanging with gang members, you're going to do gang member things whether you're a gang member or not. I tell him, 'If you hang out with shitbags, you're going to do shitbag stuff.' He gets it, but he's a kid.

"When I was in high school a lot of these guys would look up to these narcos like they were gods. Let me just give you an idea of what it was like: we would be in assembly and as soon as a Mexican flag would come in, everybody would cheer. When they started singing the American national anthem, you would hear boos.

"People are raised different. I've always known I was American and my father was always: 'Treat law enforcement with respect.' That was normal to me. To hear the boos, it was like they forgot they were Americans too."

CYAC won Edgar over not only because of the kids he met but he also liked the composition of the board of directors: someone from the National City District Attorney's Office, someone from the Sheriff's Department, police officers. The respect for law enforcement, instilled by his strict father, is something Edgar started taking ownership of as an adolescent. "I was in seventh grade," he recalls, "and I found out about the Border Patrol Explorers program by doing my own research. I've always had some sort of fascination with law enforcement. It's something I wanted to do: wear a gun and a badge. Playing cops and robbers, I was always the cop. It was my niche."

When he was fifteen, Edgar became an Explorer. "You get introduced to a lot," he says, "the firearms aspect of it, defensive tactics and PT. You get into the aspect of what the agency does, what their role is in the country. It was appealing to me. I got to do a lot of ride-alongs. My mentors were Border Patrol agents. I looked up to them. I really liked what they did. I was like, 'This is what I want to do.'"

When Edgar was in high school, an agent who was a K-9 handler for

Border Patrol spoke at an assembly. The man and his dog put Edgar in some kind of trance: "I saw the dog and literally right there I was like, 'I want to do that.' I like to bond. I'm an animal lover and I saw the relationship they had. I thought it was so cool, a dog that could find drugs. To be in a uniform and have a police dog—that was it, maximum."

Edgar became a Border Patrol agent at eighteen. He was, as he put it, "one of the young cookies." Fresh out of high school he immersed himself in as many aspects of the agency as he could. He took several advanced skills classes—firearms, physical training—always becoming an instructor after acquiring the specialization. It's as if the implementation of knowledge is not complete for Edgar until he has imparted it to someone else. His old coach did it, and so must Edgar.

After checking out CYCA, I go to see Edgar working the highway checkpoint off of 94—one of the four fixed interior checkpoints in the county that's been around for years. Edgar takes a break to meet with me in an unglamorous conference room in an unglamorous portable just off of the road.

"I started working as a K-9 handler in '08," he says, telling me about his favorite part of the job, "and then I became an instructor. You know, it is so much more than why a dog bites or why he doesn't bite. You get into the raw fact that a dog is a wolf, that's where they come from. No matter how much you domesticate them, they're never going to get rid of those genetics. Every dog is created different. You have to deal with what you've got. Maybe a dog will bite you, not because he doesn't like you, not because he's upset at you, but he gets frustrated." Edgar leans in closer to show off his newest scar. "I got a demo for you right here." He extends his arm across the table where we sit and pushes back the sleeve on his OG-107 to reveal the newest scar in its entirety. It is remarkable not so much for its length but because it is so very deep. "I got a new dog and he got frustrated on me. He tore my brachial muscle, I was out of work for six months. Once the dog came to after the attack, he was like, 'What's up dad?'" Edgar laughs. "He's a frustrater."

Edgar shakes his head, thinking about the frustrater and the bite.

"People who don't know me are baffled by the fact that I'm a law enforcement officer—baffled," he says. "It's not that I'm inappropriate, I just don't carry myself like you would expect an officer to carry himself. My perception of a policeman stereotype is Type A, Oakley glasses, fanny pack with a gun, tucked in shirt. That's not my style." With the bite and blood marking his neck the point is well taken. "The last thing they would think is that I'm law enforcement. That's cool. I like that.

"Unfortunately, because of that, there are many times when things are mentioned around me that I probably shouldn't know. Man, if I had a dollar for how many times I was out and heard, 'Hey, do you have any cocaine?' I'm like, 'No, bro, I don't!'" Edgar laughs, shaking his head. "You can't be a law enforcement officer 24/7. If you were, you'd go crazy. There are some people that live that way, but I choose not to. You'd go nuts.

"Stereotypes are something I deal with all the time. I work checkpoints and deal with a lot of people. I'm very polite and very professional, at least I think so. A lot of people say, 'Awesome tattoos!' 'Great tattoos!' But sometimes they say, 'They allow you on the Border Patrol with tattoos?' And I say, 'Yeah, I think I'm good to go.' If I were a guru banker making millions, no one would care.

"I've had a couple old people. 'I can't believe you have that many tattoos, yuck.' And I say, 'I'm sorry you don't like them.' Or they say, 'It's very unprofessional.' And I just smile and say, 'I'll be sure to take them off next time I help you out, okay?' That's all you can do with it. I tell a lot of people, 'Just to let you know, take a look at the newspaper and make sure that everybody who kills somebody has tattoos.' I use that a lot. It makes people think. Most of the people who slit throats in Mexico don't have any tattoos. Get past the stereotypes.

"One time I was walking into a Shell station and going to get something to drink. I'm walking in and I had a little girl, say six years old, she walked up to me and I saw her and my first thing is smile. So I smiled at her. She comes up to me and goes 'fuck you.' I looked at her and I said, 'Really?' I saw her mom and she was laughing. I said, 'Congratulations, you're teaching your daughter very well.' I said, 'Is that the kind of example you want to set for your child?' She looked at me and actually didn't know what to say. I said, 'I really hope that doesn't continue because you're going to increase the bad.' Some people you can't teach. They won't learn."

I ask Edgar what exactly he'd like to teach them. He starts listing the realities of his routine experiences: "In the summertime we run into dead bodies on a daily basis, every other day. And sometimes you save people without even knowing. You do your cuts, driving the roads looking for signs of foot traffic, and if you see a group of twenty people, you follow them. And when you get to them, they're on their last thread already. They don't know where they're at. The smuggler is gone, he left them. They're drinking warm water. I've seen people drinking their own urine. Think about that: urine. They're in the sun, they've got a baby in their hands. I've seen it where the baby doesn't make it. You call a helicopter and they show up, but some people are so severely dehydrated, they can't come back from it. And I'll tell you this: if you start pushing tracks and you see people that are doing circles, you better get to them quickly, something is going on. They're delusional. They don't know where they're going.

"For your safety and for the safety of my coworkers, you have to be numb to some stuff because if you show up on scene and you let it faze you, you're useless to them. You have to throw up a facade. I've seen executions. I've seen murders. I've seen a six-month baby, the mother left her and tried to run to the road and came back and the baby was deceased. That baby, that one bothered me—that was hard to chew.

"I've seen a girl who was loading into the back of a truck. The driver got spooked, took off, she fell, and he ran her head over.

"I've seen all this stuff and you almost have to accept it. You have to be able to chew it. A lot of people say, 'It is what it is.' It's going to happen whether you accept it or you cry about it. It is what it is. You can never do enough for someone. You have to accept that.

"There is so much stigma to our agency. There is anti-police and anti–law enforcement in general and then you add the element of the Border Patrol and you're this big green monster that wants to hurt people. That's the rumor: 'People die because of you.' 'You're deporting the good people.' The picture in their minds is poor families running away and you're running after them with a freaking chain saw. One thing I learned from the job, you're going to get people that, immediately when they see you, they don't care who you are it is always: 'F-you.' It's hard to accept initially. We've still got an Alpha Male personality. No one likes to be talked to like that. But they're not talking to me, they're talking to the uniform. Once you get that, you get past it, you're a lot more understanding and your tolerance is a little higher. It makes you a little more professional and it has helped me. As a Latino, coming from Mexican heritage, I get a lot of questions: 'How can you do that and you're Mexican? How do you do that to your own people?' I'm like, 'These aren't my people. The people *here* are my people.' Listen, I'm very proud of where I come from, but I'm not

Mexican-American. You've got to get past that point. Mexico hasn't done a thing for me. My father is from Mexico and they didn't do a thing for him and he was a citizen. I'm American. I'm from Mexican heritage, but I'm American.

"I come up with a lot of programs for the kids, to get the agency out there, and I know for a fact we've won people over. It does make a difference. It may make a difference in a person and it may make a difference in a group. Humans are pack animals. I raise a lot of dogs and we're pack animals! And people might see me and say: hey Sandoval, he understands. But as soon as you go home, you've got this anti-this and anti-that—you're a pack animal! Are you going to argue against your pack? No, you fall into place.

"When I train dogs, they give you eight dogs. Your job is to identify them, what they do, what makes them work. We've got eight different children with eight different personalities. I've got a dog that's hard as hell. He's just a bonehead, meathead, dumb as hell, but he's good at the job. I can hit him with a cinder block on the head and it won't break the dog. I could yell at him as much as I want, the dog won't be broken. I have to use different tactics to make that dog function. Then I've got a soft dog. Walks out of the kennel real scared, real soft, so you have to be very gentle with your words. You have to use a lot more happiness, a lot more persuasion to engage the dog. Very different types of dogs—I've got to identify all these things. That's what I do with my kids. And these kids that don't have enough, they want to fight, but they can't afford a pair of boxing gloves or a pair of shoes. So we fundraise—and I give. But the most valuable thing you can give is your time. It's very true. When you're younger, you don't appreciate it, but when you're older and a father, you value your time. For you to give your time away, you know the value of it, you know the cost because you've got people chomping at the bit for it. These kids, they need you. I walk in and they're like, 'Yes, coach!' They need it, they want it, they're looking for it. They want the praise. They want to be corrected. That's what keeps me going. That's my addiction, I guess."

CHAPTER 14

I'M CURIOUS ABOUT THE PEOPLE from the rural part of the county, where there are no Explorer programs to satisfy the urge to protect the border. I am in the town of Boulevard, population 315, which is still San Diego County, though it would be understandable to assume otherwise. Boulevard is part of East County—capital "E," capital "C"—signifying its own identity. In East County, the population thins out, scattered on ranches where Brahma crossbreeds graze in the desert scrub.

I am looking for Bob Maupin and I thought I knew the way but GPS mapping is nearly useless in East County. Like the colonias to the south in Tijuana, these roads can only be understood after years of study. At one point I make *another* U-turn on Highway 94 and notice a "Help Wanted" sign for Cebe Farms. The sign was once bilingual until the Spanish portion was crossed out, mostly, but *necesita* does remain just above the number to call.

When I reach Bob's house I am certain it is the right place because there is a World War II half-track out front. There is also an incomplete Army jeep. Bob finished restoring the half-track a long time ago but he's still working on the jeep; he's seventy-eight and moves more slowly now.

He is already outside, rummaging in a toolbox, and before I'm out of the car he comes to open his gate, with his two Labrador mixed-breeds, Inky and Shadow, bouncing around him in circles, barking, forcing Bob to raise his voice: "I'm putting new wiper blades on my truck for the trip." I've caught him the day before he drives to Phoenix for a gun show. There is another gun show coming up—much closer, in Del Mar, just north of the 8 Freeway. But when I ask about that show Bob grimaces. "Del Mar is nothing," he says. "It's all froufrou."

We go into Bob's modular home and take seats at the dining table. He lives on 250 acres, and the southern edge of his property abuts the border. He has been here since his family moved to Boulevard in 1948. He was nine at the time and he remembers that his dad bought a horse. "He was about 17 hands so I would have to get on a stump to get on him. That's the one I learned to ride on—and he learned to be ridden."

His earliest memories of the border are of chasing cattle between towns along the southern edge of the county, from Potrero to Dulzura, up into the Laguna Mountains. "As a teenager, I learned to ride with the Department of Agriculture looking for hoof-and-mouth disease. We would ride just west of Campo and back one day, then over to Imperial Valley and back the next day. It was twelve-hour days, six days a week. We got Sunday off."

Bob is short and stalky with a flattop: "I've worn my hair like this since 1955," he says, "because I was planning on a career in the Marine Corps. See, when I was a youngster I was always getting beat up by the bullies, being a little guy with a big mouth. A friend of mine and I decided to take judo until we found out how much it cost. On our paper routes, we weren't making that kind of money," he says, laughing.

So he and his friend decided to teach each other to fight. "We'd trip over each other," he says, "thinking we were throwing each other. And there was a great big, husky guy that used to come out of the canyons to watch us. One day he comes up to me and says, 'If you want to learn the fine art of self-defense—and it's okay with your parents—come on down to my house after lunch and I'll teach you. You're my paperboy, you know where I live.' At one o'clock I went down there and knocked on his door.

"He had a wrestling mat and he sticks his arm out and says, 'Let's see if you can throw me.' So I grabbed his arm and he lifted me off the floor. I was dangling, thinking I was going to die.

"I went down there every day after school and on Sundays. He taught me how to knife fight and a few other things. Then one day he said, 'I train Marine raiders in hand-to-hand combat and I'm leaving tomorrow for Okinawa. When you graduate from high school and turn eighteen, I want you to join the Marine Corps, go through basic, go into infantry and then look me up. For a little guy, you're pretty damn good at this, so I would like you to be in my outfit.'"

That was the plan until Bob met Dorothy Jeanette. She didn't like the idea of getting married to a military man who might be sent off to fight in a faraway place like Korea. She tested him when they first started dating, to see if he held military aspirations: "She said, 'How come you have a flattop?' I said, 'Well, I couldn't get all the hair on my head into a football helmet.'" Bob often clarifies his dry humor with an aside: "That was a little fib."

Bob never did go into the Marines but the flattop, the mark of a Marine, always remained. He enjoyed fifty-seven years of marriage before Dorothy Jeanette passed away last year. She spent some of her final days lecturing him about finding someone as quickly as possible. "She told me that I would need to get on with my life," he says. But I spent a great deal of time getting myself into a real deep depression because after all, since high school we had been together. Then my dainty daughter said, 'If you don't do what Mom told you to do, I'm going to come down and kick your butt.'"

Bob is now dating an old friend from the high school reunion committee. "I'm seventy-eight, she's only seventy-six. She's a youngster. My daughter said, 'Dad, if you take sixty years off your lives, you're eighteen and she's only sixteen and you can get in trouble!' I said, 'Okay, smartass!'" He laughs, shaking his head at her sense of humor, which she inherited from him.

Bob stares out the window in the direction of the nine-foot primary fence between the two countries, at the edge of his property. "You can see the fence—you can practically walk right up it," he says, pointing out how the corrugated metal nearly serves as a ladder.

Back when Bob decided to marry Dorothy Jeanette instead of joining the Marines, Border Patrol started keeping statistics of apprehensions at the southern border. In 1960, there were 21,022, and generally that number climbed over the next few decades, reaching 745,820 in 1982. The next year, the number ballooned to 1,033,974. Over one million apprehensions along the entirety of the southern border, spread out over nine sectors, but nearly half the arrests were made in the San Diego Sector. There was no other sector that even came close—next was Del Rio with 83,733. So Border Patrol's presence was ramped up in urban areas around San Ysidro to the north and Zona Norte to the south, where nearly all of the crossings took place. This forced more foot traffic into East County where most of the border had no barrier at all—only barbed wire in a few spots.

Bob wasn't the only one who started noticing people crossing onto his property. Families throughout Boulevard, and in neighboring towns like Jacumba Hot Springs and Campo, those who had grown accustomed to the isolation and quiet of East County now regularly encountered small groups of migrants walking across their property—maybe it was a handful, maybe as many as ten, often it was all men. Sometimes it was Bob's daughter who had the encounter, or Dorothy Jeanette.

By the early 1990s, activists like Bob had come together across East County. A group called Light Up the Border tried to draw attention to the crossings by regularly gathering at night to shine their headlights into Mexico. That was when Duncan Lee Hunter, the U.S. congressman who represented much of East County at the time, helped obtain the old military landing mats to start building the primary fence at the edge of Bob's property.

But from there things only got worse. Apprehensions continued to rise all along the southern border. Under Bill Clinton's administration, the federal government doubled the budget for border security with a focus on the San Diego Sector. In September of 1994, Attorney General Janet Reno announced the launch of Operation Gatekeeper. The initiative brought more fencing, more stadium lights, and more OG-107 uniforms to a 14-mile stretch of the border between the Pacific Ocean and the Otay Mesa desert. And with each phase of Operation Gatekeeper, the crossings in East County intensified—as did the estimated number of migrant deaths, with more and more of them facing harsh desert conditions. The annual estimated total of deaths has jumped from 180 to 412 in the last twenty-three years.[1]

The groups of ten that Bob had seen walking across his land before 1994 became packs of thirty, off-roading in cars. Bob says he saw fewer hungry, wandering individuals looking for work; more guides, corralling large groups and drug shipments.

"There was a cattleman south of us," recalls Bob, "and we would converse as well as we could. I didn't speak Spanish and he didn't speak English, but I would meet him out there checking the fence and he would be doing the same thing on the Southside.

Then the cartel told him not to go by the border. He was pushed away, and the people on the Southside, they became very macho, how they presented themselves. Guns are illegal in Mexico, but I've heard automatic weapon fire down there."

"Have you ever experienced shots from across the border?"

"A kid missed me by about four feet. He had a gallon of water. I pulled my rifle out. The first round on all of my guns is a hollow point. So I shot at the gallon and it exploded. All he had left was the handle. He found out that I am a much better shot than him and he made a brand-new trail south.

"I don't get excited. I think things through. If you don't, you'll get killed. That's what I was taught."

Bob has tachycardia, an unusually fast pulse rate. It has calmed a bit with age but not too long ago, Bob says, "my pulse was 100 whether I was asleep or awake, and doing calisthenics it would never get higher than 112." He is a charged but steady man. "I've got a T-shirt that has my philosophy: 'Keep calm and return fire.' I'm always prepared." Bob lifts his shirt to reveal the .40 caliber Glock at his hip. "If that doesn't work—this one, I just got." And he points to .308 caliber Armalite Rifle leaning against the wall.

Apprehensions at the southern border swelled to 1,643,679 in 2000, and a few years later private citizens started arriving to serve as lookouts for illegal crossings. "There was a group of people who formed, called themselves Minutemen," Bob recalls with a raised eyebrow. "I found that quite a few of them were really weird. They did not know how to handle themselves. They all wanted to carry guns and that can lead to a lot of problems. I didn't want them on my property."

So Bob formed his own group. "I talked to one of the resident sheriffs out here, a good friend of mine. He said, 'Bob, you have to do a citizen's arrest for trespassing. They claim they don't speak English and you don't speak Spanish other than taco, burrito, and enchilada, so you tell them, in English, they must turn around and go back. But they won't do that. Then you put them under citizen's arrest for trespassing. Call the Border Patrol and turn them over to the first badge that shows up.'

"So I had some guys that helped us and the Border Patrol started calling them Maupin's Marauders. There were maybe five or six of us on any given night. I would come home from work about 7 p.m. and my wife would feed us all. We'd stay out until one or two o'clock in the morning. We were in camouflage and face paint and we had some hides. We had some people that helped us that weren't supposed to be here. They were military, active duty. Word got out to Pendleton and the Silver Strand. They taught us how to go through the brush without making any noise, without being seen. And when we caught a group, they would just fade away.

"I didn't use the word back then, but what we would do is set up an ambush for these people coming across. We would catch a group down in the creek bed and somebody would have to walk up to the house and Jeanette would call the Border Patrol. Then we started using radios to communicate with the house. We would catch anywhere from thirty to a hundred a night and turn them over to the Border Patrol.

"It used to be all of the new agents that were assigned out here, they came to get to know me because I had a Sherman tank and they wanted their picture taken with it."

Bob might not wear the uniform but that doesn't stop him from offering perspective from the inside. He knows names, he speaks the language—*bandit, Southside.* He's been collaborating, building a rapport with the Campo Border Patrol station for decades. "I used to let them know if I was going to be out of town and there would be an agent stationed here by the house 24/7 for Jeanette."

Bob says agents served as recruiters for Maupin's Marauders: "More folks started coming up saying, 'We'd like to help you.' Border Patrol told a couple of the Minutemen who could handle weapons to my satisfaction, 'You don't really belong with these people. You need to go out to Boulevard and get ahold of Mr. Maupin. He's really trying to do something.' So they came out and we got familiar.

"The coyotes bought places to cross from the Mexican military. Nobody wanted to buy the place just south of me because they couldn't make any money. If they came across, they knew they would get caught. I had my own Vietnam-era sensors. They're seismic so we would know where people were going. What we used to do was light them up with really bright flashlights and then turn them off. We were all wearing yellow shooting glasses so it didn't affect our night vision. Those people were blinded. They would run into each other, falling down. We always had somebody that spoke pretty good Spanish and they would tell them to sit down and put their hands on their heads. I finally learned to say that much in Spanish."

About ten years ago, Bob put up a second fence, chain link with razor wire on top—$20,000 of his own money. "That has slowed things way down. They still cut holes in it, but it takes a while." For years, he's gone on daily patrols along the fence, wearing a bulletproof vest, flanked by Inky and Shadow. I start to ask what he thinks of The Wall but he answers before I finish the question: "I love it. Have you ever seen the one they built in

Israel? That's what I'm looking for. If we get a good wall behind my place, I won't have to wear that bulletproof vest anymore.

"You know, some progressives—communists, or whatever they call themselves—are trying to buy property along the border to stop the president from building a wall. These idiots don't know anything about the sixty-foot easement."

It's hard to know who, exactly, Bob is talking about when he says *communists*. For instance, Bernie Sanders, he says, is a communist, but so is Hillary Clinton. For Bob, this word seems to refer far more generally to the enemy and, very likely, an idiot. The sixty-foot easement he spoke of is easier to decipher, as it refers directly to the Roosevelt Reservation, established by a 1907 presidential proclamation, which gives the federal government access to a strip of land right up against the international line. The easement runs along the entirety of the southern border—with some colorful disputes, of course—from Brownsville to the Pacific Ocean.

Bob's enthusiasm for The Wall, the country's enthusiasm for The Wall, comes after a steady decline in border apprehensions over the last seventeen years. Of course circumstances and episodes sometimes drive up the numbers for one particular month or season, there are spikes with heavier traffic in cooler weather, but there has been a downward trend in the numbers for nearly a generation. By 2016 apprehensions had declined 75 percent from the high established in 2000.[2]

The nightly patrols by Maupin's Marauders are no more; Dorothy Jeanette, Bob's Jeanette, is gone and Bob's knees can only take so many early morning walks with Inky, Shadow, and his Armalite Rifle. The place is mostly quiet. "I haven't seen anybody cross in quite some time," says Bob. But still, his sense of danger retains its intensity—inevitably, like his pulse. He still puts on the bulletproof vest when he's out looking for new holes in his chain link fence.

Bob maintains a shooting range on his property—not a business, just a place for friends and family. It's popular with members of the military and all levels of law enforcement, the men and women protecting the border with overlapping jurisdictions and variations on the same, basic militarized look. But they come to Bob's range as citizens, keeping their OG-107s at home. "The new bloods," Bob tells me, "all call themselves Marauder Ranch Hands.

"You know, Mad Dog Mattis? He's a Marine general," Bob tells me. "And he has a saying that goes something like this: 'Be cordial to everybody you meet and figure out how you're going to kill them while you're looking at them because you may have to.'"[3] Good fences may or may not make good neighbors; for Bob, it remains to be determined.

"The press here in San Diego calls everyone out here 'vigilantes,'" he tells me. "Well, the Hollywood version of vigilante is a mob of people hanging someone. Originally, before Hollywood got ahold of it, out here in the West a vigilante group was a group of people who caught murderers and bandits and such due to a lack of law enforcement. Well, yes, that's me—I agree with *that*."

Bob tells me he once caught a Palestinian crossing and the way he says *Palestinian*, it sounds inherently threatening. So I asked if he feels threatened by someone *because* he is Palestinian.

"I'm too stupid to be afraid of anything," he says. "I'm kind of a weird guy: I consider myself an American. It's not really highly thought of anymore. A lot of people have to be hyphenated now like African-Americans that were never in Africa, Italian-American, Mexican-American. I'm just an American. I believe the hyphenated people ought to go back to the country that they claim they came from and see how they like that. To me, this is an invasion of our country. If you don't come in through the front door and assimilate, I've got no use for you."

"How does somebody assimilate?" I ask.

"Become an American."

"And how would you describe an American?"

"Pride in your country, pride in your service. Don't look for anybody to give you a handout, take responsibility, earn your own way."

Bob's definition of an American, its emphasis on responsibility, reminds me of the most important thing Giselle Haro told me she's learned as an Explorer: *taking responsibility*. For her, it meant owning up to her mistakes; for Bob, it is earning his own way. The American sense of responsibility is self-centered in the truest sense: we define responsibility not by how we contribute to our communities but by our self-sufficiency within those communities. For us, responsibility has never meant building a civil society; it has always referred to pulling yourself up by your own bootstraps.

CHAPTER 15

I LEAVE BOB'S PLACE AND start winding my way back toward San Diego on 94. Just west of Campo I pass a Border Patrol agent—*another* Border Patrol agent—and I make eye contact with her ever so briefly. Moments later she swings a U-turn in her SUV. She rides up behind me and tailgates for half a minute or so then flicks on her siren. I pull over and she approaches my window.

"Hi there," she says. "Are you lost?"

"No."

"Ah, okay. Are you a Realtor?"

"No."

She nods, looking stumped. Apparently if someone is not familiar he must be lost or prospecting—the possibility that he might be trouble is a third option, and the agent broaches it gingerly: "What *are* you doing in the area?"

"I'm just driving back from Bob Maupin's," I say.

She takes a half step back, indicating surprise. "Ah, a Ranch Hand!"

I tilt my head, ambiguously.

She smiles. We shake hands and part ways.

CHAPTER 16

IT IS THE LAST SUNDAY in September. The new fencing around the prototypes went up a couple of weeks ago, and in the days since, construction has felt imminent. Details remain closely guarded but this weekend the county let revealing information slip with temporary No Parking signs up and down Enrico Fermi Drive and the surrounding streets. The fine print on the signs includes the dates of the twenty-four-hour no parking zone, which is set to go into effect in three days. The exact date—Tuesday, September 26, 2017—seems to indicate that work really *is* about to begin.

Border Patrol has confirmed that the winning proposals are selected. Six companies will build eight prototypes. Two of the companies had *two different* proposals chosen. All of the prototypes will either be concrete or concrete and other materials. While "other materials" is remarkably broad there will be no surprises—steel is expected.

The companies in the competition all operate in multiple states and, in some cases, multiple countries. They're accustomed to the big government jobs—major highways and bridges, courthouses and prisons. They are rich companies. One of them, Caddell Construction, without admitting liability, easily survived a $2 million fine to dispense with allegations that it defrauded the federal government,[1] which one might assume would make the company ineligible to bid on government jobs, but apparently this is not the case. The builders are also well-connected companies: Fisher Sand & Gravel, a company with former executives convicted of everything from tax fraud[2] to possession of child pornography,[3] has been championed by North Dakota congressman Kevin Cramer for years.[4] Texas Sterling Construction Company is a subsidiary of a larger company that has done work on five different airports. W. G. Yates & Sons built a Border Patrol station big enough to detain 380 people. And KWR Construction already counts the National Park Service as one of its clients.

All six of the winning bidders are under strict orders not to speak to The Media. None of them are based in San Diego County. They're scattered across the country in Alabama and Mississippi and North Dakota. The sixth builder, ELTA, is a subsidiary of IAI, Israel Aerospace Industries, which describes itself as that country's largest defense company and "a global leader in the field of Intelligence, Surveillance, Target Acquisition and Reconnaissance, Early Warning and Control, Homeland Security, Self-Protection and Self-Defense, Fire Control applications and Cyber Defense and Intelligence application," most of which is, directly or indirectly, related to the endgame of a 30-foot-high barrier, 1,954 miles long. According to ELTA's website for their North America division, the company is committed "to providing solutions to the nation's warfighters."

Russ Baumgartner and the other local builders I spoke to earlier all seem relieved that the process is over. Not only were state politicians pushing to punish those who took the job, but protesters started showing up in office parking lots. Outside the entrance to R. E. Staite Engineering, one protester left a sign that read: "This company is selling its soul." I don't know which is more discouraging: the selling of a soul, or the view of corporate personhood that goes far enough to give it a soul.

I reconnect with six local bidders and they all say they want to put the experience behind them, but there is one who is willing to meet with me. Rod Hadrian owns a construction company called Tridipanel and he's been working with concrete for twenty-five years.

He asks me to meet him up in Del Mar and somehow, impossibly, I find myself at another Denny's. Somehow it's crowded again. Luckily Rod arrived early and got a table. His salt-and-pepper hair is slicked back and he wears a black Hawaiian shirt with loud yellow palm fronds. A woman sits beside him. She has short, curly hair and her lips are pursed, as if protecting something.

As soon as I join the table, Rod stands and announces he's going back to his truck for a sweater: she's cold and he's a gentleman. Suddenly it's just her and me. She sips her coffee; I squint at the menu.

Since I am here to talk to Rod about work I start there: "So, do you work with Rod?"

She doesn't answer. She sips, contemplating the question, and suddenly

I worry I have it all wrong so I offer another option: "Or are you his better half?" She raises both eyebrows, rethinking her response, and just to make sure I stumble in *every* possible way I add, "Or both?"

I make a mental note to stop asking closed questions.

"Or neither," she offers with a biting tone but she does a little shoulder shimmy, which makes me think it might have been a joke.

I laugh, nervous, and say, "Or neither. Just a friend?"

Then suddenly she declares, "I'm *supposed* to be his girlfriend."

I nod, and joke, still nervous: "Depends on the day, huh?"

"Yeah." She confides that she does not appreciate the fact that she's been "shoved" in the back of the restaurant. She wanted a table up front, nearer the sun-splashed windows, but the hostess said she was seating another party there. Now I realize this woman has been eyeing the group sitting at the table where she wishes she was sitting. I tell her they look like a boring bunch anyway. We bond over the fact that we are not *them*.

Rod returns with the sweater; she smiles and takes it from him. He's not yet fully in his seat by the time he's talking to me: "I want you to go on my website." He tries to pull it up on his phone but the pages aren't loading the way he wants them to so he goes to his photo album instead. "I built houses in Egypt," he says, showing me images. His voice is deep but with a nasal quality, like he has a built-in low-grade cold. "Cairo. I've done stuff in Israel and stuff in Belize. I've done stuff all over. I've done every kind of building you can imagine: schools, colleges, government projects, custom homes, commercial buildings, everything."

Most of his projects are concrete. He started working with the material back in the 1960s, when he first migrated to California from Michigan. "I learned how to do the lathing and the fostering," he says. "And probably twenty-three, twenty-four years ago I got involved in the cement applications, spraying the cement, shotcrete. I got to be an expert at spraying."

Rod shows pictures of a house he's been working on for himself in Cabo San Lucas, a resort town at the southernmost tip of Baja; it too is a concrete structure. Not only the house itself, but so many features inside. "I want you to look at the bathtubs," he says, "the sinks—I did it all myself, actually. I'm pretty hands-on, all this radius stuff. I'm almost close to getting done. I go in spurts. Look at the shower! I did that myself. I made the soap dishes, everything." There is pride and salesmanship and concrete in all that Rod does.

He is in his seventies now and spending more time in Cabo, as are so many Californians who went down to build homes and buy condominiums. Rod's a regular at the Container Bar, which, as the name indicates, is constructed out of the shipping containers that have hauled down all the building supplies and tiles and countertops. The Container Bar is on the water's edge though Rod tends to stay ashore: "I'm done swimming," he tells me. "I'm too old." He prefers to stare out at the water while sipping a mango margarita. "My workers, they all go swimming and I usually just hang out in the bar." A picture comes up on his phone of two men who worked for Rod on the house in Cabo—and other projects. "There's my guy," he says, pointing at one of them. "His brother works for me here. My guy's from Mexico City. So I love the Mexican people."

And more pictures, this time of a home he built on the Big Island of Hawaii. "This is all done with the panels," he says. "We built some houses on the Rappahannock River there in Virginia with these panels."

"Panels?" I ask.

His hearing aid may or may not be working; he keeps leaning forward, rocking our uneven table so he can cup his hand around his ear. Thankfully each time he does this it spills a little of my coffee and I get to wipe it up instead of drinking it.

"The panels," I say again. "Tell me about those."

"Well, I found this system," he says. "It was in Long Beach several years ago. This gentleman was building these special houses in a couple of days. They are *insane*. It's a special concrete system. So I ended up doing one in Hawaii. It's *insane*. I'm telling you these houses are burnproof, hurricane, everything proof."

Suddenly the woman sitting next to Rod, who had contented herself with eyeing the table where she wished to be sitting, or she wished the people to not be sitting, or both, says to me, "You should be doing a book on disaster-proof homes."

I look at her, a bit unsure.

"It's insane," says Rod. "I'm just telling you. It's insane what's happening—"

She interrupts him: "*Then* you would get a book that would *really* sell."

I have absolutely no faith that I could or should write a book about disaster-proof homes and I have absolutely no faith that a lot of people, or any people, would buy such a book by me. But still, damnit, I must ask, probably at my own peril: "You say it's 'insane,' Rod—how is it insane?"

He starts to answer but so does his supposed girlfriend and they end up overlapping:

"Well, the system that I have," he says, "I can tell you stories forever—"

"—that's the book you should write—"

"—about disasters, earthquakes—"

"—it would save a lot of lives—"

"—firestorms, hurricanes, I mean, you name it."

And suddenly I understand what is insane: the sales pitch. *Insane* is Rod's buzzword for the concrete system. I'm willing to bet Rod didn't use the word in his written proposal for The Wall but in his oral arguments the only word that can do the trick, over and over again, is *insane*. And his girlfriend, his supposed girlfriend, so sweetly plays the part of overwhelming enthusiast. I sit and listen to them overlap while the entrepreneurship courses through their veins. I admire their pride, their belief in the product. Now *that* is a book. The story about their undying belief in their product, their indefatigable will to bring it to market and become one of those staple stories we tell, the one about Sam Walton, or Henry Ford, or Ray Kroc. To write about that enterprising will, that kind of inextinguishable dream—*now* we're on to something.

"And this panel system," I say, "this was your design for The Wall, right?"

Rod nods, reluctantly, like I just brought up the bad news he had managed to forget. "I knew I had a really, really small chance," he says. While Rod has enjoyed a successful career as a concrete specialist and general contractor (as measured by a second home in a resort town) he knew two things about submitting a bid for a prototype: one, he was way too small to land the job on his own and, two, he had the perfect system to build The Wall.

"I can talk about The Wall forever," he says, rolling his eyes. "I really got involved in it. I can talk your leg off, actually—I talk too much. It's a bad habit."

I turn to his girlfriend: "Is that true?"

She raises her eyebrows and smirks, and I *think* we're sharing a joke.

The system, Rod says, is officially called the 3D cementitious sandwich panel design and it has three main components: fire retardant foam caged in heavy wire mesh, which is then encased by spray-on concrete. Just as Rob discovered that day in Long Beach, the concrete sectionals can be assembled in just a few days. He liked the panels so much, *believed* in the design so much, that he became a distributor for the system. "If you stood one of my panels up," he says, "you can put a 200,000-pound load on top. And when you bond them with a wire mesh and then you spray that wire mesh with more cement, you have a total concrete structure. It's indestructible. You're not going to break it down. We have ballistic testing, fire testing."

The panel system was designed by EV Group, a multimillion-dollar, multinational company with headquarters in Sankt Florian am Inn, Austria. But Rod doesn't work directly with the mother ship. There is a North American manufacturer and, as fate would have it, it is in Mexico. It is a company called Grupo Block Mex, which manufactures the panels in Mexicali, a couple hours east of Tijuana. If Rod's bid had been selected it would have come with the glaring irony that, instead of paying for The Wall, Mexico, or at least a Mexican company, would be *getting paid* for The Wall.

"Now there are many companies that manufacture the panel machinery, similar machinery," says Rod, "but it's made a little bit different to bypass patent restrictions. They're in Venezuela. There's one in Caracas. There's one in Argentina. They're all over the world. But—" Rod leans forward and taps the side of his head. "I have the best machinery that's ever been designed for this in my head and I can put it on paper for half the cost." And now he's nearly whispering: "It's a better patent, it's a better panel." He straightens his back and returns to full voice: "But I don't have the money to do it. It's just one of those kind of things."

The girlfriend jumps in again: "He's not advertising well." Then she leans in to Rod and whispers: "You're not advertising well enough. It would be a big best-seller. It would be—" She cuts herself off and raises her eyebrows.

"I'm just telling you, the system is unbelievable," Rod says. "It's just never been marketed. I've probably done more marketing than anybody and I'm a little-bitty guy.

"Are you *that* small?" I ask. "You submitted a bid to build The Wall."

"That started out as a joke if you want to know the truth," he says. "It was a joke. Because the general manager of the plant is in Mexicali—Juan is his name, he's a good friend of mine after all these years. And I sent him an email one day. I said, 'Juan, I have a job bid coming up that you might be interested in.' " Rod pokes my arm to make sure I get the joke. " 'It's a large job,' I told him. And so we started joking and finally I said let's bid on the wall."

"What was his reaction?"

"Well, he knows me, I'm half crazy. He said, 'I don't think we can sell it.' I told him, 'we can get the job.' I said, 'I'll sell it to the government. You can inflate the price.' " Rod smiles and pokes me in the arm again. "So it started as a joke and it went on and on. *And* my last name is Hadrian. Hadrian built that wall across England. And I thought, you know what? Maybe I can get somebody to look at this."

So Rod went about trying to get the attention of the bigger players in the industry. Armed with the possibility that his ancestors might have built a wall across the entirety of modern-day England in order to fortify ancient Rome, Rod approached some of the biggest commercial builders in the country to tell them about the panel system and see if anyone wanted to submit a bid with him. "The really bigger companies had a connection with the government," he says. "I mean, some of these companies did billions of dollars' worth of work. I was hoping that I could partner with somebody like that and at least sell them my expertise and the building materials. To think that you're going to be some little guy and turn a bid in and have somebody look at it, it's not going to happen.

"I tried to figure out who the real big guys were, the real bidders. And the bigger they were, the less they would talk. I couldn't even get my foot in the door. Other than Parsons." Rod managed to connect with the Pasadena-based company Parsons, which generates a few billion dollars in revenue every year. They do large infrastructure and defense work, from building 150 health care centers in Iraq in 2004, to engineering missiles and rockets. Rod's son-in-law is an executive with the company. He was able to put Rod in touch with one of Parsons's head engineers. Rod sent over samples of the foam core caged in the thick wire mesh. Draft pages were shared. The contours of a possible bid began to take shape. "But," says Rod, "after a while they decided that they were going to pull out. My son-in-law told me they didn't want all the negative stuff, the negative press."

Even though Parsons pulled out, Rod felt like he was too far into the process to give up. "It kind of left me hanging there but I still sent off a pretty good package. I had cost to install, everything. I got written quotes to spray the shotcrete." As Rod describes the proposal, he takes out a pad and starts sketching. "They were going to be 20-foot-long sections. I didn't really need a footing, the wall would have held itself, but they wanted the footing six feet down, reinforced, so nobody could dig under it. I was going to put additional rebars because they wanted to make it to where you couldn't cut through the wall. They had all these stipulations—oh, they kept adding and adding and adding. But I had this thing figured out. I could have done this wall for $3 million a mile—maybe $3.5, max—which was, like, dirt-cheap. My product is lightweight. It's easy to move. I have an insane amount of testing on it, everything they could ever want. It should have been all they needed. And I know I was way under everyone's bids. But I never got any feedback. They never got back to me."

Rod takes a sip of his coffee and continues, "The truth is, I was in over my head. I didn't have the office personnel to do this. And you know what? I didn't really care. I just—Trump wanted to do it and I'm a contractor." Then he turns a little mean, as if to break up with the person who just broke up with him: "It was never going to happen, anyway. The 2,000 miles is never going to happen in a hundred million years. But people don't get that. They're sitting there in Nebraska or Montana. They don't get it."

Despite his bid, despite his belief in 3D cementitious sandwich panel design, Rod says that the country would be better off focusing on policy instead of The Wall. "They've got to do something with this immigration law. I've had a lot of Hispanics that worked for me and friends and a couple of my guys have got kids here, I've seen them. They're illegal. I've got some guys that are illegal that are good family friends of mine. I treat one of them like my son. He's in college now. He wants to pay taxes. He *wants* to pay. He wants to be a citizen so bad, but he'll never be a citizen. And now they're talking about this Dreamer thing for the kids that have no blemishes, they're perfect, they get good grades—goddammit, make them citizens. Get the tax money. They want to pay, but they can't. They want to pay. Take their damn money!" Rod pounds the table to put the final point on a very American reason for amnesty: *take their damn money*. The original sin is lost revenue, unrealized potential earnings.

"I know I could have done it," Rod says. "I'm an expert at this." He sighs, knowing his fate has already been determined, and says, "I wanted to write a book, you know. I failed to do it but—"

His girlfriend jumps in again: "You should have him cowrite it," she says, pointing at me.

"I need to sit down and put the book together," Rod says. "It'd be pretty easy to do with what I've got. But I never could do it. It's just not what I do."

"Well, *he* could cowrite it," she persists, pointing at me again.

I smile at her but say nothing. She purses her lips and looks away. Rod shakes his head then: "Trump said he didn't want some little Mickey Mouse wall. He wanted a real wall. For what they're trying to do, I swear to you this thing was unbelievable. A lightweight concrete building system with insane strength. My system, it was made to do that wall. I'm telling you."

CHAPTER 17

THE ONLY WHISPERS ABOUT VIOLENT protests are coming from law enforcement—like the Border Patrol agents I overheard at sector headquarters. I've asked half a dozen leading activists about it and they all say they're staying away. "I think Trump *wants* to see people protesting these prototypes," one of them told me, "and we're not falling for that. We're not sending people into the middle of nowhere to protest in a field—not for the theater of the administration."

If there is any real threat of violent protests it's in the San Diego neighborhood of Barrio Logan, thirty minutes from the prototypes, just up the 5. "I don't know if you heard, but we had the white nationalists at Chicano Park," says Victor Ochoa. He's sitting in Por Vida, a coffee shop on Barrio Logan's main commercial drag, just a few blocks up from the park. The visitors Victor is talking about billed their event in the park as a "Patriot Picnic." It was not the first such gathering in Chicano Park, just the most recent.

It was September 3—exactly three weeks ago. I heard about it only after the fact; it flared up in a matter of days. Victor was there. He is an artist who's painted several murals in Chicano Park and he's been involved with the place from the beginning. He pulls out his phone and shows me an emailed invite for the picnic that fell into the inboxes of park activists. The invite describes the event as lunch and a tour of the murals throughout the park—or, as the organizer Roger Ogden put it, a chance to "peacefully view these anti-American, brown-supremacist murals in a public park."[1]

An invite to "peacefully view" the murals is hard to square with Ogden's public comments that Chicano Park should be brought down.[2] Once his invite circulated among community leaders in Barrio Logan they organized a demonstration to protect the park. Activism has always been essential in the neighborhood, worked into the grid with electricity and gas. In 1910, Mexicans fleeing the start of a revolution settled in the area. "My great-grandmother landed this side of the border in 1918," says Victor. "She crossed over to the U.S. side illegally. She was a Christian and during the Revolution they were being persecuted. My grandfather had been working as a bureaucrat but when he got here the only job they would give him was sweeping the casino."

Barrio Logan was mostly residential working-class until the 1940s when the naval base to the north expanded, cutting off the neighborhood's beach access at San Diego Bay. From there, a series of rezoning plans in the 1950s and 1960s transformed the neighborhood into an industrial zone. The residents were squeezed into shotgun row houses on narrow streets between the factories, plants, and canneries where so many of them worked. In 1963, new sections of the 5 Freeway cut right through the neighborhood, and in 1969, construction of the San Diego–Coronado Bridge cast parts of Barrio Logan in shadow. So goes life south of the 8.

During construction of the Coronado Bridge, the city promised the residents of Barrio Logan a park, a consolation for the noise and pollution and degradation from an overhead freeway and bridge and decades of industrialization. Approval for the park was finalized in 1969 but no action was taken. The following year bulldozers showed up under the Coronado Bridge to put in a parking lot. Activists began organizing, students walked out of class, and an occupation of the site began. The city eventually relented and agreed to take action on the promised park.

Artists like Victor saw canvases in the concrete pillars supporting the bridge. In 1973, they began painting murals that capitalized on the grandeur of the structures—some are as tall as twenty feet. Over the next five decades, Chicano Park grew into a patchwork of playgrounds, gardens, basketball courts, and skateboard ramps between the pillars-cum-gallery. In 1987 the artwork was formally recognized by the city of San Diego, and in 2013 the park was added to the National Register of Historic Places.

Victor is credited along with others on *Quetzalcóatl,* one of the originals from 1973, a collage involving mythical images—a pyramid, a serpent.

Thirteen years later Victor completed another mural in collaboration with a nearby elementary school, assuring himself a place in park mythology by freeing dozens to experience that childhood impulse to write all over the wall.

"I've always been drawing," he tells me, sipping on his dulce de leche latte. He wipes the frothed milk from his mustache. Victor is a big man with the frame of an offensive lineman. He's dressed in a T-shirt and shorts—a white fedora is his only flourish and it's all he needs. "My mom said that I was drawing even when I was five years old. In fifth grade I actually remember drawing Nikita Khrushchev and Kennedy in a boxing ring." As a teenager Victor designed posters for the United Farm Workers. The first was for a boycott of Safeway. "I remember the first time I met Cesar Chavez," he says. "It was 5:30 in the morning at a protest in front of the Safeway. He saw my poster and said, 'Beautiful work, my child.' He said it in Spanish and I still remember how he put his arm on me and the way he said it, it was like he was Jesus." Victor laughs when he says this but it's clear he means it. He went on marches with Chavez and, years later, was part of the committee that established Chicano Park.

Most of the murals in the park either tell or test stories of the past. There are revolutionaries on horseback, activists tilling soil with bulldozers looming in the background, portraits of political heroes from the Spanish-speaking world—Che Guevara and Fidel Castro. Several murals show indigenous people from across the Americas; one features an Aztec man wearing plumage, standing in the South Bay up to his knees, staring out at the water with the Coronado Bridge sweeping overhead—so many images like this one merge different periods of time. One mural includes that ancient symbol used by so many ancient cultures, including the Aztecs, the swastika, a reclamation from the Nazis who stole it in the twentieth century.

Chicano Park is, in many ways, the apotheosis of Hyphenated America that Bob Maupin calls an invasion. The artwork goes well beyond hyphenation: some of the murals conjure La Raza, a phrase that is literally translated as "the race" but is generally thought of today as something more like "the people," a phrase that has evolved to represent the complex identity and culture shared by those whose ancestors were both Spanish colonizers and the indigenous people of the Americas. La Raza is an idea that pervades the artwork, as is Aztlán, the ancestral home of the Aztecs, described in inexact geographic terms—maybe it extends up through the Rockies, maybe all the way down to the southern tip of Baja—whatever the exact lines, Aztlán is a landscape that renders the Mexico-U.S. border irrelevant, it is ancient access that preempts more recent assimilation requirements.

So it makes sense that Chicano Park was the site of the Patriot Picnic. When the day arrived, Victor and others made sure that fellow demonstrators encircled every concrete pillar to protect the murals, as well as the bronze statue of Emiliano Zapata, who stands watch over the playground. "We had, like, six hundred people show up," says Victor.

His estimate might be inflated but not by much. Local reports gave credit for hundreds and that certainly looked to be the case in published photos and posted videos.[3] Whatever the exact number of park protectors, they dwarfed the low turnout of patriots.

The picnic, which, Victor says, amounted to a couple of large pizzas, commenced at a table painted red, white, and green like a Mexican flag. He isn't sure how many patriots there were but he pulls up a few videos from the day that were posted online. It is hard to get an exact head count on the patriots in the first video we watch because a couple of them seemed to loiter with a certain lack of commitment and I can't tell if they stayed. It wasn't more than five or six, maximum, and they were all men.

A street cuts through the park and, initially, hundreds of demonstrators were on one side with roughly six patriots on the other. There was yelling back and forth before the pizza boxes were even open.

In one video you can hear the patriot who's doing the filming ask, "How do they even know it's us? Do we have anything Trump-related on? I mean, how do they know who we are?—I'm just curious." He wasn't asking me but if he were I would have told him he was easy to pick out because he filmed his own entrance into the park—as did the other patriots, their strut well documented. But one of the patriots offered up a different theory about how they were so easily spotted by the demonstrators. "Hatemongers," he said. "They're hateful people."

A line of San Diego police officers stepped into the street between the picnic and the demonstrators, fanning out at arm's length to form a wall between the two camps, facing the demonstrators. The barrier emboldened the outnumbered patriots; they raised their cameras higher in the air. Two of them scanned the crowd for familiar faces; one pointed out someone and said, "That guy's definitely Antifa," referencing the hard-left militant group. "I bet he's here trying to dox us," the other patriot said, laughing off the possibility of having his identity splashed across the internet.

One patriot asked of no one in particular, perhaps those he knew would watch his posted video, "This is the way we are treated in our own country?" And he really punched the last three words: *our own country*.

"We're just here to see the murals," they each said, more or less, variations on the same theme, overlapping:

"Can't I see the murals?"

"I just want to see the murals."

"Why can't I see the murals?"

"Man, you can't even go into your own park."

After a while the patriots weren't so much using the table for a picnic but occupying it as a base, abandoning the pizza altogether with their attention fully on the demonstrators. The trolling was flagrant—one of the patriots started singing "Easy Like Sunday Morning"—and it was working; the demonstrators turned hotter. Posters bobbed up and down, everything from "Love has no borders," to " Nazi-Fascistas, No Pasarán!" The crowd inched closer to the picnic in imperceptible increments, slow but certain. Sometimes a section of the front line of demonstrators would flare with a bigger advance and the officers shuffled their stances accordingly, a fluid border responding to the realities on the ground.

It went on like this for ten minutes or so, everyone standing around, yelling, flicking each other off. The moment felt like an Andy Warhol vision: no one was doing anything, per se, and nearly everyone was filming it.

At a certain point, Roger Ogden, the picnic organizer, who looked to be in his sixties, walked into the street and stood right behind the officers, peering over their shoulders, over the top of his readers at the larger crowd, waving and smiling as he recorded their reactions. Demonstrators swarmed around him just the other side of the police line. They were, in the words of Victor Ochoa, "The biggest Chicanos I've seen in a while. I said to myself, 'I haven't seen those guys in such a long time. These guys are chingaso.'"* The demonstrators in the front line surged forward, readying for a fight. Adrenaline rushed into the patriots' voices as their confidence

---

* "Chingaso" translates to something like "ready to fight."

shifted to uncertainty. "There's a lot of them, careful," one said. "These guys think they're tough. It's gonna get live here, guys. Gonna get live!"

"You can come to my city any time," another patriot yelled at the demonstrators. "I'm not going to kick you out of *mine* the way you kick me out of *yours*." Then, creating inconsistencies in his own narrative he added, "I got more guns than all you motherfuckers!"

Raw nerves seemed to take over and the moment rocked, capable of tipping in any direction. In one video, an officer walked up to Roger Ogden and said, "You guys have made a statement. Now I need you to get out of here."

"So get us out of here!" said one of the patriots, answering for Ogden and the rest of the group. No one argued.

"I will get you out," the officer told him. "Get your stuff and let's go."

The patriots, looking relieved, closed up the pizza boxes as the police formed a tight circle all around them. The security ring began inching out of the park. The demonstrators locked arms, reluctantly making way for the officers. "We're just a group of people who want to eat pizza," one patriot said on his way out.

There was a demonstrator walking backward, directly in front of the slow-crawl of officers, and he yelled directly at one of the patriots, taking his turn to troll: "You're not even white!"

"What the fuck are you talking about?" asked the patriot in question, waving his arm in the air, trying to let his skin speak for itself.

The demonstrator smirked and said, "That's not *real* white."

One video ends with a patriot yelling just before he gets into his car: "See you again soon."

Victor puts his phone down on the table and shakes his head. "Nobody," he says, "is going to fuck with the park."

He pushes his fedora back off his forehead and looks out the window of Por Vida, in the direction of Chicano Park.

We sit for an hour or so and every few minutes someone comes over to shake Victor's hand. After decades of painting all over the world, from Barcelona to Havana, his work is widely known and he basks in this fact. His ego is naked and something about its exposure helps unleash a generous core. Victor is a confident guy who is fun to talk to, and willing to do so with just about anyone.

While he is primarily a muralist he has done other work including big installations. He grew up on both sides of the border and it is a prevailing theme in his work. "I'm a complete border phenomenon," is his refrain. In the 1990s he did an installation of an open door—frame and all, with the key left in the lock—at the Mexico-U.S. border. He also worked on a collaborative project called Border Sutures. "We had an RV," he says, "and we rode around and we put these giant staples all along the 2,000-mile border."

The line between Mexico and the U.S. is not the only border Victor considers in his work. He did a project involving a reimagined fragment of the Berlin Wall and he completed a mural in Northern Ireland. "I painted in Belfast with the IRA," he says. "This was in the '80s. It was interesting to see the amount of disrespect that they were getting out there; language, culture. All of that shit. I used to call the Irish white Mexicans." Victor laughs and sips from his cup. "They say that Che Guevara was Irish, his dad's name was Lynch. And, you know, I never thought that I would be friends with so many white people, but—" And here he stops to smile at me, "—you guys are cool."

A question occurs to me but it feels too awkward to ask: how does Victor know I'm white? It seems a stupid question because I have never been perceived any other way. But my question isn't really about me as much as it is *for* me—and the White America that I grew up in: how do we define white? Skin tone is the obvious answer but it doesn't work in all cases. There are, as the gleeful demonstrator pointed out to the disgruntled patriot, people with dark skin who identify as white and could easily be perceived otherwise. Ethnicity doesn't work either because, as Victor said, Che Guevara was partly Irish and it is safe to say he never identified as white. Something about how we define white seems to be fluid too. There were generations of Americans who did not consider Italians white but, now, do we perceive Joe DiMaggio any other way? For immigrant families like DiMaggio's, the process of becoming American was the process of becoming white. And there isn't a reliable legal definition for white because, in the courts, it has historically boiled down to *not* being black. One drop and you're disqualified. *White* seems to have no objective definition because, in the end, it defines nothing other than our prevailing perceptions. Our perception of beauty, our perception of who should be the boss, our perception of who can become rich. At the inception of the U.S., the land-owning men who envisioned independence controlled the wealth of the newly formed Republic, they determined what was beautiful in the eyes of the new Republic, they decided who was included in *we*. It was a small set, the patriots, easy to identify by skin tone, and so white was shorthand for power and dominant culture. But, slowly, *we* has opened up to a more complex population. First to those men without landholdings, then to the men brought from Africa against their will, then to women—each gained suffrage and slowly, too slowly, each gains in the pursuit of wealth, in the grip of power, in our shared ideas of beauty.

"The patriots—whatever the fuck they call themselves—they will be back," Victor says. "Mark my words." He takes a sip of his latte and grimaces. "These hipsters, man, they make this shit too sweet."

I ask him if he feels more comfortable on one side of the border or the other. "We have a house here and a house in Tijuana. I'm comfortable both places," he says with some hesitation. "I'm so comfortable there though. I've built a three-story structure and my studio is up on the third floor. I have a little park across the street. I have WiFi, I got Netflix on my TV— fuck everything else!" He laughs. "I have a sense of community that I love in Tijuana.

"I don't know, sometimes I don't really like to come to San Diego. You know, even when my mom was ninety-three years old and I crossed her over, she would shout, 'Viva Mexico!' In Mexico, she actually looked like she breathed different and everything. I don't know if it's just imagination of freedom and that you don't have a gringo overseeing you or trying to step on your neck. I think a lot of people feel like that.

"My dad came from Sonora and he was like a *trampa*, he would call himself. He was on the railroad trains—hobo, I think, is one of the other terms people use. It was common in the '40s to do that. He was an orphan and he would ride the trains and get jobs in different places. I think he went as far east as St. Louis. He was a big dude and he had big-old arms— nobody would fuck with him. He was a Zoot Suiter, a pachuco, he was street fighter trained. Pachucos used to wear brass knuckles, switchblades, chains, pipes and then they would have triple-soled shoes to kick. They loved to dance too. My dad would go to Tijuana to party and dance. That's where he met my mom. My grandparents didn't really like my dad because they thought he was a streetwise guy who just roams around without a home. And it was mostly true. He finally eloped with my mom and brought her up north. They traveled around for different work. During the war, they *wanted* Mexicans over here. My mom worked on the Pullman trains, she worked making uniforms as a seamstress, she worked with food, packaged walnuts and all kinds of stuff. My dad was always working in different industries like meat processing. They did some farm picking. They got a chance to cruise around.

"Eventually they settled in East L.A. That's where I was born. I remember going to school and there was no Spanish at all. I remember my parents didn't want my sister and I to speak Spanish. They didn't want us to say that we were Mexican. It wasn't that they weren't proud of it, it was just that they were undocumented and they were afraid. Immigration officers used to run around like gangsters in trench coats. I remember them coming to the house with big .45s, bulging. That was in 1955. They booted us out, actually. I remember my dad took me to the opening day of Disneyland in 1955—I remember that shit. I had my Davy Crockett shirt and my raccoon hat, a pop-gun. And it was later that same year we got kicked out. I remember when they came to the door. We had something like four days to pack up all our belongings."

Victor's family was removed during Operation Wetback, a federal program for large-scale deportations of Mexicans who had crossed illegally into the U.S., or those who had stayed in the country after their bracero, or manual laborer, contracts expired.

The braceros had been coming into the country legally for over a decade under a program that allowed the agricultural industry to hire them temporarily. It began during World War II when many men left the workforce for the battlefield. Women stepped up—and so did migrants. The Bracero Program made it legal for Mexicans to sign short-term contracts that guaranteed minimum wage (30 cents an hour), adequate food and shelter, and other basic rights like access to water and medical care.

Over the course of twenty-two years, the program brought about five million migrant workers into twenty-four states.[4] Many were men separated from families, living in substandard housing, holding contracts that were often not enforced and so did nothing to protect their livelihood or health. The historical record is crowded with contemporaneous testimonials about wages being paid late or not at all, unsanitary living conditions, and no access to doctors when doctors were badly needed.[5] Woody Guthrie wrote a song about the braceros, so did Phil Ochs. "While your muscles beg for mercy, bracero," sang Ochs, "In the shade of your sombrero, drop your sweat upon the soil."

Eventually the program became injurious to just about every person and institution except for the U.S. agricultural industry: domestic workers got squeezed by the braceros who worked for less money; the braceros had worthless contracts; the Catholic Church fretted about the vices overtaking the lonely workers separated from their wives and priests; Mexican wives raised children on their own; and the government of Mexico saw one of its greatest assets, a thriving workforce, noticeably weakened. Beyond the hundreds of thousands of Mexicans who entered the U.S. legally every year there were countless others—literally, no one was counting—who crossed illegally and began lowering wages even more than the Bracero Program had.

By 1954, World War II was long over; men were repopulating the workforce: it was time for women and migrants to return home. Operation Wetback commenced in May of that year, organized at the request of the Mexican government, which was eager to stop hemorrhaging workers—although it was the U.S. government, as one might guess, that decided on the name and tactics for the operation. "Our work contract's out and we have to move on," sang Woody Guthrie. "They chase us like outlaws, like rustlers, like thieves." Federal immigration officers, imprinted in Victor Ochoa's memory with trench coats and bulging .45s, emptied Mexican communities across the country.

"I was seven when we were sent back to Mexico," Victor says. "I was always fighting with the kids there because they were always calling me 'gringo' because my Spanish was zero. I had to be put back into first grade. I made it through elementary school in Tijuana and then I came back to the U.S. on my own in junior high. I always knew I was a U.S. citizen but I had no money and I was living in people's garages. It was terrible. My parents were really poor. In those years, they were averaging $20 a week. They could survive in Tijuana but what could they give to help me go to school?

"It was really hard because all the kids on this side of the border all had brand-new clothes, new shoes, new everything. For the first time I go into school and my collars were worn out and shit like that.

"I went to Montebello Junior High School and they didn't want you to speak Spanish. And everybody was Mexican!" Victor laughs. "Everyone was affected by the oppression," he says. "The people were so *oppressed* it was almost as if they were brainwashed into looking down on Mexicans. The Mexican communities where I lived—Montebello and around there—they didn't call themselves Mexican. And they told me that I was too Mexican. When I came back on my own, my Chicano attitude clashed with the U.S. I would always hear shit about Mexico, like Pancho Villa being a bandit. And I'd say, 'Yeah, he's a national hero.' I was always on the defensive.

"You know, I'm going to write a book about all of it one day: *Chicanosaurus at the Border*." He laughs, half serious, half joking. "I grew a lot during those years," he says. "My mom would buy me the real long pants and I would roll them up. When you're poor, you're poor. That was a big thing for me to readjust to being in the United States."

I can't get *Chicanosaurus at the Border* out of my head—the image it conjures. Victor has created the perfect mythological iteration of himself to confront the idea of assimilation. Partly human, partly supernatural, Chicanosaurus tests the bounds of *we* in all our founding documents. What began as a small group of patriots—landowning, Anglo men—has grown into a sprawling society including the likes of Chicanosaurus. He has never been mistaken for white nor wondered if someday he might be. The perception of white as power and wealth and beauty is dated and irrelevant to Chicanosaurus. Yanked back and forth across the border, now he rises above it, sure of who he is: yes a U.S. citizen, yes Mexican, but, in the end, the one and only Chicanosaurus.

I wonder if one day he will rise beneath the San Diego–Coronado Bridge. There are more pillars to paint. Victor suggests I walk down the street and take a look at the most recent mural—a good friend of his just finished it.

I tell him I'm on my way to meet a minister who runs a church service at the border so I might not have time.

"You mean Friendship Park?" he asks.

"Yeah," I say. "You know it?"

"You should ask for Enrique Morones—he's always there on the weekends. "

"Who's that?"

"Enrique started Border Angels. They go into the desert to leave water for migrants. They also raised the money for the new mural. Go see it, go, go," he says, shooing me out of the coffee shop in the name of art. I hustle down to the park for a quick look at the new mural. There are many scenes but one stands out—near the bottom, at eye level: migrant workers walking across a parched landscape with jugs of water in their hands. They move toward a shining city on the highest point of a green hill in the distance. The Wall stands between the workers and their destination, and The Wall is where the earth changes abruptly, from barren to verdant. That city on the hill, that gleaming free market, is protected from the workers who approach it. The story of America, country of immigrants, has always been set in the land of capitalism, where competition drives all. And the competition doesn't just entice immigrants; it entices the most enterprising immigrants. Those who, like the patriots before them, are willing to do whatever it takes to stake a claim with determination as their deed. The "brainwashing" that Victor described among the Mexicans in Montebello was nothing more than assimilation into America, which, after assimilation into the idea of white, is assimilation into capitalism. Limit the competition by shutting the door behind you, for God's sake. Climb the ladder. Get the title, no matter how the land is acquired. Prove your sense of *responsibility* by putting up a fence and fending for yourself.

CHAPTER 18

BEFORE THE WALL, BEFORE THE secondary fence and the primary fence, there were no barriers along the Mexico-U.S. border. The international line took six years to survey after the Mexican-American War. A binational commission completed the process in 1855 and the U.S. government erected fifty-two modest stone obelisks along the border with about three miles between each of them.

Over the next few decades, local disputes about the exact position of the line persisted from the Pacific Ocean to the Gulf of Mexico. Several of the obelisks were damaged or went missing. A binational resurvey of the line commenced in 1891 and it took three years to complete. The U.S. government restored the obelisks that had survived and added hundreds more, raising the total to 258.

The 1891 survey reasserted the line established in 1855, correcting some errors along the way, but disputes continued. The U.S. installed additional obelisks to mark the line more precisely, and by the early nineteenth century there were 276 of them. That number grew to 442 by 1976, and in 1984 another 51 were added.[1] In a way, the process of building The Wall has played out as a 162-year exercise in connecting the dots.

The obelisk known as Monument 258 is in a place called Friendship Park, a pavilion on a bluff overlooking the Pacific Ocean. Pat Nixon was there when the park opened in 1971. At the time the only fence was barbed wire strung between cockeyed stakes. But even that was too much for the first lady, who praised the park while lamenting the barbed wire. "I hate to see a fence anywhere," she reportedly said before stepping into Mexico to shake hands.[2]

The Friendship Park pavilion is just one small section of Border Field State Park—1,316 acres managed by the State of California and the federal government. Like most of the county's coastline, the beach at this park has a lot to flaunt—soft sand, approachable surf, sunshine most days of the year—but it's often desolate. The public has access to the shoreline, but the nearby parking lot is closed most of the year due to flooded roads and stingy budgets, so the walk to the sand is often over a mile and a half. Crowds really only gather on weekends, when Friendship Park is open to the public from 10 a.m. to 2 p.m.

I am on my way up to the pavilion with John Fanestil. He is a Methodist minister but skips the collar, sticking with blue jeans, a button-down shirt, and a wide-brimmed lifeguard hat. John is a former Rhodes Scholar and a founding member of a small coalition that works to preserve public access to Friendship Park. He says the fight goes back at least as far as Operation Gatekeeper, the 1994 border security program implemented in tandem with NAFTA. "Before NAFTA," John says, "people would come into the U.S., work for a while, and go back home. With Operation Gatekeeper, we took what had been, for many people, circular patterns of migration and we turned it into a one-way street."

NAFTA gave U.S. industries what they hadn't had since the Bracero Program: large-scale *legal* access to the cheapest labor in the region. The manufacturing jobs shifted to the maquiladoras of northern Mexico. NAFTA allowed the border to open to the flow of products while Operation Gatekeeper helped close off the border to the flow of people. And while the federal program was designed to stop illegal crossings along the entire southern border, most of the fencing and stadium lights and additional agents in OG-107s went into patrolling 14 miles from the edge of the Otay Mesa desert to Friendship Park at the Pacific Ocean.

"The idea was to lock down the urban crossings," says John, "on the assumption that if you made crossing the border difficult enough people would stop coming. They just grossly underestimated what people were willing to risk in order to get to the United States for the jobs that couldn't be moved to Mexico. After Operation Gatekeeper, once you got into the U.S., you didn't want to go back. It became too costly, too dangerous. So you stayed. Border crossers became immigrants. And once you stay, the next natural thought is how do I bring my family to be with me? That's when significant populations of Mexicans started popping up in really every major city in the United States.

"And pre-9/11, George W. Bush and Vicente Fox—two conservative presidents—were openly talking about the next phase of NAFTA and drawing analogies to the European Union and saying obviously we have to do a lot to equalize standards, we need to invest in Mexico, bring the standard of living up. And this was not controversial, it was mainstream conservative orthodoxy. And 9/11 changed the tenor of everything. It's night and day on either side of 2001.

"Now, most of the 9/11 hijackers came in through Canada, legally on visas. So if the reaction really was to 9/11, directly, it would have been more logical to take a closer look at the visa processes. But instead we focused on the southern border and Customs and Border Protection got folded into the newly formed Department of Homeland Security. That was a defining moment in the border story: everything becomes national security. There is nothing that is not national security. Prior to 9/11 the border was not conceived of by U.S. policymakers in national security terms. Or if there were policymakers framing it this way they were outliers. There was no one pushing that agenda until 9/11."

Talk of a barrier on the southern border went from, say, Pat Buchanan's 1992 presidential run, to actionable planning in the years immediately after 9/11. The federal government seized nearly four hundred acres from California at Border Field State Park. In 2008—and again in 2011—the Department of Homeland Security announced that Friendship Park would be closed in order to allow for construction of more substantial fencing.

"Before 2008 Friendship Park was very much a wide-open binational meeting place," says John. "There were no walls or any kind of infrastructure other than a chain-linked fence. You could see through it very easily. There was access 24/7. People would come up all the time to see their friends or family, exchange gifts. People would eat together and there were all kinds of vendors selling tamales and candy and ice cream and trinkets. It was kind of a marketplace almost. Border Patrol tells us that there were drugs being trafficked across the border. I'm sure there were at some points. But the vast majority of visitors were just here to meet up with people on the other side. The drug-peddling claim was just total bullshit.

They needed a plausible cover story to close the park. Technically anything that comes from Mexico into the U.S.—officially material of *any* kind—is supposed to go through a port of entry and be examined by a U.S. customs officer. And so to move things across the border between ports of entry is technically a violation of U.S. customs law. So the fact that people at this park would exchange gifts, would have meals together, Communion, was a problem. In the eyes of U.S. customs law the Communion bread is contraband."

After Friendship Park closed in 2008, Michael Chertoff, then the secretary of homeland security, used a rider from the 2005 Real ID Act[3] to suspend "any and all laws deemed necessary to expedite construction" of planned border fences. Chertoff waived more than two dozen environmental, labor, and Native American preservation laws. "There was a Native American site over here." John points back over his shoulder as he continues hiking up to the pavilion. "They just plowed over that." The secretary of homeland security, an unelected official, is the only person with the authority to grant such waivers and dozens have been applied to barrier construction projects all along the southern border.

By 2011, three layers of fencing were up at Friendship Park and it wasn't clear if Border Patrol was going to continue to allow public access to the pavilion. "We negotiated a compromise," says John. "Friendship Park would be open on Saturdays and Sundays for a few hours but in exchange for access they said, 'Well, we're going to put up wire mesh so people can't pass things back and forth.' And they said, 'If you keep passing Communion through the fence we'll kick you out.' We imagined that over time they would loosen things up but they've remained very strict about it, which is frustrating. They won't let people hug there. These families come from long distances, haven't seen each other in years and all they get to do is touch fingertips. It's crazy.

"There's a garden off the eastern edge of the pavilion where there's no mesh but there is a rope line to keep everyone eight feet away. There you can see each other clearly but can't touch. And so we're saying, 'C'mon you guys, at the end of the day, just let families go hug at the garden before they leave. Let them give a good hug and a goodbye kiss.' They won't go for that.

"We're always trying to create more access. Right now our approach is: while you are prototyping all these ridiculous walls, why don't we prototype Friendship Park? An architect who works with the coalition to protect the park is developing plans to make the pavilion truly binational.

"We're anticipating that those prototypes will attract more attention to the border. And we'll try to attract some of that attention to Friendship Park. In our minds, it's a place where the border is always being created. This place has always had the capacity to demonstrate what a more human border can look like." John says this as we approach the initial fence leading to the pavilion—the first of three, where a Border Patrol officer stands watch and reserves the right to ask to see identification.

I look down at the beach and the sand is not dotted with footprints but marked by Border Patrol ATV tire tracks, arching with the shoreline. Eventually the tracks break in two directions; one set heads up toward the grassy bluff where we stand, and the other keeps close to the water, directly approaching a row of steel bollards sticking out of the sand. Each bollard stretches 20 feet into the sky and they're placed far enough apart to slip an arm through but not much more than that. The bollard at the end of the row, in the water well past the breakers, stands as the westernmost marker of the border between Mexico and the U.S.

John and I continue forward, passing through the open gate in a second fence. I ask him to point out Enrique Morones from Border Angels. John squints into the small crowd of thirty or so and says he'll keep an eye out for him. "Enrique has worked with the park coalition for years now," he says. "But he sort of has a separate conversation going with Border Patrol." This intrigues me but before I can get further clarification, John marches off to say hello to someone at the third and final fence, made of 20-foot-high steel bollards covered in wire mesh.

I hear music coming from the Mexican side of the park, an acoustic guitar with a crooning male voice. I move closer to the steel bollards, hoping to see him through the mesh. The gusts off the ocean give minor relief from the heat. Standing at the very base of the fence I can see that it is rusted over, both the bollards and the mesh. Visitors to the park greet each other from either side by pressing a pinky between bits of scored wire, small bulges of fingertip managing to touch.

Standing right next to the 20-foot-high structure makes it look even taller. It is hard to know, precisely, what it is in front of me. The combination of the bollards and wire mesh seems to be mid-metamorphosis: not yet a wall but something past a fence. It feels like the best possible representation of our rhetorical *mis*representation of what kind of barriers are possible at the border. We debate The Wall, but on the ground there are seven hundred miles of various barriers already in place and none of them resemble a wall. It is a hodgepodge of designs and materials, tested across time and environments. Border Patrol agents and border people in general often bounce back and forth between the two words in conversation, *wall* and *fence*, presenting them in tandem as if separated by a slash. It gives cover, acknowledging both the border as it is becoming, *fence*, and our mythology about the border, *wall*, but the two are never reconciled.

I stand a few feet away from Monument 258, which is about fourteen feet tall, carved from marble. It used to be called Monument 1: the original survey team worked west to east but the 1891 survey moved east to west. The border is not static and neither is the way we mark it.

The obelisk has a triangular dome top and text etched into its base, something about commemorating binational cooperation. I bend down to get a closer look but the message is difficult to read because the obelisk is on the far side of the wire mesh. Border Patrol positioned the third fence at Friendship Park just north of the monument, cutting off access to the carved stone and the collaboration it commemorates.

I look again for the musician but, like Monument 258 and all else on the far side, he remains obscured, screened off by the wire mesh. I catch fragments of his bright blue shirt and smile; I catch fragments of the picnic tables and the stall where mango is sold, cut and dusted with chili powder. The stall is under an awning, which also gives shade to a few rows of elderly women and men taking in the afternoon from the semi-comfort of plastic chairs. There are far more people on the Mexican side, probably closer to a hundred. Behind them is a bullfighting stadium that seats more than 21,000. Foreign journalists seem to refer to the structure more euphemistically as a "sports complex," but to anyone from Tijuana who has ever mentioned it to me, it is the bullfighting stadium.

Not only is the crowd smaller on the U.S. side but several people look like me: lost and curious, unfamiliar with the scene. I pull up Enrique's image on Google and scan the crowd for him. Meanwhile John has started unloading the contents of his backpack, which include the body and blood of Christ in the form of a squeeze pouch of grape juice—alcohol is not permitted at Friendship Park—and a small dinner roll in a Ziploc bag, indicating John knows there won't be many takers. He unfolds a woven cloth, about the size of a doormat, and spreads it out on the ground, right up against the wire mesh. After he sets a wood cup and plate on the cloth he punctures the juice pouch with a plastic straw and lets the blood drain into the cup; the plate gets the body once it's broken. John reaches into the backpack again—it's starting to feel like Mary Poppins's bag—and pulls out a Bible along with a wireless microphone that networks with speakers set up on the other side of the fence.

John tests his connection—"Uno, dos, tres"—and goes right into greetings: "Gracias y bienvenidos!" He announces, in Spanish and English, that the service will begin in twenty minutes. As he speaks his microphone keeps cutting out—for a second or two, here and there—but he's used to it. Each time he repeats the interrupted sentence without hesitation and rolls forward with his remarks. John gives the crowd a brief description of the service: the scripture and the message, the Communion and the fellowship, but he emphasizes the brevity more than anything else, as if trying not to scare away the hesitant, the park visitors who have clearly stumbled into something they did not anticipate. He tells them it's okay to just watch, not everyone has to participate. "No requirement of church membership," he says, repeating it like a refrain.

The sound system is blasting and the speakers are having a hard time handling it; John's voice is loud and dented, garbled in spots. Same goes for Guillermo Navarrete, his counterpart on the Mexican side, who adds a few announcements of his own at the twenty-minute warning. After they've both put down the microphones John introduces me to Guillermo through the wire mesh. They've been doing this weekly service since the park reopened in 2011. "Before six years ago," Guillermo tells me, "I never think about migration." Not only does the mesh obscure him but so do his sunglasses and his thick mustache. There's a lot of crowd noise; some of the park visitors shuffle away while others settle in, and the musician is going again with his guitar, so I have to press my body into the mesh to hear Guillermo. He tells me he's been in Tijuana for forty-three years, working for most of that time as an Episcopal priest. "Six years ago, a missionary invited me to come to the Tijuana River and have another view of how humans treat each other. That moment touched my heart." The Tijuana River is an intermittent body of water that feeds into the estuary surrounding much of Friendship Park. The riverbed snakes east, weaving up and down between the two countries. Inland from the estuary, the river is dried out most of the year, save for the wastewater that flows out to the ocean. It is usually a shallow, narrow stream at the base of a concrete canal built to manage the river during heavy rains. The canal has become a de facto encampment for deportados, Central Americans who have been deported from the U.S. and lack a safe home or the money to get home or both. They live in obscurity on an international line, stateless, and after meeting some of them Guillermo was changed. "I was a religious pastor," he says, "but now I am a social pastor with no congregation, with no offering. But work on social issues provides me a very good time because it's about human justice." Guillermo tells me that he raised money for a project that gave deportados psychological counseling and access to social workers who helped with jobs and housing. The program reached fifty people before the money ran out.

Before we part, Guillermo says, "Let me give you a kiss," and he presses his pinky to the mesh. So I do likewise. Moments later, I hear a man moving through the crowd, passing out flyers, looking like he's selling something. Suddenly he asks, "You do yoga?"

It's a question I'd rather avoid so I delay: "Me?"

"Yeah. Next Sunday here at the park. It's binational yoga. It's free. We do it on both sides." He points at my notebook and asks, "You're a journalist? I'm Enrique Morones." He asks me if I know Border Angels. I tell him not yet. Just then Guillermo begins quieting the crowd so Enrique leans in to give me his phone number and email address. "Next week," he whispers.

Guillermo begins by introducing a group of deported mothers who have U.S. citizen children on the far side of the border; they are part of the crowd of elders parked under the awning on the Mexican side, which also includes deported U.S. veterans. After introductions Guillermo delivers his message, speaking in two- and three-sentence clumps, breaking occasionally to give John time to interpret in English.

The man in the bright blue shirt picks up his guitar again for a brief musical interlude then John takes the lead, reading from the book of Jeremiah. "'The days are coming' declares the Lord, 'when I will make a new covenant with the people. . . . It will not be like the covenant I made with their ancestors. . . . I will put my law in their minds and write it on their hearts. . .'" John looks up from the scripture and continues without notes: "So it seems God likes to work with human beings through covenants. There are many covenants that are spoken about in the Bible. The creation itself is called a covenant. Here with the prophet Jeremiah, God is speaking to his people about a different kind of covenant. Up until this time, the covenants have been covenants of laws. But Jeremiah talks about a different kind of covenant that will be made in people's hearts. It turns out that covenants of law are not sufficient for God. We, as human beings, we cannot make laws that are truly just. Our laws always have flaws in them, they always come up short. And so we, as a people of faith, have to look beyond the law. Here on Sundays we gather as a church and we are in a place that is dominated by the laws of humankind. We come looking for justice, knowing we will not find it if we look only to the laws made by man. We have to search for justice in our hearts, and find justice with each other. We make our own justice. We come not as a people of law. We come as a people of heart."

John invites everyone to raise a hand to the wire mesh. Not just anywhere but find some hint of flesh, some extremity of a pulse. As everyone does so, John says a prayer, and provides a big silent space for everyone to lift up confessions of the mind and heart. The sound of the earth takes over, as waves crash below and pelicans break in; after a while, so does the musician, only now it's just the faint strum of his guitar, no vocals. He continues as background while John and Guillermo offer Communion. The sacraments are given concurrently but can't be shared because of the wire mesh, and even if the two men did devise a way to pass the transubstantiated body and blood of Christ, it would still be contraband. The sound of the guitar is the only thing that manages to slip through.

Finally there is a benediction, the end of which is run over by the sound of a Border Patrol ATV rounding up the bluff just beyond the pavilion. It is a reminder that we are standing in a security zone. No matter what our hearts may say, they remain under the jurisdiction of the law. The security zone extends 14 miles to the east where the real-world fencing runs out and construction of the prototypes begins—in two days.

PART 2

CONSTRUCTION

CHAPTER 19

I AM IN A VAN with a dozen reporters and photographers. We're maneuvering around the road signs just past Enrico Fermi Drive, all variations on KEEP THE HELL OUT. The sentry under the bright yellow tent to the side of the barricade is uninterested, as ever. He doesn't even look up until the Border Patrol agent behind the wheel taps on the horn to say hello.

There is a buzz in the van, probably because it's air-conditioned. The sun pierces the tinted windows but the sweet streams of freon protect us for the two-mile drive across the desert. We stop just outside the chain link fence at the construction site. Everyone pops out of the van and puts on a compulsory hard hat and reflective vest. Just past the fence there is a viewing area of sorts, encased by cement barricades, keeping everyone about fifty feet away from the works in progress.

It is 92 degrees and there isn't a cloud in the sky to keep the sun away. Immediately everyone feels the absence of air-conditioning and begins working quickly. *The San Diego Union-Tribune* sent a photographer but he's looking a bit out of sorts—the desert is not his usual beat. He's got a checklist and he'll be the first one back in the van. The photographer who "usually shoots for Getty" hits up the reporter from *The Washington Post* to see if his editor is sending a photographer or if they're looking for images. Email addresses are exchanged—the gig economy extends to every extremity of the country.

The photographer from Toronto's *Globe and Mail* sets up his drone, talking about "getting the feel" for the controls with a couple of other guys who have yet to "play with one." They give him a few feet all around, probably because he's wearing his own specialized reflective vest that reads:

AERIAL MEDIA PILOT
DO NOT DISTURB

He gets the thing going and it pierces the ear with a high-pitched vi-
bration, sounding and feeling like an oversize robotic fly. "We're doing a
time lapse," he says, shouting over the mechanized beast. He controls the
thing in the air for several minutes, brings it back down to the edge of the
cement barricade in front of him, checks the footage, then sends it back up.

At one point, a man working on the prototype for Fisher comes over
carrying a drone of his own. He starts talking to the guy from the *Globe
and Mail*, mainly planning out how to avoid a collision in the sky. After a
minute or so, agent Eduardo Olmos starts drifting toward the men, likely
to remind them that contractors are not allowed to engage The Media; but
they see him approaching, like an umpire breaking up a meeting on the
mound, and the guy from Fisher peels off.

Agent Eduardo Olmos is the lead media wrangler on the scene, a patrol agent halfway through his two-year rotation as a public affairs officer
for the San Diego Sector. He is a natural fit for the position: a tight tuck
on the shirt, belt appropriately at the navel, hair slicked and parted, always
ready for the camera. He is affable but official. "Guys, remember," he says
to the photographers, "don't zoom in on the faces of PD and workers."
Each time he rigidly enforces the rules he does so with a conciliatory tone.

He stands back of everyone and watches them work, small talking here
and there. He's just back from a vacation in Mexico City with his wife. "I
had never been." says the Tijuana native. "I expected this chaotic scene.
But people are very respectful, professional, very curious, very educated.
They are very positive," he says with surprise in his voice. "A lot of entrepreneurs, even if they're just selling chips. Spent a couple thousand with
the hotel and everything but, you know what? It was worth it. The food is
amazing. Now I'm following a couple of restaurants on Instagram."

Eduardo drifts in and out of the conversations between the photographers and reporters, there's a lot of familiarity in the group. It is the first
week in October, construction has been going on for several days now and
a few of the photographers are coming out regularly.

"Weren't you just here yesterday or the day before?" one asks another.

"Yeah, Wednesday."

"You're having way too much fun! You're going to have a helluva farmer's tan."

"I already got it!"

Ralph DeSio is on-site too, taking it all in. He is a longtime public affairs specialist for Border Patrol, a senior civilian employee, not an agent, much more blasé with reporters, inclined to say things like, "D.C. is my puppet master so they keep me busy." He is not as well groomed as Eduardo, nor is he as diplomatic. The two make for an inverted pair with the young agent often reining in the old-timer.

"The very first day," says Ralph, watching the construction in front of him, "they had an incident where somebody fell into a hole." He laughs and so do the photographers and reporters in earshot.

Eduardo cuts in: "Fortunately, he wasn't injured."

"But it wasn't a good first step," Ralph says. "The start of construction and somebody falls into a hole—I think it was forty feet deep," he says with a jeez-like buzz of the lips.

One reporter follows up, a bit incredulous: "Forty feet?!?"

Eduardo nods, reluctantly confirming the depth of the hole. "He was fine, he was fine," he adds. "He went back to work, he went back to work." He keeps repeating his words, as if to shoo away the story.

But Ralph won't let it get away: "Thank God. Otherwise that would have been a bigger story: First Day, Someone Dead," he says, laughing.

Eduardo breaks in with another reminder not to zoom in on any faces. I start asking Ralph questions because I like his answers. "Have you been getting any rocks thrown over? I know you guys say that's a big issue."

Ralph takes a moment to answer and Eduardo steps nearer to hover over the conversation. "Southside is aware of what's going on," Ralph says. "And they're likely patrolling that area—"

"They are," Eduardo says. "It was confirmed yesterday. And actually, that is a pretty tough neighborhood so they're usually there."

The gate to the construction site opens and the truck with 4,000 gallons of water appears. When it crosses in front of the viewing area it does so with enough distance to keep the spray off the cameras but close enough to hit everyone with a wave of refreshment.

Two photographers crouch behind tripods, framing shots, and one of them says, "They'll still find a way to get over."

"It's a crazy waste of money," says the other.

"To build here on this flat soil is one thing, but you go twenty miles east, it ain't happening."

A staging area is clearly delineated for each prototype but only two are taking shape so far. One is made of four concrete panels, each 30 feet tall, lined up edge-to-edge. On the north-facing side of the panels, the bottom third of the wall jets out at a sharp angle and becomes three times as thick as the top portion.

The second prototype is made of five concrete panels, also edge-to-edge. A thick mesh wire extends across the top, pitched toward Las Torres with crisscrossing razors on the end. It could easily pass for an oversize version of the walling around most prisons—if not for the faux stonework on the north-facing side of the model.

There is no signage to indicate which prototype belongs to which builder. One of the reporters asks Ralph if he knows which is which. He squints and says he's unsure. He suggests that Border Patrol number each staging area. It would save him from having to remember and it would allow all the reporters and photographers to pick favorites: "I want number one!" he says. "I want number two!"

Just as he gets the game show feeling across, Eduardo steps in to clarify that contractors have been asked not to put any signs up around their prototypes. "We don't want this to be about advertising," he says.

Ralph shrugs: there goes that idea. He looks bored and suggests to Eduardo that they fire the van back up. "Anyone want to use the blue house before we go?" A couple of guys head for the porta-potty while everyone else packs up gear. I start back to the van, just behind *The San Diego Union-Tribune* photographer. Eventually everyone's in and we make our way across the desert. Eduardo keeps driving past Enrico Fermi for a mile or so, to the spot where everyone left their cars outside the no parking zones.

I parked at the nearby Border Patrol station so Eduardo gives me a ride back with him. In the parking lot he switches out his van for an SUV and offers to let me join him for a patrol in the desert.

We head east, into the mountains, where the roads are often narrow and bending with a steep drop on one side. "Of course these views are spectacular," Eduardo says, pointing out his window, more focused as tour guide than driver. I would prefer to see both of Eduardo's hands on the wheel but I keep my mouth shut. "All-weather road, this road," he continues. "Makes a *huge* difference. Before we had to hike everything. We had access to this area by foot only."

Part of me feels this should still be the case—I'm not exactly sold on this "all-weather" designation. We wind our way through the mountains as close to the border as we can get. At least that's what Eduardo tells me, and I have to take his word for it because we have gone far beyond the primary fence and there is no barrier to mark the line. There is only continuity in all directions: the brownish hue of granite stone defines everything. There are jagged granite canyons below the road and sharp granite peaks above us—some are precariously topped by cockeyed granite boulders. Small spider trails, used by agents on ATVs, are all over the place, with even fainter trails worn only by feet. The Otay Mesa Mountain Wilderness where we ride is open to the public but we don't see anyone along the way. After an hour or so, we turn back to the west and wind our way down the mountain. The open desert levels out and this is where the primary fence begins—or ends, depending on the direction one is traveling. "In the past we had an issue with vehicle drive-throughs," Eduardo says. "Vehicles full of drugs or migrants just driving through into the U.S. So the primary fence has actually helped us stop that—or control it."

Beyond that, Eduardo doesn't have much good to say about the primary fence, the original. Its limitations have been well documented. Not just that the corrugation of the metal provides a boost for anyone wanting to get over the barrier but also that the solid panels block agents from seeing any activity that might be swelling on the other side. "Those slits that you see on the bottom of the panels—of these panels—" Eduardo taps against his window, pointing at a particular spot. "Those are made by us. That's just so we can see if there's anybody gathering on the Southside."

The panels are all numbered, a rushed spray-paint job in various shades of white. "If I have something going on in Panel 1185, I can call anybody out in the field to meet me in that spot."

Eduardo's phone rings. He recognizes the number and decides not to pick up. He says that with construction under way he's having trouble keeping up with all the media requests. "Everybody has shown an interest in the prototypes," he says. "'We want to go to the site,' and 'I want to have an interview.' There's worldwide media interest. We're not able to accommodate individual requests. I've been telling the reporters: 'We're going to take a group of reporters at a time.' That's just going to make it a lot easier." Eduardo is a gatekeeper for THE gate, and he's enjoying it. "It's going to be hot for a little bit," he says with a smile.

As we ride west along the Roosevelt Reservation, Eduardo always answers my questions with respect—perhaps too much: he keeps calling me "sir," which doesn't work for me because I'm not the one in uniform and I can't be *that* much older than he is. "You see it right there, sir," he says, pointing out the windshield. The road ahead is completely smoothed over until our tire tracks break the surface. "We keep the roads dragged so we can see any new footprints or tire marks. We have different types of drags. Some of them are just tires that we recycle from debris that comes from the Tijuana River. We also have big brushes."

Along the drive, Eduardo points out several of the colonias to the south, and each is always described as an acute security threat. There is Nido de las Águilas: "Another neighborhood that's known for smuggling," he says. And there is Parte Baja, "notoriously known as a bad neighborhood. Some of these folks are hardworking people, living their life as law-abiding citizens, but some of them are not.

"On the other side of the neighborhood, Parte Alta, kids were actually told by their parents and grandparents never to come down here, especially at night.

"There is Libertad. It's known for generational drug smuggling—the grandfather smuggled, the dad smuggled, the son smuggles now." Across from Libertad we stop and get out of the SUV. The primary fence dips low with the terrain and the road sits high, giving a good view of the colonia. Eduardo shifts back and forth between talking about Libertad in professional speak—"a challenging neighborhood"—and as someone who grew up in Tijuana near the colonias. "I lived in Otay," he says. "And I remember hearing about Libertad, how bad it was."

Eduardo points at what we both smell: mounds of trash piled up against the primary fence. "Some of these houses aren't incorporated to the city of Tijuana," he says, "and they don't have the basic necessities like trash pickup. So they'll throw their trash to the U.S. side. It's taken care of by the city of Tijuana. They gather volunteers twice a year and they pick up the trash along the border. But a couple of weeks later, it looks the same." He stares for a moment and shakes his head—part confusion, part pity—and heads back to the SUV. "I do not understand their mind-set to be honest with you."

Once we're moving again I ask Eduardo if he's seen any of these neighborhoods recently and he hasn't. For him they seem shaped by experiences working as an agent more than any old memories of the streets themselves.

Eduardo's most recent experience in Tijuana involved only the airport. He and his wife caught their vacation flight without even setting foot on the city's streets. They used Cross Border Xpress, an elevated bridge that allows passengers to enter the terminal of the Tijuana airport from the U.S. side of the border. "They do charge $16 a trip," he says. "But people gladly pay it because it's way cheaper to fly out of Tijuana than San Diego. And it's easier for a friend to drop you off there than it is for them to drop you off in Tijuana, having to deal with the border. You can also Uber it. They'll just drop you off and then you're on your way."

The bright purple Cross Border Xpress bridge is just a few miles from Libertad and circumvents not one but two fences at the international line. The secondary fence is so much more substantial than the primary but still no match for globalized capitalism—there are bargain flights to be had.

"The secondary wall is 14 to 18 feet high with concertina wire," Eduardo says, slowing down to give me a good look. The secondary fence applied lessons learned from the primary fence. It's not only taller and harder to climb with concertina wire at the top but it's also made of wire mesh that allows agents to view activity on the other side.

But more lessons were learned with the secondary fence. Eduardo explains how migrants and smugglers generally get past the newer barrier: "They'll use rope ladders with carpet or a blanket on top. They'll set the ladder and get the carpet or blanket on top of the concertina wire. And then they'll have a rope ladder on the other side too. That's a way of getting over the concertina wire.

"They also make cuts in the wire mesh. We call them compromises. They can actually pass their merchandise through." Eduardo points out a few compromises bunched together. "All these are cuts, compromises to the secondary fence. The last year fiscal year, 2016, we had approximately 550."

We continue west, from Otay Mesa into San Ysidro. The transition from one neighborhood to the other is abrupt: the industrial parks end and Las Americas Premium Outlets begin. It happens right at the spot where the Tijuana River bends north, into the U.S. The Roosevelt Reservation becomes an elevated road overlooking the river canal. Eduardo points out stadium lighting and cameras on towers high overhead. There is a lot to watch in this spot: the deportados living in the river to the south; the outlet malls to the north, along with the San Ysidro Port of Entry directly across the street from the stores.

"I can honestly tell you that I never thought I would see a Coffee Bean & Tea Leaf in South Bay," Eduardo says, his grin still carrying some disbelief. "I saw it there and I thought it was a joke."

The first phase of the mall went up in 2004 and a large part of the clientele is middle-class Mexicans. Eduardo says there have been three multimillion-dollar expansions. "This is all thanks to Border Patrol," he adds, "being able to control and manage the area." There is pride in his voice and he's sure to mention that the management company renting out spaces in the mall tells him there are no vacancies. "Nike, Levi's, Adidas— these brands would not put their name on a store and sell their product if it was back in the '70s, '80s, and early '90s. I can assure you of that." This close to the border, the sign that says *Justice* refers not to a call for immigration policy but a retailer that offers *spinkle doughnut lip balm* and *unicorn look beauty kits*.[1]

Eduardo stops the SUV at a gate built into the secondary fence. He grabs his two-way radio: "Unmarked white Suburban from Whiskey 8 to Whiskey 15, ten twelve." We sit in silence for a moment, waiting for the gate to open. As the light fades in the sky I look down into the river canal and see a small fire sparked just outside a couple of makeshift tents. It does not matter how hot the day gets, the night will always be cold. The exact spot where the river enters U.S. territory is not marked with any certainty. There is no red line painted across the canal, and the deportado encampments shrink and swell without any real consideration of the line between two countries. Their disenfranchisement extends in both directions with neither Mexico nor the U.S. willing to claim the people subsisting in the place between. Interactions are limited, mostly with the Tijuana police who clear out the canals periodically, pushing the deportados south, reasserting the unseen line.

"We don't have the area completely locked down," says Eduardo. "But I can tell you that it's controlled and before it was not. Back in the '70s and early '80s and even '90s, I mean, all the way through the '90s, agents were calling it 'No-Man's-Land.'"

CHAPTER 20

IN 1977, SAN DIEGO'S *EVENING TRIBUNE* described the border scene in San Ysidro as a "high crime area that has become a combat zone." One of the headlines, from December 7 of that year: "San Diego Gains Reputation as Alien Center."[1]

David Duke, who was then the national director of the Knights of the Ku Klux Klan, drew up plans to assemble a militia, hundreds of armed citizens to help protect the border. He held a press conference at the San Ysidro Port of Entry to make the announcement. "The rising flow of color is washing over our border," he said, "washing away our culture, our racial fabric, and changing America as we know it."[2]

It was around this time that the San Diego Police Department assembled a special task force to address the violence being reported in the papers. It was the city's police department and *not* Border Patrol that put together the task force because San Ysidro is part of San Diego and the "combat zone" was driving up the department's crime stats. So they went in.

Ernesto Salgado was a member of the task force. The official name was Border Crimes Task Force, though one lieutenant preferred Border Agent Robbery Force so that it could be shoehorned into the acronym BARF.

"All of us were Spanish speakers," Ernesto says, scratching at his bald head, "some were more fluent than others." He sits in his home office, still an imposing figure, even in his seventies. San Ysidro wasn't his first combat zone. He had a career in the Marines and fought in Vietnam before joining the police department.

BARF broke down into several undercover teams, he says. "We actually started in camouflage but that didn't work because we couldn't move fast enough. We decided to dress like the undocumented and became victims ourselves. You know, we would walk like the normal undocumented and hope that we would get hit upon by the bad guys. Then we would sit down and play the meek part and let them go through their threats and if it got to the point where they were going to hit us, then we would take them down.

"Terminology is very important when you say you're from somewhere and you use a word that, to us, means one thing but to them it means something else. We had to learn the slang of where we claimed to be coming from.

"Once we were saying we were from South America—I can't remember what country we said—but to them 'pisto' is money. And to us up here, 'pisto' is slang for alcohol. This one guy got to conversing with us and he said in Spanish, 'Do you have any pisto?' And we said, 'No, no, no, we don't drink.' And then they knew. 'No, no, no, you guys aren't from there. You guys are cops!' And our sergeant said, '¿Sabes qué? I've had enough of this.' And then he said, 'BARF!' And we took the guy down. From then on the preparatory command was always '¿Sabes qué?' And as soon as BARF was said, we would jump on them.

"We started on the Westside over by the Mexican airport and walked more than three miles. We went into the canyons because there were rapes, murders, robberies, assaults, all kinds of stuff going on.

"What you see now at the border is not what was there then. There were areas that had one single barbed wire. There were areas that had nothing. In some areas there was a chain link fence and there were culverts underneath it. That's what made it so easy for them to cross.

"There was this one guy we called El Loco who used to go around robbing migrants, wearing a mask. We couldn't get him—it took us a while. One night, we were able to grab him in the culvert.

"And there was another incident where we were on the north side of the San Ysidro Port of Entry. I was with three other guys. There was a lady and a fourteen-year-old girl. They were up against the fence at the culvert on the Mexican side. These two guys started assaulting the lady and they were getting ready to rape the little girl. It was in Mexico but two of the guys I was with said, 'Forget that, we can't let this happen.' They took one guy down and chased the other guy back south—our guy realized he was running with a gun down the streets of Tijuana so he came back."

As the task force continued into its second year, the arrests and shootouts began adding up, and so did the newspaper stories. Ernesto has two albums packed with yellowed clippings; he puts both of them in my lap for me to thumb through.

In the stories that were published, it was becoming clear to the public that whatever violence persisted at the border was not, by and large, perpetrated *by* migrants crossing into the U.S. but *on* them. The criminals were Americans and Mexicans already living in the region, claiming control over the migratory pathways.

In 1977 and 1978 the story coming out of the San Diego Police Department was the story of American heroes saving migrants, and it didn't go over well. "The citizenry was up in arms," Ernesto says, "wondering why we had these officers at the border when there was a shortage of officers on the street. Everybody started saying, 'why do we have officers protecting illegal aliens? Nobody cared. They were 'just undocumented people.'"

The task force disbanded after eighteen months. The officers took off their disguises and returned to the old beats. Violence continued at the border but everyone had learned to look away. There were still robberies and sexual assaults but Border Patrol contained the combat zone to San Ysidro, and the South Bay served as a buffer for everyone north of the 8. It took two decades for various border barriers to rise, driving out migrants and the criminals who pursued them, all the way to Bob Maupin's ranch or his neighbor's place or deeper still into the desert.

CHAPTER 21

I'M ON MY WAY OUT to the prototypes to see if Roque De La Fuente's name will still help me gain access—and my phone rings. It is the man himself, calling to say he's in town with time to meet. I make a U-turn and head up north, past the 8.

Predictably, Roque asked me to meet him at the Del Mar Country Club, for lunch at the 19th hole. He comes straight from the locker room, just out of the shower, and I assume this means he finished a round of play but not so. He tells me he just showed up for the shower and the food. Things are a bit complicated at home: he is sharing the primary residence in Rancho Santa Fe with his ex-wife. The divorce sounds recent or even ongoing. "Under California law," he tells me, "she owns 50 percent of everything." And he laughs a deep, dark laugh, laced with all kinds of pain.

Roque shaved after the shower and now he's bleeding. It's just a nick, almost lost on his broad, shiny chin, except the blood is stubborn, slowly soaking through the little wad of Kleenex that Roque left there to plug it up. He discovers the situation by accident with a brush of the fingers and swaps out the red Kleenex with a fresh little wad from a cocktail napkin. Despite the blood, Roque is very well composed, giving off fresh wafts of cowboy aftershave; his thinning gray hair is slicked back tight against his scalp. He wears a shiny blue pullover shirt with a pattern of scattered flags—all fictional flags, all regal and vaguely international.

Roque leans over our table, scribbling a map of Otay Mesa on a napkin. He draws several Xs and tells me that each represents a fortune he has already made—or that he intends to make very soon. One X marks the spot where he might sell property to the county for a landfill. One X marks the mile of land surrounding the prototype site, which he might sell to the federal government. "They've been trying to get that from me for *years*," he says.

When the government began putting up the secondary fence from the Pacific Ocean to the Otay Mesa desert in 2008, the Department of Homeland Security was very specific about the project extending 14 miles. The memorandums, the press releases, the waivers from the secretary of the department of homeland security all referenced 14 miles of new fencing. In the end, it was more like 13 because Roque De La Fuente did not sell the last desired parcel of land. Negotiations for the government to acquire that last mile are ongoing, which is how Roque seems to like it.

One thing that makes the 14th mile so desirable is its proximity to the spot where the government is planning a third border crossing for San Diego County. There are just two in the county now, Otay Mesa and San Ysidro, and Otay is the only commercial port, designed primarily for eighteen-wheelers heading south with raw goods, then north with finished products. Roque was instrumental in getting the Otay port opened in 1985 and since then he's been pushing to build another commercial crossing.

"Right now," he says, "they think they're going to break ground on the new port in March of 2019 and have a two-year build out. I think they'll achieve that. I mean, c'mon, Otay is the second busiest commercial port of entry between Mexico and the United States. The first is Laredo, the second is Otay, and the third is El Paso. Laredo has at least two commercial ports of entry. El Paso has at least two and we only have *one*.

"I think what they're trying to figure out is whether funding's going to come from Customs and Border Protection or the toll revenues for the facility. It's supposed to have these express lanes where it's a dollar to use when there's not much traffic, but as traffic backs up, it becomes three dollars. But first there is some technology to be worked out to make sure that this is a financial success."

There will be a lot of development in Otay if the port is realized: more logistics companies and truck stops, more warehouses and industrial parks. "That's the big catch," says Roque. "A new port of entry." He circles the corresponding X on the map several times, tearing at the napkin where it's drawn. "Priority number one."

Roque puts two more Xs on the map, each at the base of the Otay

Mesa mountains, about three miles north of the prototypes. Both of these spots, Roque explains, represent a parcel of land he already sold—one is 320 acres, the other is 687 acres.

The first of those two properties is now the Richard J. Donovan Correctional Facility, which was built by the state. Roque says it was his idea to put the prison there. Initial drawings showed plans to build it directly across from the Otay Mesa Port of Entry but Roque intervened. "They had acquired 320 acres twenty years prior and they were going to build the mother of all prisons right next to the border crossing," he says. "It was a done deal. And I said, 'Not under my watch.' We had just decided to build a border crossing. So you cross here—'Welcome to California!'— and you see the mother of all prisons? I don't believe that that is a good welcoming.

"So we basically said to the state, 'This is the wrong place to put it. Where can we put it?'" Roque feigns a quick search for ideas before continuing: "'I got the perfect location for where to put it.'" He pecks at the X with his pen. "So the State of California said, 'Done.' I was able to get them to change their minds. The governor of California, Pete Wilson, and the elected officials agreed to buy the property from me for $11 million. They were going to close the transaction in sixty days—they signed a contract. All of a sudden, thirty days later, I get a phone call and they say to me, 'Roque, we have a problem.' We're supposed to write you a check for $11 million next week. We don't have the money. You're going to learn in a week that the State of California is broke and we don't have money to pay the teachers. I said, 'Well, if you remember, I originally didn't want to sell my property. I wanted to trade with you. And you told me that the State of California doesn't trade.' So I said, 'Look, you got this property right next to the border crossing. The property that I have is three miles away: put the prison there and let me have the property next to the border.' They say, 'To be able to do that, we need to pass a bill. The State of California cannot do a trade unless there's a bill that authorizes us to do a trade.' I said, 'Well, you either pay me my $11 million or you better make it happen.' So that's basically what happened. They passed a bill and we traded. Everybody thought I was a hero because nobody knew how to put that deal together and I was able to put it together."

The story about a prison not setting the right tone for a welcome, which I thought was making for an interesting story, somehow became a story about a heroically enterprising character, which feels like a place where a lot of American stories wind up.

"Now, a second transaction," he says. "The County of San Diego wanted to build a prison too." He points at the second X at the foot of the mountains, which is now the Otay Mesa Detention Center, a private facility owned and operated by CoreCivic. "So we tell the county, 'There's already a prison right here. Adding another prison next door is the perfect thing to do. Why don't you guys go do this?' So they say, 'Okay Roque, we want to buy it.'

"I told them I'll sell it to you for $8.4 million. They said, 'We'll only pay you $6.4.' I said, 'Look, at 8.4 it's a steal.' So, guess what they did. They condemned it! And once they condemned it so they could take it by eminent domain they said, 'Forget about the offer, we're only going to give you $2.4.' I said, 'You cannot do that.' And they essentially said, 'Watch us.'

"We went to court and the jury gave me $55 million.[1] I eventually settled for $39 million. Imagine getting paid $39 million instead of $2 million—that's not chicken change," Roque says, flapping his lips. "So we sold one parcel to the state and one to the county, and we still own, today, 250 acres over there. Basically I'm the father of this whole area," he says with a grin.

Thanks to Roque, a correctional facility does not greet everyone who enters the country in Otay Mesa. They get about a three-mile reprieve before they spot it, right next to the detention center—again, thanks to Roque. He draws a big circle around the whole map and laughs: "Today the De La Fuente Business Park sits right next to the Donovan Correctional Facility. And we were able to get a power plant on our property. It was 660 megawatts. That was $1 billion that was spent there. And it's a private property, so they paid taxes. The county said, 'Wow, look! We're getting all of these beautiful property taxes.' Then they built a second power plant, 330 megawatts, nearly another $1 billion. The biggest two developments in the area have been the power plants and the prisons and we basically were part of every one of those transactions.

"And now the question is when will they finally build the third border crossing for San Diego County? They're working on it, but I have no idea what's going to happen because right now Trump wants this wall."

Roque's political endgame, it should be noted, is to defeat the president in 2020. Yes, he is planning to first run against Dianne Feinstein in

California next year but, in the end, it is all about running for president just as he did in 2016. Roque still maintains he got locked out of the Democratic primary process last time. "I said to myself, you know, there are seventeen people on the Republican ticket and I believe Trump is going to win. He's got more charisma. So he's going to win. I believe he has a lot of faults. I think he exaggerates. I think he's all showmanship, everything else that you already think or everybody else thinks—but he's going to win.

"And I said to myself, what's happening on the other side? I mean, people have to make a choice between him and who's on the other side. For all practical purposes, they basically said Hillary's going to be our horse. So I saw an opportunity. I said, you know, I can compete against Hillary, Sanders, and Martin O'Malley. It will be a lot easier for me to beat three people than for Trump to beat seventeen. And eventually, it will be Trump against me. And it will be his business judgment versus mine, his manners versus mine, his curriculum vitae versus mine. And I actually thought they played it correct on the Republican side. They allowed him to compete, thinking that he had no chance. On the Democratic side, they didn't allow shit."

While Roque was on the Democratic primary ballot in forty states, and six territories, he wasn't allowed to participate in any of the debates with the major candidates. "They closed the doors," he says. "They said this guy has bilingual, charisma, business judgment. He can be toetotoe against Trump. And maybe people might want to see a fight between him and Trump.

"Look," he says, "trying to build a fence or a wall is the most stupid thing ever. It makes sense to put a fence between Tijuana and San Diego, between Calexico and Mexicali—between the cities—but not where there are deserts and rivers."

Perplexed by his opponent's missteps, Roque shakes his head: why waste your time on The Wall when you can advocate for more ports of entry? More specifically, *commercial* ports of entry. Roque's push for the county's third crossing is not so that asylum seekers can be processed more expeditiously or so that more passenger vehicles on the way to grandma or school or work can avoid hours of waiting; rather the new port is needed to bring more goods to market more quickly. Express lanes for eighteen-wheelers bearing down on the border with a schedule to keep.

After an hour or so, we get up from the table. On the way out Roque stops here and there, shaking hands, waving across the patio of the restaurant. I watch him work the crowd, following after him, and I will confess that I never even saw a bill for our lunch—the sight of money can ruin the atmosphere at a place like the Del Mar Country Club—so, presumably, my food was added to Roque's big tab in the sky.

As we wind our way through the wood-paneled hallways of the clubhouse, past the room with the big screen TV and card tables, past the pool and the banquet halls, Roque tells me a story. It is from 1978, that first time he and his father bought land in Otay Mesa. "Some people brought us 4,000 acres for sale," he says. "And I did an analysis of the deal and I brought it to my father. 'Father, they're offering this property for sale and I did all the numbers and this property has unbelievable potential.'" He really punches *unbelievable*—his jaw jets out, his voice sinks low, and his back goes erect. "We're basically buying this property for 10 cents a square foot. And this property has the potential to eventually be $10, $20 a square foot. So I brought the guys to my father.

"We met at his house, my father said, 'Okay, tell me what you want to do.' And they said, 'The property's worth $28 million. You put in 14 and you'll own 50 percent and we'll own 50 percent and we'll become partners.' I told my father it was a hell of a deal and we should do it. And after the guy finished his sales pitch I thought it was a done deal. But my father ended up saying, 'Thank you but no thanks.' The guys were shocked. 'Why not?' 'I apologize,' my father says, 'but I don't have partners, I've never had partners and I'm not prepared to have partners. Thank you very much.' I was *really* disappointed.

"Then, two years later, the people filed for bankruptcy. And the property was in bankruptcy court—they were up to their necks in debt. All of a sudden we showed up in bankruptcy court and we were the successful bidders." *All of a sudden*. Roque has a grin on his face and it reminds me of the smirk on David Wick's face when he confessed that some in the business had, from time to time, referred to them as "grave-dancers."

"And the important thing," Roque says, continuing, "is what my father told me earlier, when the people made the offer he rejected. At that time, I asked my father, I said, 'Father, I brought these people here. I recommended you buy it, and you didn't buy it. Why?' And he told me, 'Well, one of the guys' names is Vinnie A—. He's Italian. And the rumor on the street is that he does business with the mafia.'

"Well, in reality, there's no real mafia in San Diego and this guy's not from the mafia. But he is very successful and because he has an Italian name, they can *make* him part of the mafia. My father said to me, 'I agree with you, this property has huge potential. But I have worked so hard to get to where I am. I have worked so hard for my name and my reputation that now, if I buy this property with this guy, people are going to say I made my money with the mafia.'" Roque laughs and says, "And I'm telling you," pointing straight at me, "he's not from the mafia! But it was the perception!

"So we bought the property in 1982 and we bought it for $13 million. It turns out that my father was technically right: instead of buying it at $28 million, and owning 50 percent, we bought it in bankruptcy court for $13 million and we owned 100 percent."

By now Roque and I are standing in the front lobby of the club. He stopped before we stepped outside so he could emphasize this last part of his story. The smile on his face is so fixed, his body is so unmoving as he basks in the bankruptcy court bargain, I can't help but notice how his stillness nearly matches that of the statue over his shoulder. Mounted on a block of marble at the main entrance of the Del Mar Country Club, it is a Blackamoor, or it is Blackamoor-inspired—whatever its artistic cate-gorization, it is a bust of an African man with jet-black skin, his eyes are expectant and his dress seems to be that of a worker, a servant. He reminds me of the story Roque was originally telling, the one about how his father turned an Italian into a caricature. But again the story has changed, and now it's about one businessman outmaneuvering another. Roque's father was "technically right" because he managed to get rid of the competition *and* secure the lowest possible purchase price. Just as $1 a square foot be-came $2 a square foot, the expectation was that $13 million in bankruptcy court would one day generate twice that in sales and leases. Probably even more. Roque learned early to always expect more.

CHAPTER 22

IT IS THE SECOND WEEK of October and construction is moving faster. Now four of the prototypes are really taking shape. A blue steel panel—five feet wide, 20 feet tall—is set into place on top of a 10-foot-high concrete base for the ELTA model. There still are no company signs around any of the staging areas, no advertising—save for Roque's Truck Net billboards in the background—but Border Patrol has confirmed where each builder is working.

Texas Sterling and Caddell were the first two models going up a few days ago, and now ELTA is not far behind. Caddell is one of the companies building two prototypes and their second model is coming along. It is the first to use something other than solid concrete panels at the base: 30 bollards stick out of the ground with a few inches of daylight between them. Each is about 10 feet tall and looks like it's made of rusted steel. I can't be entirely sure of the material because today I'm relegated to standing on the roof of my rental car, trying to peer over the chain link fence around the construction site. I managed to get onto Roque's land but Eduardo Olmos and Ralph DeSio aren't around and I can't get past the last fence without them. The guy manning the gate won't even let me use the blue house, as Ralph likes to call it, so I head north a few miles up to one of the truck stops on Otay Mesa Road.

I grab a coffee and sit in the parking lot for a while, watching trucks pull in and out. I read a few pages of Ursula K. Le Guin's *The Left Hand of Darkness* and write down one of her questions:

—*"What is love of one's country; is it hate of one's uncountry?"*

Exhaust from the eighteen-wheelers shoots into the sky, hanging over the flat desert; in the distance, brown smog nestles up against the mountains. A woman comes over the loudspeaker letting the driver waiting for shower #8 know that it's ready. The sun's glare obstructs the green road sign hanging in the intersection, and palm trees stand at attention in the still air. Just down the road I can see the control tower for Brown Field Municipal Airport, a former naval air station converted to a commercial runway for small aircraft—the place where Roque earned his pilot's license, ascending thousands of feet into the air to get a good look at the place where he would build his fortune.

A text comes through on my phone. It's from Civile at the loft, asking if I have any job leads for him. I told him I would let him know if I came across anyone looking for handiwork. It's been several weeks since I last saw him so I drive over to the Christ Ministry Center instead of texting back with a disappointing answer.

When I arrive, Civile is again in his room, at his desk. He has managed to get a broken laptop up and running for himself. He opens a browser to show me that it's working, but each page takes a while to load because the machine has an old, slow processor. I tell Civile I don't have any leads for him and he reminds me that he's a hard worker, a certified electrician and plumber. I assure him that I have forgotten none of these things. "And remember," he adds, "I don't give money the first place in my life, okay. If I do then I will never have enough. Let me give you an example," he says, pointing at the laptop in front of him. "Yesterday I dreamed to get this computer. It has 100 GB. But tomorrow I might think to get another one, 500 GB. When I get 500 tomorrow I will hope to get another one, 1 TB. Because every day, the more you progress, the more your problems increase."

Civile is still waiting for his work permit and can only take informal, cash-paying opportunities and there aren't many. He is knocking on doors in the neighborhood, looking for odd jobs while the interest compounds on his bond. His debt is still marked by the GPS monitor shackled to his ankle—the right ankle; the device on the left ankle is the one from the U.S. government. Everything in Civile's life is just as it was when I last saw him. The only new thing, he says, are the faces around him: a recent arrival from Cameroon, and two others from Honduras. Civile speaks Spanish so he's been showing them around the facilities, around the block, the bus system, the travel patterns he has come to memorize.

Civile tells everyone he meets: he is willing to do any work that comes his way. "The U.S." he says, "don't build with only Americans." Civile is, of course, referring to his own capacity but he's also referencing the history of labor in America. He is aware of what James Baldwin called the "sturdy, peasant stock" that has always fed capitalism a steady diet of free and cheap labor. They "picked cotton" wrote Baldwin, "and dammed rivers and built railroads and, in the teeth of the most terrifying odds, achieved an unassailable and monumental dignity."[1] Those teeth of terrifying odds chomp at the Christ Ministry Center. The people like Civile who have been living here over the past two years, they are waiting for the chance to become a part of the sturdy, peasant stock, for the chance to get ahead of the competition and land the backbreaking work that makes the American economic system thrive. Some of the most important contributors to capitalism are the unsuccessful capitalists.

After Civile and I part ways I stop into Bill Jenkins's office. He mentions there's a family in the neighborhood that's moving and they might pay Civile to help load furniture into a truck. Christ Ministry Center is in Normal Heights, one of the San Diego neighborhoods just south of the 8 where rising housing costs are driving a lot of moving in and moving out. Some of the old bungalow homes have new windows and fresh paint jobs, refinished fences and 240-volt outlets in the driveway for car charging. Bill hopes more neighbors might help find ways for Civile to earn money. "But," he acknowledges, "not everyone in the neighborhood has always been thrilled that we opened this place up to migrants."

He tells me a story from very first days when he opened the loft, as 6,000 Haitians were crossing the border. Back then, Bill says, the sidewalks around the old church were always crowded. Children filled the grassy courtyard while new mothers and their infants took in the sun from the steps leading into the sanctuary. "We averaged three hundred in the building a day," he told me. "So there was a constant stream of them going down 33rd Street to the grocery store or the 7-Eleven down on the corner—a constant stream."

Most of the neighbors supported the shelter; Bill says they brought food and clothes. Some raised concerns about sanitation with such crowded conditions, and Bill promised to maintain necessary standards, making sure everyone had safe, clean places to shower and sleep and eat. But there were concerns in the neighborhood that weren't so easily addressed. "Some of the neighbors got *really* upset," Bill recalls. "A lady down the street, she was giving me holy hell on the phone. She said, 'These are homeless and they're taking our tax dollars.' I said, 'No, they're finding jobs. They're going to be paying taxes.' I couldn't get through to her. Finally, she said, 'But it's running down our neighborhood.' I said, 'Really? Let me ask you a question. I want you to be real honest. What's more important to you: the value of your home or a human life?' There was dead silence for about ten seconds. She came back and said, 'The value of my home.' I said, 'Thank you for being honest.' And that's just one example. These are people within the shadows of the church. They're my neighbors.

"Yes, it might have been an inconvenience to the neighborhood but I think it was a time to test whether we are who we say we are. I hope we passed the test. We had many churches, many nonprofits, labor union advocates, activists who came alongside us, but the city, the county, the state, and the feds gave us not one red cent to help. But we got through it.

"I had an experience one day when I walked through the loft and everyone was eating. We must have had sixty or seventy people in there. It's a very small space and I was having to do this 'Excuse me, excuse me' thing," he says, rolling both of his shoulders in tight. "It was almost like a voice said to me, 'Quit looking at them as a mass of people. Stop and look in their eyes.' That was a transformative experience for me. I quit referring to them as 'the Haitians' even though they are Haitian. I quit referring to them as refugees even though they are refugees. I quit referring to them as immigrants or asylum seekers. They are immigrants and asylum seekers, but they're human beings, they're individuals. *That's* the way I look at them now."

Whatever Bill has seen in the eyes of the individuals he has met, the people living in the loft remain The Haitians to many of the neighbors who have been assured a certain trajectory for property values. The refugees, the immigrants, the asylum seekers, the abstracted, the mafia, the criminals, the bandits—whoever that is beyond the pale—*they* are a threat to that trajectory.

Bill updates me on life with Harry, the five-year-old he and his wife are fostering. "He's still with us," he says. "We hear he might be sent to Florida to live with some extended family, but while he's been with us, he's brought joy and laughter and love into our home which we desperately needed.

"I have no biological children, but little Harry is as close to anything

I've ever had. It came at a late time in life but he's stolen my heart and won't give it back. He's really thriving right now. He's learning English really well; we're getting him potty trained. He's playing with other children."

Bill and his wife would like to adopt Harry. He crossed the border with his mother but she is no longer able to care for him. His dad is still in Brazil and supports the idea of the adoption but the U.S. government has not yet decided if it will deport the boy. "We hope he can stay with us forever," he says. "We'll see.

"You know, when you take someone in, you open your home and you open your wallet and you open your heart. To me, that's welcoming strangers. That's who Americans have been. I'm afraid there is a new message being sent out: that's not who we are anymore. I am very, very worried that a whole new standard has been set."

CHAPTER 23

EVEN AFTER MONTHS OF LOITERING around the prototypes I still meet new agents patrolling the area. When I began, I anticipated a set crew but there are always more faces. Just the other day I encountered an agent in a jeep at the barricade near Enrico Fermi. I mentioned a nearby hiking trail in the mountains that I had heard about and asked for directions; he told me he just moved from Pennsylvania and didn't know the trail. Then he apologized and zipped away.

"We used to know every agent by name," says Donna Tisdale. "We don't know them anymore."

I've driven to East County again, this time to meet Donna, who is a good friend of Bob Maupin's. We sit at her kitchen table. She lives outside the town of Boulevard. Like Bob, her property abuts the border and, like Bob, she has experienced years of people running across her driveway in the middle of the night. There are two signs on the road that leads to Donna's house. One reads, "WE DON'T DIAL 9-1-1" and the other reads "IF YOU CAN READ THIS YOU ARE IN RANGE."

Donna tells me she and her husband don't have a close relationship with the agents at their local station like they used to. "They relaxed the standards of the Border Patrol," she says. "They were trying to beef it up, adding so many agents."

"Hiring standards?"

"Hiring standards. It was awful."

"You noticed a marked change?"

"Yes, unprofessional behavior and agents that, if you just met them, you wouldn't trust them and they wear a badge."

"Do you know any of the Border Patrol agents now?"

"There are a few. But they brought in agents from other areas who didn't know the locals."

I asked her if she could remember a specific time when she felt this shift and she says, "We used to leave our curtains open. We would never close our curtains because we are outside people. Then one time they wanted to put the scope truck on our property to watch the border. My husband said, 'Sure.'

"The scope truck is a truck with a big piece of equipment in the back—a night vision scope. They parked it out back and an agent said, 'Come on out and I'll show you what's going on.' They zoomed in on the house with the camera. The agent said, 'Let's check that house over there.' And we saw our neighbor walk out of the garage, walk around the corner and go to urinate. There was a little cat walking around his feet.

"My husband came home and said, 'We've got to close all the curtains.' They're supposed to be watching the border and you think they're watching the border, but they may be bored and look at what's going on here. We don't know the agents anymore."

CHAPTER 24

WHILE I'M STILL IN EAST County I meet up with Jill Holslin. We drive to the border outside the town of Campo so she can show me one of the lesser-known fences in the county. Outside the town center, the roads lose their names, their certainty. We drive over sagebrush, winding our way toward the rusted primary border fence. In the open terrain, the primary fence is a useful compass. The desert surrounds us but the fence interrupts the infinite, marking north and south.

Jill stops the car just short of the Roosevelt Reservation. We are a few hundred feet away from the southern terminus for the Pacific Crest Trail—the beginning of a 2,650-mile, grand excursion north, and the only nearby spot marked on most maps.

As we walk toward the primary fence, I notice another barrier in the foreground. Not really a barrier, more of a failed cattle fence. There are metal posts, about four feet high, holding up barbed wire, but the effort is sagging in various places, completely collapsed in others. Tangles of wire are half buried in the sand. Small metal placards dangle from the wire, here and there, like ornaments on a Christmas tree.

I approach the fence and grab one of the metal squares in my hand. It has writing engraved on it; it's hard to make out at first with the sun glistening off the silver surface but eventually I find the right angle and catch the text:

AS YOU PASS THIS POST
YOU ARE AMERICAN
NOT MEXICAN-AMERICAN OR

AFRICAN-AMERICAN-BUT AMERICAN
YOU WILL NOW DEFEND AMERICAN
FREEDOM! FOR YOUR FAMILY,
YOUR CHILDREN, YOUR HERITAGE!

I grab another placard, to see if it carries the same message. Yes, but no:

WE HAVE ROOM FOR
ONLY ONE LANGUAGE
ENGLISH ROOM FOR
ONE SOLE LOYALTY
THAT IS TO THE USA
IT'S FLAG A CITIZEN
OF THE USA ONLY

This one takes a few readings; the capital letters, spacing inconsistencies, and lack of punctuation make it seem rambling. Perhaps it *is* one long, wayward thought. Or perhaps this is a remarkable poet who eludes me. But the latter seems unlikely, as most of the messages seem to have a rather arbitrary presentation of the text:

REAL AMERICANS DO NOT BARGE
ACROSS THE BORDER LIKE THUGS TO
LOOT, PILAGE AND ABUSE OUR
HOSPITALITY. THEY COME THE RIGHT
WAY, DO RIGHTLY AND LEARN
OUR LANGUAGE AND BECOME
LOYAL AND TRUE AMERICANS
THEM WE WELCOME

Jill has come out here a few times to get photos of all the messages, which isn't so easy with the direct sun and shiny surface of the placards. She has counted more than fifty different messages but some have disappeared, stolen by rain and wind and visitors. Still, dozens remain and most read as strident announcements about assimilation. Some say it will not be possible, no matter how it is defined:

GO HOME AND STAY THERE
GOD BLESS AMERICA

One placard simply reads:

DROP DEAD

And the one next to it reads like a roll call:

MULHOLLAND FIGHTING CLAN 41-06
WWI 4 CLANS MEN
WWII T CLANS MEN
KOREA 5 CLANS MEN
VIETNAM 2 CLANS MEN
SPECIAL FORCES WORLD WIDE
13 CLANS MEN

I do not know what "T" means, with regard to the "WWII Clans Men," but if the last line is meant to be a sum total then I suppose the "T" could be a typo, perhaps an abandoned effort to write out "TWO."

Some of the placards just have names engraved on them, with the feel of a memorialization or a major donation. Some of the names come with home states or cities or neighborhoods. There is one placard from Alice H—of Brooklyn, New York, where I lived the better part of twenty years. I tried to find Alice after seeing the placard—oh, I tried. But I couldn't find you, Alice. I can't help but wonder if I've ever passed you on the street or sat next to you on the subway. Maybe you were the one in the lawn chair across from Farrell's Bar & Grill in the summer. Or the mean one at Community Bookstore on 7th Avenue. Whoever you are, Alice, you are some 2,800 miles from this place and still you send this message:

MY DONATION HELPED TO BUILD
THIS FENCE WHICH IS BEING
ERECTED AND MONITORED TO
PREVENT UNATHORIZED CROSSING
FROM MEXICO INTO THE UNITED
STATES OF AMERICA

The message is more expository than rousing but the phrase on that last line, *States of America*, now that's something I'd like to consider, Alice. Did you plan that? Or was that just part of this big exercise in haphazard line breaks? Perhaps it was a volunteer who engraved all these messages, someone too overworked, too tired to think anything of separating *United* from *States of America*. But it has got me thinking, Alice. Perhaps we should contemplate the various states of America. There is the liberated state, for instance, represented by Revolutionary War, the divided state represented by Civil War, the imperialistic state represented by Dirty Wars, the capitalistic state represented by Trade Wars, and various other states, all of which—it would seem, Alice—are defined by war. Were you the one I saw on the bus reading Amitava Kumar's novel, *Immigrant, Montana*? Do you remember the passage where Kailash contemplates U.S. engagement in the 1990 Gulf War: "There was alternative energy for everything in normal, comfortable, American life—television, air conditioners, light, heat, cars. There was only one enterprise that needed such a colossal infusion of energy that no alternative to oil would work—and that was war. A tank could move only seventeen feet on a gallon of gasoline. This war was a war to ensure that America could continue to make war."[1] It feels like our only constant state, Alice, is one of conflict. Perhaps this is why we have accepted the border as a combat zone. Perhaps your hope in this hopeless barbed wire was not in vain: yesterday work began on the fifth prototype.

The mention that the fence would be "monitored" helps to better understand what otherwise appears to be a senseless undertaking, it indicates a bigger vision than the half-buried fence. In 2010 a man named Jim Wood started the Border Fence Project. At the time he was a forty-five-year-old web designer slowed, but clearly not deterred, by Parkinson's disease. He traveled two hours south regularly, from his home in Orange County, to do, he said, what the federal government could not: keep the migrants out and catch all those who got in. While Congress debated what the militarization of the border should look like, Wood raised money for cameras, patrols, the barbed wire fence with the placards—all installed in East County where Operation Gatekeeper had driven much of the migrant traffic. It wasn't just the fence but the monitoring—patrols with two-way radios, motion detectors, cameras, and the capacity to stream footage on the internet twenty-four hours a day. Wood said anyone in America could help monitor the border. Anyone, that is, who took a test to get the password-protected footage. The test covered how to gauge threats from migrants. One of the questions asked, "Why is it good to note if migrants are carrying big bags?" If one guessed the answer to be that big bags are more likely to have drugs in them then one could gain access to the footage.

But Wood found out what the Army Corps of Engineers and various law enforcement agencies and Bob Maupin had already discovered: the East County landscape is not for patrols and equipment. The days climb to 123 degrees in the summer, dip below freezing in the winter, and during the wet season the floodwater washes out the so-called roads. Wood's solar-powered cameras that routinely failed because of water damage and windswept brush was enough to set off the sensors. The project was abandoned after less than a year, and Alice—Alice, you stopped getting what you paid for.

CHAPTER 25

A COUPLE OF DAYS LATER, the short stark messages on the placards are the ones sticking with me: *Go Home And Stay There, Drop Dead,* the Clansmen head count. And the *120-mile* drive that Jim Wood routinely made from his home in Mission Viejo to organize the Border Fence Project in the desert.

I make that very drive, trying to find Wood, but his trail in the real world is even more faint than online. Driving back south from his hometown, I pass through the city of Escondido, where a twenty-foot-tall cross stands on a small mountain. The cross is, for many, the most recognizable landmark in the city of Escondido—definitely for anyone whose travel patterns involve the 15 Freeway, which passes right by the white monument with beveled edges. The history of the mountain itself complicates what might otherwise be interpreted—casually, from the fast lane—as a religious symbol. In the 1920s the local chapter of the Ku Klux Klan held its initiation ceremonies on the mountain,[1] and in 1966 a local Lions Club paid to build the cross in the same spot.[2] Today it is maintained by an organization called Let's Light the Cross, Inc.[3]

There are tremendous views up on the mountain. Escondido is in the northern section of San Diego County, which, like East County, exists on its own terms and gets proper designation as North County. Historically it has been agricultural, strawberry fields and avocado trees, and despite some industrialization it is still mainly wide open and green, particularly from the foot of the cross. But perhaps it wasn't just the scenery that drew the Klan to the perch: the mountain is formally known as Battle Mountain because it is the historically recognized sight of the 1846 Battle of San Pasqual[4] in the

Mexican-American War. The Battle of San Pasqual was a rare and stinging defeat for the American forces at the hands of the Mexicans.

"When you consider the lost battle, I don't think it's a coincidence that the Ku Klux Klan chose that mountain," says Ricardo Favela, who lives in nearby Fallbrook, where he grew up. He has spent his whole life studying the history of the area—and living through it. "When I come from San Diego and I pass that mountain, I'm like, okay: I'm in North County," he says, laughing.

I meet with Ricardo at a coffee shop—more accurately *the* coffee shop—in his hometown of 30,000. He points to one of the roads leading out of Fallbrook, called Ammunition Road, which, fittingly, arrives at the entrance to Camp Pendleton. Much of the land now used to train Marines, including Navy SEALs, was once a complex of cattle ranches owned by a man named Pío Pico, who was the last Mexican governor of California and someone who fought in the Battle of San Pasqual. "Pico was very significant in California history in that he opposed the U.S. occupation," says Ricardo. "He and his brother were the two that were at the head of the resistance.

"A lot of the communities in Fallbrook sit on former Mexican ranches. But we're not taught about who the families were in school, what their contributions were, that they were actually the first settlers in the area. There's been a constant, unbroken presence of Mexican people in this community. You can't say the names of certain communities without speaking Spanish—even San Diego, to say it correctly, you have to say it in Spanish. The space might have become part of the U.S. at a certain point, but that didn't mean that we went away. I think it's so important to recognize and celebrate and uphold that because it changes the narrative that we're foreign—which is based on myth, not on historical accounts. We're not a foreign people."

Ricardo grew up playing in avocado trees where his father picked fruit. The family migrated from Durango, Mexico. Fallbrook appealed to Ricardo's dad not just because of the steady work but the landscape. "He liked the nearby mountains," says Ricardo. "They reminded him a lot of home."

The white cross, however, was very American. "I grew up being ashamed of my family," he says, "of speaking Spanish, of eating the food that we ate, telling people about what my father did. And that's just something that you grow up with—I mean, that's just the climate. Unconsciously you have to respond to it.

"In the early '80s, Tom Metzger was the Grand Dragon of the Ku Klux Klan, meaning he was head of the statewide Klan. But he felt that he didn't go far enough. So he created the White Aryan Resistance—and this was all based here in Fallbrook. When I was in high school, the White Aryan Resistance members, the skinheads, they would make their leaflets, their literature, put them around campus. And often, they had cartoons of Mexicans in the most vile way that they could depict us, right? So we saw open hostility, open violence, calls for violence, against our community. And we saw a lot of that whole narrative of Mexicans being foreign.

"Some of our parents were being attacked in the groves. They called it 'beaner bashing.' On the weekends, the white youth would go out and look for a worker in the grove and beat them up for fun. I remember two guys talking in the locker room. One of them says to the other, 'Hey, what are you going to do this weekend?' The other guy says, 'I'm going beaner bashing. Want to go?' The other guy says, 'I'm grounded.' I mean, it was that type of conversation—like he was going to the movies.

"And since then I've tried to understand why it is—if our community contributes so much and is such a cornerstone of the local economies—why are we disparaged? Why are we treated the way we're treated? What does it take for our community to get the respect that we deserve?

"Everything that we still hear today is the same exact narrative, the same exact talking points that I heard from Metzger, from other groups—or we hear it from right-wing politicians. It's the constant narrative that we don't belong here. For me, the narrative of the border is that narrative, Metzger's narrative, the Klan's narrative."

When Ricardo was still a young kid in the 1980s, older teenagers started organizing and formed United Pride. "They believed that if we tucked in our shirts and picked up trash and painted over graffiti and we did service for the community that that would eventually change people's minds, change what they thought about us, and eventually change the relations in the community."

One of Ricardo's older brothers got involved. "They were also looking at history, they'd talk about history. They said, 'Mexican history goes back thousands of years, there's great civilizations there. We have something to be proud of.' I grew up being ashamed of who I was. And now I'm being told there's so much there to be proud of."

There were other chapters of United Pride in Escondido and farther south in Encinitas. "The Chamber of Commerce, at one point they declared United Pride Day in Fallbrook because of the good work the group had done. But then one of the youth that was part of this organization was being harassed by law enforcement and the community thought that the sheriffs crossed the line. The white community, the Chamber of Commerce, sided with the sheriffs. So that division, that social division, came up to the surface again. And the youth started questioning themselves: we've done all this and we're still not getting the respect, we're still not getting the change we set out to get.

"And that was what sparked me and I said to myself, 'This is what we need to figure out. What are our basic human rights?'

"Although we're seventy miles away from the border, we are impacted by vigilantes, by CBP's and the DHS's policies. I mean, we're all affected. There's constant Border Patrol activity in this area. I see more Border Patrol on a daily basis than I see local sheriffs. They come to our communities. And we're at the far end of San Diego County near the place where Riverside County starts so there's a checkpoint here. In order to keep going further north, we have to cross that checkpoint. We have family members that live in Riverside. We have family members that don't have documentation. Anytime we want to travel to visit family, we have to keep that in mind. Then there's a checkpoint in San Clemente on the 5 Freeway. It's like a beehive here. It's the nucleus of Border Patrol.

"People don't understand that the border is a region. It's not just a line where they're just going to line up agents. In communities like Fallbrook, seventy miles away, even going to Riverside and Orange County there's Border Patrol, all the way up to Disneyland. I don't think people associate communities like Disneyland as part of the border. Most folks think of the border as being at the line, being down in San Ysidro or south of the 8. But the border resurfaces, right? And any discussion of our community is always linked to Border Patrol and immigration. And we're constantly tied to that concept that we don't belong here, that someone needs to be supervising us all the time. The concept that we're a foreign people."

CHAPTER 26

A SEDAN LABELED *Department of Homeland Security Police* approaches the prototypes and rolls to a stop in front of the all-concrete designs from Caddell Construction. An officer gets out of the car and puts on a bulletproof vest. He takes several steps toward the Caddell then turns back toward the car, and, as he does, a cell phone emerges from the passenger-side window, held by another officer who is, apparently, willing to snap the shot but unwilling to get out of the car to do so. The officer in the bulletproof vest gives a thumbs-up and rugged smile for a count of three then drops both, takes off the vest, and gets back in the car. A moment later they continue down the line, coasting the Roosevelt Reservation in the direction of the Pacific Ocean.

CHAPTER 27

WHILE THE GOVERNMENT'S REQUESTS FOR proposals required security plans from the builders, I haven't seen any private muscle on the scene. It's the public sector that continues to provide the security detail. The stream of drive-bys is steady—San Diego police, Border Patrol, California Highway Patrol, they are looking more bored and aimless by the day.

I am taking in the action with Jill Holslin again, from a mound of dirt in Las Torres, and I see two Border Patrol agents to the east, trotting toward the prototypes on horses, but they pull up well short of the action: not only are there no protesters to wrangle but the vibrating din of construction doesn't look like it sits so well with the animals, so the agents turn back toward the mountains.

It is the third week of October and now there is progress on all eight prototypes with six looking nearly complete. KWR Construction and W. G. Yates are the two builders getting late starts. The KWR model, which might very well be the last one to get finished, is only the second design to feature bollards at the base. The other six have solid concrete bases.

Aurelia comes over to where Jill and I are standing at the primary fence. She says she's still looking for the perfect frames for the pictures that Jill gave her. "Thank you again," she says, in Spanish. Then she adds: "And don't forget you are not the only one with a camera." Aurelia is smiling as she says this, pointing up at the Border Patrol cameras mounted on top of a tower that's at least 40 feet high. Jill laughs, "Right," and we all look up at the cameras. There are several lenses, all fixed at different angles to capture 360 degrees. The tall column of scaffolding is so tall it dwarfs the prototypes; the surveillance is so out of sight it's easy to forget about—though lately there have been more reminders. With the mounting boredom within the security apparatus, Border Patrol agents have taken to phoning Mexican federal law enforcement when they feel like the cameras and the stares from Las Torres are too much. This prompts the Mexican federal authorities to send out Tijuana police to chase us away.

Maybe fifteen minutes after Aurelia's warning an officer arrives in a pickup. There are two men in the bed of the truck, cuffed with their hands behind their back. The officer hops out in a thick bulletproof vest and—without saying anything to Jill and me—climbs onto an adjacent mound of dirt, not quite as high as ours. In order to see the action he must step onto the very tips of his toes. After tiring of that he finds a rusted-out spot in one of the landing mats and peeks through it, tracking the last blue steel panel being placed onto the ELTA model. There are six of the panels and, one by one, each has been carefully inched into place by a telescopic crane. This has been going on for a few days now. Each piece takes several hours to place perfectly and secure with rivets.

Work on most of the designs is being done with large panels of steel and concrete, which are fabricated off-site, hauled in, hoisted up, and methodically lowered into place. It gives the scene grandeur—not quite *Fitzcarraldo* but, still, man's quest to conquer nature is there, in the heavy sway of the steel, dangling from a giant hook set against cirrus clouds.

After a few minutes, the cop steps off the mound and asks Jill and me what we're doing at the fence. Jill lifts her camera and tells him in Spanish that she's a photographer and that she takes many pictures of the border. I tell him I'm just watching the show. "Es como ver teatro. ¿No?" I say, unsure if I have that just right. He gives me no reaction and seems annoyed that he's been sent over to make us leave.

"What are you writing?" he asks me in Spanish, looking at my notebook.

"Soy escritor. Estoy aquí trantando, trantando—"

He interrupts me immediately and turns to Jill, keeping it Spanish: "Do *you* speak good Spanish?"

Jill says, "Yes," and steps forward.

"What are you reporting about?" the officer asks her.

"I'm an artist," she says, "so this is a long project for me."

"Okay," he says, "the thing is, you can't be here along this line because it can be misinterpreted that you want to help people cross over, make tunnels or holes. That's the reason."

"Got it," Jill says. "Did Border Patrol ask you to come over?—do you have an agreement with them?"

"Yes," he says, "I report anything that goes on here and if I need support they send people over to the international line. For example, we've had situations where they even send out helicopters for support. We've seen smugglers and raiders and they send out help and support."

"Do you think this agreement with the U.S. is a good idea?" I ask.

"Yes," he says, "it's good. The wall? No. The wall, no, but having the Mexican police coordinated with the U.S., yes. There are a lot of people who try to cross, looking for a better future, but there are also a lot of people who are using people to make a profit. There are a lot of smugglers. I'm one of the leaders here and we receive a lot of threats. We avoid Facebook, anything like that for our own safety. So if you are going to work here I'm going to ask you to be careful because there is also a group of people here who can take away your camera. So do it from a distance and take care of each other, so you don't have any problems while doing your work."

"Very well, yes," says Jill. "This is just a project for me, I'm not helping people cross, I'm not a smuggler."

The officer likes Jill's declaration and laughs. "You're not a smuggler, huh?"

"No," she says, laughing with him.

He looks at his watch and starts back toward his truck, still tickled by the idea of Jill as a smuggler. The two men in the back of his truck have been silent for the whole visit. Both of them are cuffed and look exhausted. Jill guesses they were caught trying to get across the border. The men have fully surrendered, staring hopelessly into the bright sun emerging from the clouds. It is early October, early fall, but it feels like summer. The dry heat lingers with Santa Ana winds on the way, raising the possibility that even the smallest ember might be fanned into an uncontainable flame. The threats of fire, drought, flooding, earthquakes and aftershocks run in cycles in Otay Mesa. It could make one think twice about building the prototypes in the California desert—a decision questioned by most of the contractors I've met who bid on the job: Why not Arizona or Texas? Why not a border state with politics more friendly toward The Wall, a state with lower wage demands for subcontractors, lower fuel costs, less red tape? For everything California lacked in practical terms as the setting for the prototypes, it was *supposed* to make up for in theatrics. But that was before the activists proved so unwilling to stand on their mark and light a match.

CHAPTER 28

I VISIT WITH A FEW activists to see what they're up to, if not protesting, and I reconnect with Enrique Morones, who tried to hoodwink me into binational yoga when I met him last month at Friendship Park.

Border Angels, the organization he founded in 2001, focuses all its work on migrants. Over two decades, Enrique has been the engine for the organization; his most natural role is unquestionably that of spokesperson. "I've gone on all the shows," he tells me as we settle into his office a mile from Chicano Park. "The *Today* show, Lou Dobbs, *O'Reilly Factor*, all that. Lou Dobbs would say, 'I'm not a racist, my wife is Mexican.' And I'd say, 'What does that have to do with anything? Lou, I don't know your wife. I know you and you're a racist.' I would say this on the show. Of course he would get really mad.

"O'Reilly, he would say to me, 'You call yourself Mexican? You were born in the USA!' And I'd say, 'Hey Bill, if you want to call yourself Irish or Irish-American or American, that's up to you, but I am Mexican and I'm going to call myself what I want to call myself.' That would really get him mad. I didn't do it to make him mad—it's because that's what I believe! I love the United States too, but I'm proud of my own roots."

It might have been both: pride *and* getting under O'Reilly's skin. Enrique is a professional instigator. "I became public enemy number one of the Minutemen," he says. "We did a lot of creative stuff to expose these guys and we were very successful in getting them to shut down in some communities. We would follow them around and make all sorts of noise so migrants would know they were there," he says, laughing.

"I used to have police protection for about five years. I had an undercover cop because I was getting death threats. I never talk about it because that's what they want. They want you to get out there and provoke them and I didn't want any of that."

While I don't think Enrique was trying to provoke death, it does seem that he was definitely trying to provoke the Minutemen—and succeeding at it, as evidenced by his cable news appearances that live online. He also has a habit of name-dropping: Cesar Chavez, Dolores Huerta, Ethel Kennedy— Enrique's met them all. More recently he's worked with the actor Demián Bichir. "Demián contacts me and goes, 'Enrique, I saw you in the news. I want to join you. Can I join you and do some sort of action?' I said, 'Yes, you can join me, but the action is going to be this Sunday at Friendship Park. I'm going to have the San Diego Symphony on one side of the wall and musicians from Baja California on the other.' He goes, 'Okay!' and he did join me."

Enrique points to a picture of Bichir in Friendship Park. All the walls in Enrique's office are covered with pictures, framed newspaper clippings, posters—a museum of Border Angel press. Boxes full of Border Patrol paraphernalia are stacked in one corner: Border Angel stickers are $1, Border Angel bracelets are $5. There are no big donors here, this organization sweats for every dime it raises.

Enrique has been organizing events at Friendship Park since Border Patrol reopened it in 2011. In 2013, he was involved with getting a gate at the pavilion opened so that the first lady of Tijuana and the fiancée of the mayor of San Diego could greet each other in a symbol of binational unity. Just before the ceremonious moment, someone grabbed Enrique and pointed out a man whose daughter was also in the crowd but on the south side of the fence. Enrique was told that the man had never had the chance to embrace his daughter. When he heard that, he approached the man: "I go, 'Listen, we don't have time: put on this Border Angel T-shirt, don't say anything, just pretend you're part of the ceremony. And I want you to be standing next to me when they open the door.' He was all nervous, but then all of a sudden, the door opens, it was the first lady of San Diego and this guy with the Border Angels shirt was standing right next to her. His little daughter sees him—she's on the Tijuana side but she goes running up and jumps into his arms. That was not planned."

Enrique points at a giant photo of the moment in a framed newspaper clipping.

"I was hoping something would happen but it wasn't planned. We were all stunned. Afterward, the chief Border Patrol agent for San Diego, he pulls me aside and says, 'Enrique, I could have arrested that little girl. You didn't say that was going to happen.' I go, 'We both know that would have been the worst decision in your life. That image of a little four-year-old in handcuffs for hugging her dad?' I said, 'I didn't know that was going to happen and that was a beautiful moment.'"

The chief was not persuaded because he didn't allow the event the following year. It wasn't until a new chief was appointed to the San Diego sector that Enrique saw a chance to restart the conversation and, eventually, persuaded him to let Border Angels organize a "Door of Hope" event where people from either side of the border could embrace during a brief fifteen-minute ceremony, closely supervised by agents.

Since that day when the daughter ran into her father's arms, there have been five Door of Hope events. Enrique's always pushing for more. He's trying to organize a soccer game too. His relationship with Border Patrol is tricky, he has to balance instigation with persuasion, honey and vinegar. "Because of that relationship I have with the Border Patrol," he says, "we've been able to do a lot of things."

Enrique has to keep his inner provocateur checked, which is why, he says, he is not organizing any protests. Border Angels is trying to channel the rage by organizing water drops—hikes to remote locations to leave behind jugs of water for migrants.

Enrique was doing water drops on his own before he started Border Angels. For him, the practice goes back to the 1980s when he was introduced to migrant farmworkers living in the canyons of Carlsbad, in North County. He brought water to them and a few years later, when Operation Gatekeeper drove migrant traffic to East County, Enrique started making water drops in the desert. Friends joined him and, eventually, he formalized the effort by creating Border Angels. "We're kind of like the Navy SEAL team," says Enrique. "Because we're on the front lines and we can respond right away." The viewpoint that the border is a security zone feels so very established when even the activists pushing back on the idea speak in such militaristic terms.

I tell Enrique I want to go on a water drop. He asks for my email address and I write it down for him. "Be ready to go early on Saturday," he says. "And get plenty of rest the night before. You'll hear from my team tomorrow with all the details."

A few days later, about a hundred people are gathered outside the Border Angels office at 6:45 a.m. To start any later would make the journey too hot. It is already too hot but, in a few hours it will be dangerously hot. Everyone signs waivers, which comes as no surprise. The email to all of the water drop volunteers read like it was meant to scare away as much as inform. Here's an excerpt:

> It will feel VERY HOT. Keep in mind, the temperature and lack of shade could present health difficulties for those sensitive to heat and sun exposure. We will have safety monitors equipped with umbrellas and electrolytes, but that can only do so much for those with a low tolerance. For those that are sensitive, we advise you not to attend. We also advise those with serious health problems not to attend, and those recovering from surgery. Please use your best judgement when deciding whether or not to attend. If you are unclear, please consult your physician.

I should underscore this is a *brief excerpt* from the email; there were other paragraphs with other warnings: Don't come if you are in the U.S. on a temporary visa from Iran, Libya, Sudan, Syria, Somalia, or Yemen; don't come if you have DACA status.[1] Try to drink three gallons of water in advance of departure. If you can't come, don't worry, there is a waiting list. Each month an average of one hundred people sign up. In November of 2016, four hundred people signed up.

Organizers get all of the volunteers to huddle up for announcements. There are lots of twenty-somethings, couples and clumps of friends. Jacqueline Arellano is the first organizer to speak. "Thank you guys for stepping up," she says. "A lot of people dropped out. It's okay. It's going to be very hot and we understand," she says, as if to suggest it's not too late.

Jackie tells us she is the proud daughter of once undocumented parents. She is from the Imperial Valley, to the east where we'll be hiking in a couple of hours. "Just remember," she says, "however hot it is, it does not deter migrants." She reminds everyone that the gallon of water each person holds just might "spare a human from painful death by dehydration." But Jackie is also realistic with the volunteers: some of the bottles disintegrate in the hot sun before they're discovered by the migrants who need them; some jugs are slashed by Border Patrol agents and activists who do not want them to be found. Jackie mentions a viral video of one agent dumping out gallons of water—"you've all probably seen it," she says, as a few people pull out their phones. Jackie says she recently found fifty slashed jugs while scouting routes, and that another organization that does water drops in Arizona, No Mas Muertes, has found 3,000 slashed jugs in the last three years.

Jackie asks everyone not to post videos or pictures while we're on the water drop. "In fact," she says, "everyone should go into airplane mode—no GPS tracking. Some groups who slash the bottles closely monitor social media posts. And when you post something, when you check in on Snapchat, Instagram, or Facebook, it geotags you and that's leading people directly to where our gallons are. Please, please do not post anything while you're on route. Take plenty of pictures but don't upload them until you're back here."

After all the warnings, the volunteers are put into groups of twelve; each will hike to a different location and leave behind jugs of water. Carpools are arranged—I cram three San Diego State University freshmen into my rental—and we drive seventy miles east to the Shell gas station in Jacumba.

Upon arrival, I am assigned to a group led by Jonathan Yost. He is thirty and his army green fisherman's hat protects most of his face from the sun—but not his long red beard, which almost becomes translucent in the direct light. He wears only a T-shirt and shorts, exposing several tattoos.

We huddle around Jonathan and he introduces the two guys who will be our safety monitors. One of them runs through a tutorial with the group: "Let's talk about the internal and external things to watch for," he says. He tells us that we're looking out for rattlesnakes, brown recluse spiders, and scorpions. "Don't go climbing off into the boulders. Looks tempting, but that's where those critters hide out. And don't pick up any trash. Scorpions love to hide under it." He reminds us to answer the following questions honestly every few minutes: How am I feeling? Am I dizzy? Am I feeling nauseated? Am I losing my balance at all? These are questions that should not leave our minds. One of the safety monitors mentions that they'll be carrying first-aid kits, highlighting that the kits include tweezers. "To get cacti out of your leg," he says, "if that happens."

Jonathan distributes printed directions to the exact spot where we will be driving into the desert from the gas station. It is mid-morning and the sun is much higher now, bearing down on us. "We need to go now," Jonathan says. He tells everyone to drive in a caravan. "Bumper to bumper," he insists. "It might be overkill but I don't want anyone to get lost. It's the last thing we want to happen out here."

We get back on the 8 heading east and take the first exit onto the 98 toward Calexico. We drive just over seven miles down the desert road in a tight pack that reminds me of a funeral procession. Two big rigs pass us going the other way but otherwise we have the desert to ourselves. We make our last turn onto a dirt road called Coyote One. The sign marking the road, which is peppered with bullet holes, is the last we see, and after half a mile the dirt becomes much more sandy. Our caravan slows to a deliberate pace, allowing the lead driver to veer left and right in pursuit of the sturdiest-looking parts of the road. I am the third driver and can feel my tires spinning out in a couple of spots but I manage to power forward. Then there is one divot, pure sand, and the car behind me gets stuck. I honk my horn to alert the cars in front. All the drivers stop and everyone wanders over on foot to take a look at the stuck car.

As we stand there, staring at the half-buried back tires, we all begin to sweat. Then the driver grabs a piece of cardboard from his trunk and uses it like a shovel to clear out some of the sand around the rear tires. Others survey the area for whatever loose, flat rocks can be gathered and arranged like paving stones. We build two small tracks, one for each tire, trying to give the rubber a surface to grab. The driver gets behind the wheel again and, with four of us pushing against the back of the car, he gases it. The car lurches forward but does not rise completely out of the ditch. The stone tracks are obliterated by the weight of the tires and sand has closed in again.

We are more exhausted, our sweat is caked with dust, and more frustrated, more determined to win—so we try again. We gather bigger, flatter rocks and build stronger tracks. We squeeze one more person around back of the car to push while the driver taps on the gas. Again it doesn't work, which frustrates us more but we try again.

After half an hour, Jonathan announces that there is time for one more attempt. If it doesn't work, we'll have to move on and come back to free the car the next day. Otherwise the window of time to complete the hike before the noon sun will close. So we put a different driver behind the wheel, with a different touch, and once more we push, harder still—grinding teeth, grunting, cursing, every last current of energy. The low-riding, stubborn, motherfucking Honda Civic finally relents, lifting out of the sandy ditch.

Everyone gets back into the cars, the caravan continues down the road for another half mile, and the journey is completed without further incident. The road ends and it's time to get out of the cars and start hiking.

Jonathan sets the speed as we start into the canyon. "Don't charge ahead," he says. "We're doing this together and everyone moves at a different pace." We inch forward and, despite our deliberate steps, one of the volunteers asks to stop after just a few minutes. She's feeling dizzy, unsteady. She keeps looking up into the canyon at the rocks we are about to climb, and the sight of it all seems to suck whatever energy remains in her. Jonathan gently puts his hand on her back and says, "It's okay." She gets up and, with her boyfriend at her side, turns back toward their car.

Everyone else continues onward. The canyon cuts off any extended view of the landscape but sometimes the rocky walls on either side of us dip down just as we scale up a few larger boulders and, briefly, there is a glimpse of the expansive desert all around. We are just a couple of miles from the border though there is no barrier to make this evident.

The local Border Patrol station likes to know in advance when and where the water drops take place so that there aren't any unnecessary confrontations. But with more jugs slashed, Jonathan says he stopped telling the agency when he goes out.

He and a couple of other organizers scouted our path just a few days ago, setting out flags to mark the most approachable trail for us in advance. The flags are not all that mark the path; there is litter too. First it's mostly empty shell casings, empty beer boxes, empty bottles. "Be aware," Jonathan says, "the area is open to recreational shooting."

But as we get deeper into the canyon the nature of the litter changes. Clothes appear: T-shirts, shorts, pants, a couple pairs of underwear, socks— most of it caught up in thorny dried-out brush. There is a pair of shoes with images of Cinderella and a backpack covered in mermaids. There are balled-up diapers. There is plastic everywhere, empty wrappers from packages of salted crackers and nuts. Plastic water bottles at various stages of decomposition, some reduced to windswept shards. Rusted, emptied tuna cans are all along the path. All colors are in the process of surrendering. I spot a bright, partially deflated "Happy Birthday" Mylar balloon but in this landscape everything eventually turns some shade of brown.

Jonathan checks in with the group and reminds everyone that we have hiked just under a mile. "By the time a migrant reaches this point," he says, "they've been hiking for ten miles. And they're still not done. Most of them have another ten miles to go." The 8 Freeway is the ultimate destination for most; just the other side of that great divide, they are met by assimilated America and, if they're lucky, a pickup vehicle.

At one point Jonathan insists on sixty seconds of silence. "Many people have died in this area where we're walking," he says.

There is a very certain educational component to the water drop. Jonathan doesn't just want us to leave the water jugs; he wants us to have a reason for doing so. "It's about reflecting in these sixty seconds. Don't think of the thousands who have perished. Imagine one individual. What do you share in common with them? What might their name be? If they were a mother, what might they have in common with your mother? We have a connection with these people. We are walking on the same ground."

A minute passes but the silence is sustained. Everyone is too tired to talk. Except for Jonathan, who continues to check in on everyone and direct the experience a little more: "Where's all the shade at?" he asks, rhetorically. He wants us to understand how easy our task is: he scouted the path; we have safety monitors; we have tweezers in our first-aid kit.

We reach a rocky perch in the canyon where we can see out across the desert. This is where we are to leave the water. Jonathan tells us to be careful with where we place the jugs. "As you heard," he says, "we have these anti-immigrant groups and they will sometimes locate spots we have dropped and gut our jugs. So we try to be as strategic as we can because we want it to be as visible as possible for migrants but we also want to tuck it away from people who will sabotage this."

Place the water in crevasses under rocks, he says, tucked away in the shade. One volunteer hikes another few minutes up to one of the highest points in the canyon where he can position a "signal jug" just so, beside a certain boulder that obscures it from the north while displaying it perfectly for anyone coming from the south.

Everyone finds a place to stash a jug, one by one creating a scattered oasis. Jonathan is heard every now and again: "Each jug of water, in my mind, is a life."

Most write a message on the jug with a felt-tip marker. "Estoy Contigo. Te quiero ayudar a luchar. Te Amo." Almost everyone includes "Te Amo"—*I love you*. I struggle with what to write. Part of me wants to be practical and write something like *Be careful!* Or *Stay safe!* Then it suddenly occurs to me that all of my instincts are in direct opposition to the sentiments etched into the metal placards in Campo—so many conflicting messages at the border. I end up writing *Don't give up*, and then I'm disappointed in myself for being so generic—even though my words are genuine. I hate to admit it but leaving the jug on the granite stone feels a little hopeless. Part of me doubts that a migrant will get to it before it is slashed or shot at, or before it deteriorates. These are all possibilities but so is the migrant's survival. I am certain that if a migrant does get to the water, it won't be just any migrant but one of the most enterprising, one of the willful and lucky survivors of the journey. At Terrace Park Cemetery alone—just thirty minutes from where I leave the water—hundreds of unidentified migrants are buried in an open field; each life marked only by a numbered brick for a headstone. And then there are the *undiscovered*: disappearances marked in the desert only by an emptied backpack or a ripped pair of underwear, and disappearances marked not at all, recorded only in the memory of the one who remained silent back in Choloma or Soyapango, too afraid to go looking or to call the local police station. Those who arrive in the U.S. are only a fraction of those who felt compelled—by capitalism, famine, chemical weapons, or other iterations of brute force—to try.

Migration is life, and this is our reckoning. From the first pages of scripture until the end, as Bill Jenkins once pointed out to me, the story of the Bible is the story of migration. And so is the story of America and all her pilgrims. In fact, since that moment more than three billion years ago, when the very first microbes developed vision that enabled them to swim away from harsh ultraviolet rays, living organisms have been on the move so that they can endure. Migration is life.

I look around at the jugs stashed between the rocks and I try to imagine 4,000 of them—enough to fill the truck for just one run to wet the ground at the prototype site. We've left only ten jugs, and there will not be another water drop until next month.

CHAPTER 29

JONATHAN DEFINES RESPONSIBILITY AS SOMETHING beyond self, just as Bill Jenkins does—but it surprises me more coming from Jonathan. He lives month-to-month and doesn't own a car. He doesn't always have a working cell phone either. He is a college student—worse yet: soon he'll be a graduate student. His field of study is International Politics; his path to the six-figure salary that will pay down his tuition debt is, to say the least, unclear. Which makes me curious to discover his reasons for leading the water drop. He views each jug as a life—I heard that part—but I want to know about the point of origin. What drove him into the desert in the first place?

A couple of days after the water drop, I meet up with Jonathan at the Ballast Point brewery in Miramar. We are approximately thirty miles north of the border, twelve miles north of the 8 Freeway, where the air smells of eucalyptus and abundance.

The brewery was founded in 1996, which makes it a dinosaur in a very young, very crowded field of San Diego County breweries. The Grapefruit Sculpin is a rare treat for Jonathan. "I'm thirty," he says. "So I'm an older student. I've already done the partying. I've done having a lot of fun of different types and now I'm here to work.

"It's kind of a long story as to how I awoke—how I burst my bubble. Or how it was burst by outside conditions in this world. See, I graduated high school in 2004 and joined the Army, if you can believe it," he says, smiling, stroking his bushy, red beard. "I know, I don't seem like that type but it's true. I was seventeen years old.

"Well, around that time I went to a party. I had too much to drink and I passed out on a tile floor. I woke up at about 5 a.m. No one wants to sleep on a tile floor, so I decided to drive home even though I was still pretty intoxicated and I was very tired.

"It was probably only about a fifteen-minute drive. I was at a light, about to get on the freeway. Light turns green, I roll through the light and pass out at the wheel. There's this embankment with trees and a call box. I smash through all the trees, I hit the call box, and flew to the other side of a freeway. All the windows were shattered, the call box smashed the roof of the car. I was unhurt. I don't know how. So many things had to go right. Luckily it was five in the morning on a Sunday because, at one point, I was driving perpendicular on the freeway. I swerved and got control. A construction guy saw me—I had just missed him, thank God.

"There was a McDonald's right off the exit. I stopped and parked and just sat there. I didn't have a driver's license, didn't have insurance. I was an awful kid—had my parents' brand-new car.

"Anyways, five cop cars pull up. I'm awake but just sort of out of it. I don't know what the hell just happened; I just know it was bad. And all these cops come to me. One, in particular, was left to really deal with the situation. And I told him what happened. He said, 'Let me see your license.' And I said, 'My uncle was an Army ranger. My whole life I wanted to be a ranger. I'm in the Army right now. This means everything to me. I don't have a driver's license but I do have a military ID.' I gave it to him. He called my dad to come pick me up. Didn't even breathalyze me. Just let me go.

"*That's* white privilege right there. And the cop wasn't even white— which is important. It wasn't him; it was the institutional way of seeing things, *our* institutional way of seeing things. I was given some inherent legitimacy that I didn't earn. *And* that guy just happened to have been in the Army. Heck, I might have been up on a pedestal. And I didn't deserve it.

"I got a friend who is African-American who's a student at UCSD, and he gets harassed by the cops all the time because he walks back to the dorms late at night. They see him as out of place, as a threat. Imagine I had been African-American when I crashed that car. Say I even had a hoodie on. Who knows what the hell could have happened.

"It took years for that moment to sink in. You know what I was missing? You know what I needed in order for it to really sink in? I was missing the *privilege* of listening to the experiences of people who were African-American or who were Latino. You can't evolve your own identity unless you have those interactions.

"I learned so much through my girlfriend who is on DACA, she is tied in with the forefront of the undocumented, millennial activist movement, which is very aggressive in its approach—and I mean that in a good way. They're saying, 'We've been around too fucking long and we need to take action.' Seeing her work and doing my own work with Border Angels really started to open things up to me.

"I call myself a servant to migrants—*not* an ally. I'm a servant. I'm going to let them tell me what to do. You know, a lot of my girlfriend's friends are really hard-core activists and they do not like white people. Which is a little ironic because she is with me. It's accepted because I understand my place and I listen. And they say pretty harsh things about white people that 99.99 percent of white people would freak out on. And I won't say anything. Every now and then there is someone new in the group and they look at me and say, 'Aren't you offended?'

"And I say, 'No. Why should I be offended? I was never personally attacked. Also a lot of this is true and—most importantly—it's *their* experience!'

"It all comes back to that fragility we have, that white fragility, that tendency to be defensive or afraid of being called racist, instead of working to *erase* racist tendencies. To some extent we all have them, these preconceived notions that aren't accurate; these tendencies happen automatically. The trick is to challenge them. If we say, 'No, that never happens to me,' we're never going to evolve. That brick wall *is* white fragility. We need to break it down because we *do* still have preconceived notions and white people *do* benefit from the past, in macro and micro ways. Don't see it as: you are guilty. That's your choice to see it as you are guilty. Just shut the fuck up and listen to others and digest what they say. Stop taking everything as a personal attack. Take it as the reality faced by others."

Soon after the car crash, Jonathan was discharged from the Army. He enrolled in college for a while but it didn't work out. After the accident he dealt with rounds of depression and anxiety, reenrolling in school and dropping out again. "I ended up in a psych ward several times," he says. "It was rocky. My condition—something broke within me. What broke? I don't know. Maybe part of my ego. I'm not quite sure. But this whole identity of me in my bubble, as a separate entity from the rest of the world, it just kind of burst, and I was able to get through my own suffering. And through my suffering, I was able to really empathize with other people.

I had this drive. I had no other option as a fellow human being. I started getting more involved, volunteering—not just giving aid of some sort, but really trying to serve people who are taking control of their own lives. And I started challenging people around me to be more empathetic and really humanize all of these things that are going on.

"You know, borders, they're meant to create *us* and *them*. They are meant to create *the other*. And the human cost of that is extraordinary. Just look at the language, the legal language for somebody who's undocumented is 'illegal alien.' I mean, mic drop—that's incredible. That is in the legal language! Somebody crafted that language and a lot of people approved that language.

"And even when you call somebody an 'illegal immigrant,' it seems very subtle, but the use of that word—*illegal*—it dehumanizes somebody, right? Because if you're an 'illegal' immigrant, then you are an illegal human being. If you're an 'illegal alien,' you're not even a human being. This language is used by the powers-that-be, these words are seen as authoritative, where everyone says, 'Well, if the government created this language, it must be legitimate.' You hear it again and again and again and again and again. In your mind you might not be thinking, oh, they're subhuman, but things are operating beneath the conscious mind. That influences your behavior, inevitably, whether it's your thoughts or your verbal behavior or your physical behavior. So it's important to counter that language. These are fellow human beings."

CHAPTER 30

I SEE THREE MEN WALKING toward the primary fence in Las Torres. They are professionally dressed in collared shirts tucked into belted pants, and they approach the border single file. One after another, each of them climbs the fence, balancing himself at the narrow top for a moment while swinging one leg over, then the other, and each man lands in the U.S. with a dusty thud. Aurelia is sorting bottles just a few feet away but doesn't even look up. The last of the trio takes the time to urinate while waiting for his turn. Once he gets over, he joins the others on knees in front of four Border Patrol agents who cuff them and confiscate their shoelaces and belts.

The prototype site turns out to be a popular place to cross into the U.S.—increasingly so, it seems. I've seen it happen at least half a dozen times in the last couple of weeks, generally in the late afternoon or early evening. People from all over the world approach one of the dirt mounds in Las Torres, usually one with a couple of stacked tires so they can use the extra elevation to get up and over the corrugated metal. When they land in the U.S. there is no running or hiding. Each person immediately surrenders to the nearest Border Patrol agent and declares the intention to seek asylum.

In recent months videos have circulated online, many posted by immigration lawyers who accompany asylum seekers to ports of entry where they are denied the right to ask for asylum—it's not that they have been denied the request for asylum but that they have been denied the opportunity to *make* the request at all. The fact that this is illegal under federal law[1] and international law[2] is not the question. The question is whether or not anyone, the world over, has interest in enforcing one of the laws. And while that question remains open, more and more asylum seekers are jumping over the fence in lieu of using a port of entry because crossing into the U.S. illegally forces an interaction with a Border Patrol agent, which affords a migrant the opportunity to initiate an asylum request. Las Torres is where the secondary fence ends, leaving only the primary fence to get over, which is much easier, even if it lands everyone in the shadow of the prototypes.

Whenever I watch people approach the primary fence and realize they are about to jump over, I am instantly frustrated by my lack of French or Hindi or better Spanish so that I might speak with them before they cross. But it might not even matter because no one ever looks interested in stopping to talk. The moment usually seems to be about approaching the fence directly and getting over as calmly and quickly as possible.

Sometimes I get to the primary fence and there is the feeling that someone has just crossed over, and sometimes it's not just a feeling—there's evidence. One day Jill Holslin and I find ripped-up documents at the base of the fence. There are eight distinct piles of torn paper on the ground and some of the pieces bear the names of Indian nationals, all men, all with the surnames Kumar and Singh; they also left boarding passes for international flights to Mexico, twenty-day humanitarian visas from the Mexican government, wire transfer confirmations, transfer papers. There is a cell phone nearby, weighting down a 50-peso note on a rock—about two and a half dollars. The cell phone is dead and, at first, the idea of a migrant leaving behind any cash at all seems odd but then it's hard to imagine what good the 50 pesos would do him moments later in the back of a Border Patrol sedan. And the temporary visas, giving the men permission to stay in Mexico legally, no matter how briefly, would not have aided their asylum cases in the U.S.

A young woman approaches the fence with a toddler, a boy. She is dressed in dark jeans and a brown T-shirt; the boy wears jeans that are too big for him and a bright green shirt. They are with two men—one tall, the other wide. The wide one wears a tank top that reveals his arms, which, likely, were once muscular but have now turned fat. The men give the woman a boost over the fence, steadying her while she gets both legs over. This happens in a matter of minutes, no panic, no effort to be inconspicuous—just an anxious laugh from the woman at the top of the fence when she catches a glimpse of her descent. Once she lands in the

U.S., the men drop down her large purse then lift the boy over, into her arms. The woman reaches up to grab him and lower him to the ground. The two of them clasp hands as they approach three agents standing near the W. G. Yates model. After the two men in Las Torres get the woman and boy over the fence, they immediately fade back into the colonia.

CHAPTER 31

"ME? I'VE CROSSED MANY, MANY times. I've crossed . . ." Ernesto pauses, wanting to be thoughtful with his estimate: "I've crossed about a thousand times," he says in Spanish. I look at him with some disbelief but he raises his eyebrows and nods, standing by his statement. Then he goes back to chalking his pool cue.

Ernesto doesn't tell me his last name because he spent years working as a pollero—a coyote, a guide—for migrants looking to get across the border. In the pool hall where he stands in jeans and a bright white, zip-up sweater, there are about twenty tables lined up in two long columns with a wide aisle down the middle. It is a dark pool hall, as are most, but the more games there are, the brighter the place gets: the woman pouring drinks flicks on a fluorescent light over another table every time someone hands over enough pesos. It depends on the time of day but generally forty or fifty does the trick for an hour.

The hall is in Zona Norte—downtown, hotbed Tijuana, where the cables suspended from the city's signature two-hundred-foot white arch chirp in the wind, echoing across the sky like arcade lasers. There is no sign for the pool hall and it doesn't seem like a business looking to advertise; the faithful clientele is mostly a settled bunch. I am with Jill Holslin, who is the only woman in the hall besides the bartender. We get plenty of sideways glances and open stares. We are acutely aware of the fact that Jill is the only female patron and that we are the only two white people in the hall. The man standing at the end of the bar, clutching the rounded wood edge for balance, smiles and waves at us before sending a couple of beers our way. "He's a pollero," Ernesto tells me. "He's still crossing people." Jill and I have yet to interact with him beyond initial eye contact. His eyes are entirely bloodshot, and he is the only person in the place who is obviously drunk. In fact, there is not much drinking going on: a few beers, a few shots of tequila, but mostly it's concentration flowing through the hall. What's more, there is no smoking. Not only is there no smoking but signs on the walls instruct the men to inform on others caught in the act:

**Si usted mira a
alguien Fumando
Dentro De este
establecimiento
Denuncielo**

Denuncielo—report it, denounce the act.

It is afternoon and the crowd is light, about twenty-five guys, scattered, mostly old-timers, several with canes. Ernesto says most of them worked for years in the U.S. before retiring in Tijuana. "There's even a professor!" he boasts, though nearly everyone he points out did manual work: agriculture, construction, custodial services—part of the "sturdy, peasant stock" that Baldwin wrote about, part of the class of individuals that builds, maintains, cleans, and repairs America, generation after generation.

Chairs and cocktail tables line the perimeter of the hall. There is billiards and pool; the tables with pockets are at the back, and the very last table, turned perpendicular to all others, seems to be the marquee spot: no matter how much the action in the hall slows *that* table doesn't stop—nor does its small crowd. The onlookers form a circle that I dare not enter. Occasionally I get to pass by on my way to the bathroom, where the smell of disinfectant is losing to the smell of urine.

Around 4:30 in the afternoon the crowd grows—and shifts. Not only more guys but they are mostly younger, busting off work, clad in T-shirts and Dickies—covered in paint or dust or both, carrying their own pool cues cushioned in black cases. They greet each other as they slip into three-fingered gloves, each of which fits snugly over the thumb, index, and middle finger. Once they're warmed up with a few practice shots, some approach the bar to order drinks.

Tonight there is a tournament and, as it gets dark outside, more players start streaming in. The buy-in is 50 pesos with a 2,000-peso payout—about a hundred dollars, half of which comes from the house. A man dressed in black pants, black T-shirt, and a black vest approaches each available table to take a brush to the baize then drag a soft cloth across the wooden edges. He spits frequently, a tic of some kind, tiny darts shot straight at the floor. No signs about reporting *that* to the authorities so I look the other way.

Soon almost all the tables are taken and the place is bright with fluorescent light. "Here in Tijuana," Ernesto says, "there aren't a lot of people who can get you across anymore. Yesterday I was in here with some people and they're pretty much the only ones in all of Zona Norte: El R—, El A—. These are their nicknames, of course. El C—, he moves a lot of people, near Jacumba, Yuma."

Ernesto draws one of the first games of the tournament. The full weight of one of his big hands lands on my shoulder and he tells me with a stern smile to stop with the questions about crossing for now. "This isn't the place," he says, and he wants to concentrate on winning 2,000 pesos. So Jill and I watch him play instead. He makes quick work of his first opponent and survives a few rounds but eventually gets eliminated.

Later on, Jill lets me restart the conversation with Ernesto at her apartment. She lives in the seaside neighborhood of Las Playas in a spacious two-bedroom with breezes on the patio. The monthly rent is $300. She would easily pay $2,000 a month for the same place anywhere along the coast in San Diego County.

When I ask Ernesto to tell me about his experiences as a pollero he interrupts to ask, "You want to pay me $5,000?" Then he laughs, and when I try to join in, when I try to figure out if he's laughing *with* me or *at* me, he stops, confirming the obvious. So I stop too, and in the silence I realize he actually wants me to answer his question.

"I'm sorry," I tell him. "I don't have any money." I go on to detail my embarrassing earning capacity as a writer but he's not convinced. I do, after all, remain white. I tell him that a lot of people would like to know about his experiences, which is equal parts truth and self-projection.

"I don't want fame," he tells me. "I want money." He laughs then shakes his head. "I can give you an entire book with everything that happened in my life. You can interview a lot of people from the border but not a person like me who knows a lot. I know what happens in the hills, the polleros—I helped many, many people cross."

He gets lost in his own thoughts for a moment, distracted from the issue of payment for the interview. "You know, I have a lot of cousins in Mexico who don't really understand what it's like on the border," he says. "It's a novelty for people in central Mexico. If I post a picture of that border online, do you know how many likes I'll get from people in central Mexico? Not from people in TJ, but people in, like, Guadalajara, Puebla, Chiapas. It's because they've never seen this. They wonder what it's like, the border."

Soon Ernesto is telling me about his very earliest experiences in the business, how he started out as a driver, or a cholo as he calls them—one of the young, tough guys dressed in a flannel with a bright white T-shirt underneath. The driver—the cholo—he insists, represents the entry level in the economy of crossing.

Ernesto grew up in Mexico City but arrived in Tijuana in 1997 and crossed into the U.S. soon thereafter. "The person who got me across," he says, "one day he went where I was living in Los Angeles, looking for drivers, and no one wanted to go. I told him I'd do it. I started in June 1997. I was about to turn nineteen. He took me to San Diego and I started driving people to Los Angeles two to three times a day.

"I would cross Border Patrol checkpoints in a truck with people hiding in the back. I was a driver in the car, nine months," he says. "And then, walking across for five years." Most of the enterprises today are run by large cartels that subcontract the work, not only drivers but also the polleros who physically lead the migrants, the pollos, across the international line.

"I crossed on foot at Tecate, Tijuana, El Hongo, Jacumba," Ernesto says. "Each week, I'd cross at least a hundred people. In Tijuana, you could only cross when it was foggy or rainy. In El Hongo we had a cabana where we'd shower. Tecate I would cross thirty-five, forty people through the hills about three or four times a week. When it got too hot, we'd have to go back. We'd wait a day or two, and if it wasn't possible we'd stay in the hills and someone would bring us food.

"I had a path. Sometimes we'd walk backward so that our footprints showed we were walking the other way. Sometimes Border Patrol would see us and chase us. When it would get hot in one place, we'd go somewhere else.

"You have to be ready. If you see that a lot of border agents are headed your way, you have to tell a few pollos to wait at a certain spot, and then you leave another group at another spot, and others over there. And then

I'd go far to not be near them. Sometimes Border Patrol would come after all of us, and I'd start running. They wouldn't catch me—I was nineteen years old, they couldn't get me.

"Border Patrol, they check along the path, and they know how many people there are. Just with the footprints, they know how many people. They'd catch some and say, 'There are thirty-five. Two are missing.' Border Patrol is really—" He taps his head, "—they're smart. I always changed my shoes. I'd buy tennis shoes or cheap boots and I'd change so they can't recognize my tracks again and again.

"I met some white guys at a ranch in Potrero on the U.S. side. I would get there and drop people at the ranch, and they'd take them to San Diego. All of the white kids would take three people in their own cars to San Diego. Someone would pay them, and I'd walk back through the hills. I'd drop people off and head back to Mexico. In an hour and a half, I'd get to Tecate. I'd have more people waiting there, and at night, I'd cross again."

Ernesto's network used cell phones but he was careful never to carry his because possession of the flip-up StarTAC would be a clear sign he was a pollero and not just another pollo looking to get across. Crossing the border without documentation is a misdemeanor; aiding others in the effort to do so is a felony. "If Border Patrol caught us with the phones," he says, "they would take us to jail. So we would leave the phone buried in the ground.

"At that time, in 1997, we charged $700. In '98, we charged $1,200. In 2000, we charged about $2,000. When I crossed six Chinese people, walking four hours, I got $14,000. Now, it's more."

Ernesto says part of the fee always went straight to Grupos Beta personnel. Grupos Beta is part of the federal immigration enforcement authority in Mexico. It was created in 1990, ostensibly to provide aid to migrants at risk but the agency does not have a good reputation with human rights advocates like Amnesty International[1] or polleros like Ernesto. "They are animals," he says. "If the federales or judicial police caught you, that was another thing. But the ones who were real dogs were Grupos Beta. They would hide and grab you as you were walking. If you only knew. One time, we were in Tecate. We got there, and there were two Oaxaquitas with a jug of water. 'Hey, we came with someone but he left us,' one of them told me. 'Can you help us cross?' I said, 'No, I can't.' My cousin said, 'Let's take them.' Turns out, they were from Grupos Beta."

"Disguised?" I ask, a bit incredulous.

"Disguised! That's what they would do. In 1997, 1998, 2000 every fifteen days, I paid $1,500. He would call me by phone, the guy from Grupos Beta. I would pay, but I wouldn't go. He knew me by phone but not by face. I would send someone. He would give me a name, and that was the password for fifteen days. If the police got us in Mexico, I would tell them the password, and they'd let us through.

"And when we'd start going in the hills on the Mexico side, the bajadores* would come out with guns. They'd come out and say, 'Who's the guide?' I would tell them it was me. They'd move me aside, and they'd rob everyone. They never did anything to polleros, just to the people. That's why I would tell people, 'Bring money, and I will hold it for you, because bajadores will come out and they'll take your money. But they won't touch me.' Some of them, they'd tell me they didn't have any. But they'd get $1,000, $500 stolen. I would say, 'I thought you didn't have any?' Some people would give me their money to hold, since I knew them, and further along the way I'd give it back. But most people don't trust polleros. That's why you have to find someone you trust. Some people sew the money inside of your clothes. That's how they were able to cross. I've seen everything. I saw a woman keep money in her wig."

After a few years working as guide for someone else, Ernesto started dealing directly with clients. "You know, if you cross a person, that person is going to give your number to their family, for example, from Michoacán. And they're going to get to Tijuana and they'll look for you. And you create a customer base. First I worked with someone, with a boss. Then I started working on my own.

"I crossed a lot of family and friends from where I'm from, Mexico City. Many of them are in New Jersey, New York, most of them are in Los Angeles. They used to come here for a few years at a time, then go back to Mexico, then they'd come again. So I'd help them cross, then in a few years, do it again.

"See, you have an operation: I rented a house in San Diego where people would stay. I had cars, los cholos—las cholitas gorditas too. At the time, we'd charge $1,500. Someone who would drive for me, we'd pay $150 to

---

* Rip-off crews.

$200, but the driver would use his own car. And when I supplied a car, I'd pay them $120 or $100—and I would use cheap $700 cars.

"We have to pay the person who watches for the Border Patrol checkpoint too. Then we also have to pay for the house in San Diego. You have a house in San Diego where you take them and you have cholos who travel north. They would drive the pollos to their homes and then they'd bring me the money. The pollos pay when the cholo takes them to their house. But sometimes, the cholos would follow the pollos, rob all of them, take all of that money. A few cholos in Los Angeles would take pollos and drop them in Tijuana, so that they'd have to cross again. For a while, that was happening a lot. Now, the pollero has to send two or three people with the cholos because they will try to rob. Also now in some places, like Nogales in Arizona, pollos have to pay up front because of the cartel, Los Zetas. I know because I have a friend who works crossing people near there. Now they charge $6,000 or $7,000, through the mountain. Through La Línea[2] they charge $11,000. Coming by the ocean on a boat they charge $14,000. It used to be three hours, now it's seven hours because they have to go further north to avoid the agents patrolling the water."

Ernesto continued to work as a pollero, even as he grew his own operation. He had a new son to care for and the hard work increased his personal profits. In his prime he pulled in $5,000–$7,000 a week.

But Ernesto did not remain nineteen forever and, eventually, Border Patrol agents did start catching him when he ran. By 2011 he was well into his thirties with forty-three arrests for crossing the border illegally. It was enough to give him second thoughts about the business. "I didn't want to do it anymore because Border Patrol got me too many times."

So he ended his operation and started looking for other work. In recent years he's done different jobs—the pool hall is always a good place to get leads. For a few years he sold cars, buying and fixing them up to unload at a higher price. Then he started doing handyman work. "I really like working in construction and doing flooring," he says. "Finished concrete."

There are a lot of guys like Ernesto in Tijuana, he pointed a few of them out in the pool hall. Many of the men who wore boots and hard hats also have experience in the crossing industry—drivers, guides, lookouts, fixers. Some, like Ernesto, were eventually scared away by too many arrests; some were pushed out by changes in the industry. Like all other sectors of globalized capitalism, the business has seen much consolidation since the end of the twentieth century. As Ernesto pointed out in the pool hall, there are only a few polleros in Tijuana now, and many of the crossings in Arizona and Texas are organized by more sophisticated cartels, which have merged their human- and drug-smuggling operations. Just as there is little room for a small-time concrete man like Rod Hadrian in the big business of prototypes, there is not much room—and too much risk—for a small-time operator like Ernesto in the big business of border crossings.

He has just turned forty and is earning $400–$500 a week working construction jobs, supplemented by occasional billiards tournament victories. He used to feel certain that he needed to get back to the U.S. but not so anymore. "I have more clients here each year," he says. "I didn't use to have this many. I think in six or seven years I'll have more customers and I'll earn more money. I won't need to cross over. That's what's going to happen: I do good work and, little by little, I get more customers.

"You know, right now, a lot of people are coming back to Mexico from the United States. In reality, life in the U.S. is not like it used to be. Right now, you can have a good life in Mexico, too."

CHAPTER 32

AFTER SPENDING THE MORNING WATCHING construction from Las Torres, I start walking back to the Otay Mesa Port of Entry. If I'm not with Jill, I am often on foot in Tijuana—rental companies are persnickety about customers taking their cars into Mexico. Besides, being on foot suits me: from a car, the city is a montage that leads to quick answers; on foot, it's all complications that lead to better questions.

It is about four miles from Aurelia's place to the Otay crossing. The only real challenge is the first mile or so, getting out of Las Torres. The most direct way to do this is to stay on the dirt road up against the primary fence. It is a dusty road when dry, muddy when wet, and really it's only wide enough for one-way traffic, though it often moves in two directions. What's more, this uneven dirt road turns into the main commercial checkpoint at the Otay port so truck drivers who know their way around Las Torres like to get on the approach early. Any pedestrian willing to share the road with the eighteen-wheelers and other neighborhood traffic should stay out of the way and prepare for lungs full of dust or clothes covered in mud, depending on the time of year.

It is late October but still no rain and the dryness, the endless dust remains the issue; each time an eighteen-wheeler passes I lean up against the fence and raise my jacket over my nose and mouth and wait it out with my eyes closed until I can sense that the swirl of particles is thinning. And then I continue, trying to stay as close as possible to the fence, but the heaps of trash that agent Eduardo Olmos pointed out on the U.S. side of the barrier are also on the Mexican side of the fence and it makes for challenging terrain. Sometimes there is a burned-out vehicle to circumvent but the smaller pieces of garbage are the trickiest part; there are so many unsteady surfaces, mushy spots, and variations in elevations—all of it camouflaged by the same layer of pale dust that covers everything. There are a lot of difficult odors too. A used diaper smells bad but a used diaper that has been baking in the sun for weeks is *difficult*.

One particularly difficult smell causes me to stop for a moment. I look at the uneven place where I stand and see a dirtied pillowcase under my foot; I can tell it's stuffed with something so I reach down to look inside and discover the carcass of a dog.

It is mostly trucks along the road; I see very few people as I walk, and those I do encounter are in the middle of something, usually noisy: welding, hammering, auto demolition. Then a pickup with two municipal police approaches. The officer in the passenger seat looks concerned for me; the driver looks annoyed. I wave at them and say, "Hola, buenas días."

They look at each other and the concerned one gets out to approach me. As he does, the annoyed one behind the wheel says, "¿Estas trabajando?" He nods in the direction of the notepad in my hand. I nod my head, a bit nervous to speak bad Spanish. He points at the voice recorder in my pocket. "¿Una cámara?"

"No," I say, which is true. I tell them I am watching the prototypes go up, making notes.

The concerned one asks me for ID and he does so in English. As I wrestle my passport out of whichever pocket it's buried in, he says, "¿Cómo estas? Officer Chávez."

"Nice to meet you," I say. "David." In Tijuana, particularly when interacting with law enforcement, I mostly default to the first half of my first name; it estranges me from myself but it's much easier than pronouncing and explaining "DW" in Spanish. When I say "David" I do so with Spanish pronunciation—DAH-veed—and when Chávez repeats it back he does so with English pronunciation—DA-vid.

I hand over my passport. Chávez looks at it and says, "David-William," which sounds equal parts question and observation. I nod. He says, "Okay. From where David-William?"

I sigh, never sure if I should answer this question with a city, a state, or a country. Chávez sees the exhaustion on my face and answers his own question, looking at my passport: "From the States, David-William."

I nod.

"That's yours," he says, handing back my passport.

I thank him and he says, "Yeah, we're just checking around."

He speaks in a very deliberate English, like he's been taking lessons and looking for the chance to use it. I stick to my mangled Spanish, determined to break through with fluency at some point. We both cling stubbornly to the other's language, insisting on fumbling our way through. Chávez's partner remains in the truck, annoyed. He keeps the window down and I get a little relief from the AC blasting out the vents in the dash.

"How do you like the border?" Chávez asks.

The sweeping nature of his question paralyzes me. So I give quite possibly the worst answer: "¡Me gusta!" Then I try to save the comment by professionalizing it: "Estoy escribiendo un libro. Un libro sobre la frontera."

"Okay, well, the border, as you can see we got a few walls right here—"

His partner cuts him off—in Spanish—no patience for either of us: "Está trabajando para un—"

"Dijo que está escribiendo un libro," Chávez tells him. Then he turns to me: "You're working for some news station too?"

"No, no un libro solamente. ¿Periódico? No."

Then Chávez, pressured by the annoyed one says, "You working here in Mexico you have to have permit."

"Okay," I say.

"You're freelance right now?"

"No, solo estoy escribiendo y haciendo notas solamente."

The annoyed one cuts in again: "Sigue siendo lo mismo. Necessitas—"

Chávez cuts him off, nodding, telling me, "You still need the permit."

"Okay," I say. "Perdón."

"We're wondering, you see, because you are far from the city in a way, right? There are factories and towing services and big trucks and everything. It's not very safe for you to be wandering around."

"Yo entiendo," I say. "Perdón."

"Your safety, that's our priority."

"Si, si, gracias. Yo entiendo. Estoy caminando hacia la garita."

"You're *walking* there?" Chávez says, completely incredulous. "You don't have a car?"

"No, no tengo. Está bien."

The officers look at each other while I search for something to say. "Pensé que un amiga me econtraría, pero. . ." Then I peter out.

"Watch the big trucks, man," says Chávez. "They're not going to see you."

"Okay, gracias. Soy cuidadoso."

They both nod at me. Chávez turns to get back in the truck but then asks me one more question: "What kind of book are you going to write?"

Again with the zingers, Chávez! "How do you like the border?" "What kind of book are you going to write?" What kind of impossible questions are these? I respond by trying to cut to the center: "Quiero escribir sobre personas que *conocen* la frontera."

"Okay," Chávez says with a sideways glance. He wets his lips and continues: "Okay, my point of view: if someone attacks the United States I say, 'Hey, c'mon, we're brothers. I got family over there. There's a lot of relations. We're so close. And we—" he says, tapping all ten fingers against his chest, indicating "we" as the neighbors, the Mexicans, "we *respect* everybody. If you're going to put a fence, I'm going to *respect* that because you want privacy. It's your privacy, I've got to respect that. If you want to build a wall to keep it: okay. But the one thing is if you start saying that you need to build it because, hey, you are a bunch of thieves. Well, c'mon, that's different.

"There are certain things when I think about what's happening right now in the United States. Right now you're starting to separate. C'mon, the United States is *United*. United States, not just California or Arizona, we take United States to be all the states—because you have people coming from everywhere—"

"—Sí, sí—"

"—from all over the world. And not all those people are bad. Maybe some."

The annoyed officer, still behind the wheel, has officially run out of patience and rolls up his window, taking the AC with him.

Standing in the sun, sweating, Chávez continues: "But it works both ways. Some of those guys who have United States citizenship, they come here and sometimes they don't come with the best of intentions. So it works two ways!

"But we forget that. I think the point is, the point is you get scared of new immigrants, I think. But that's what makes the *United* States!"

As he talks, Chávez begins to draw something on the dusty hood of the truck with both hands. And as he punches the word *United*, he arches both index fingers toward each other on the hood, drawing what looks like a rainbow. "And now all of the trouble you are having is because you are dividing yourselves." As he describes the country dividing itself he draws his fingers away from each other, making something that looks like chaotic bursts of light, fireworks, cannons shooting in all directions. "You already surpassed the American Revolution, slavery, race and problems you had in the '50s and '60s, all this stuff—and now you're bringing it back? You got a lot of problems, guy. You got a lot of problems . . ." He trails off, like he's searching for the next thought. But then, suddenly, as if frustrated by the English language, or me, or all of his neighbors, Chávez throws his hands up—he's done. He has just laid it all at my feet and walked away, leaving his take on the divided state of America, all of its fragility, in my hands. Chávez gets back into the truck and his partner finally gets to pull away.

I continue toward the port. Just past Las Torres, the city becomes more pronounced: dirt roads give way to paved streets—wide with painted, respected lanes—just outside the maquiladoras. Each factory is tucked behind a fence and takes up several city blocks. They are set back off the street at least one hundred feet, making for a long approach to reach each gated fortress. It is early evening as I pass by, and I watch the two-way foot traffic in front of a maquiladora, workers shuffling in and workers shuffling out under the watch of a security guard. The people going in look only slightly less exhausted than the people coming out.

Looking at the signs for the international brands on the outside of the maquiladora—Panasonic, Bose Corporation, Medtronic—I am reminded of a local human rights activist who recently made the case that people should be able to move across borders as freely as products, putting it like this: "Many companies already operate as though they are borderless, almost as though they are their own nation-states. It's just crazy how companies have that power to travel across borders without any real accountability. Whereas humans aren't able to. And now I think there's a question that could be asked about how we expand human rights in this seemingly borderless economic world."

CHAPTER 33

MORGAN SCUDI, A LAWYER, SPENT two decades running maquiladoras—
"maquilas," he calls them. He describes the factories as cavernous spaces
with fluorescent lights and concrete floors. Workers are usually lined up
in long rows, he tells me, at individual stations with a sewing machine or
conveyor belt or a piece of automated machinery. And a maquiladora is not
just the factory floor; most of them are large complexes with offices, break
rooms, bathrooms, a cafeteria.

"What's the quality of all those amenities?" I ask.

"It depends on the operators," he says. "Not all are created equal."

I ask him about the documented cases I've read about: deadly working conditions, with exposure to chemicals (potassium hydroxide, which
corrodes body tissue, and acetone, which is a carcinogenic—just to name
a couple)[1] or dangerously long hours at machinery; pregnancy tests for
female workers, paid for out of their own wages;[2] unsanitary bathrooms
and cafeterias; month-to-month contracts, short-term guarantees, which
are easily broken by abusive managers.[3] Morgan says he participated in
none of that.

"How were your maquiladoras set up?"

"Well, everyone starts by putting a fence around the place," he says,
"and you have trucks of material coming in. Now, once you bring your
materials inside the gates of your factory, they're treated as if they're still
in the U.S. by the Mexican authorities. And the goods come back to the
United States as U.S. goods returned. That way you avoid any duty."

I realize Morgan means *duty* in a very strict sense here—economically—
but I can't resist contemplating his statement on a more comprehensive

scale. *That way you avoid any duty*: it seems democracy has been slow to realize this is what capitalism has done for so long now.

While the maquiladora landscape really expanded with the implementation of NAFTA, the concept of duty-and-tariff-free factories at the Mexico-U.S. border has been around since the 1960s. After the Bracero Program formally ended in 1964, the U.S. needed a new way to access all the cheap labor it had driven back across the border. The following year the Border Industrialization Program allowed for the implementation of maquiladoras.

"See, I'm a lawyer," says Morgan, who is past retirement age but still very much in the office. He is a partner in the firm he founded and brings Pepper, his French Brittany, into the boardroom where we meet. Morgan also wears a cargo vest, which seems to indicate he might take off to go fishing at any time. "But I have a cousin," he says, "who got into the maquila business at the beginning. And he got to be one of the big independents.

"See, big companies would start divisions and they would operate them under the maquila framework of taxes. The concept was that by encouraging manufacturing, particularly along the border in the frontier zone, we would alleviate some of the unemployment problems of Mexico and both countries would benefit. And the whole concept of maquila is that Mexico's bringing the hands and the United States is bringing the opportunity.

"My cousin had five plants in Mexico," he says. "I was doing some legal work for him at a large firm in Michigan. And, you know, I kind of wanted to get a job where people *made* something. So he said, you know, why don't you come down and take over and reorganize my companies. You can run them for a year or so and it would benefit me and benefit you and we'll see where it goes."

In 1989 Morgan moved to Bisbee, Arizona, then, eventually, to San Diego. Initially the operation he ran had facilities on both sides of the border with sixty employees in the U.S. and 3,500 in Mexico. "I was on the factory floor every day," he recalls. "I didn't ever talk with the line workers. I talked with all the supervisors. The training I had, it's kind of like the military. The general talks to the colonel, the colonel talks to the captain, the captain talks to the sergeant, and the sergeant talks to the men. I'd go down as far as the supervisory level. And most of our supervisors were college educated. We hired a lot of people from Monterrey Tech, which is the big school in Mexico. A lot of our plant managers had master's degrees in manufacturing. And they took their jobs very seriously. They were young, really young, and really aggressive. And a number of them have gone on to become very rich men.

"The factories were mixed-use and did manufacturing for General Electric, Eli Lilly, Cummins Diesel, Levolor. Levolor made blinds," Morgan recalls, squinting, "hard window coverings." He stops to rub his eyes and thinks for a moment. "We made, I think, 55,000 blinds a week which is hard to imagine. It's really a lot of blinds," he says, laughing.

"The question is always quality assurance, quality control. Is the process repeatable? Can you keep to a time schedule? Can you have a supply chain that works?

"For us, it was all compartmentalized. In Tijuana we had five different clients and we had one large building with five large bays."

Morgan managed maquiladoras all along the border—200,000 square feet here, 250,000 square feet there. I ask him if he knows the exact number of places he has managed over the years but he loses track while trying to add them up: "We had a plant down in—I've forgotten the name of the town," he says. "It was in a town that had virtually no employment. And my cousin went down and negotiated a deal where they had an abandoned school; he took the school over and converted it into a factory. They didn't have any fire protection. So my cousin donated a fire truck and money to operate a fire department and some money for an orphanage and school, to get those things up. And so the plant became very popular in that town." Morgan's description of the town—forgotten name, forgotten past—reminds me of the towns that companies used to build in the U.S., when it was still chasing workers in places like DeWitt, Nebraska, and Empire, Nevada—towns built around factories not unlike those that define the newer sections of Tijuana.

Whole industries have grown out of the maquiladoras, from management companies that run the facilities, to catering and security services, to lobbying specialists and worker recruitment centers.

"I found that the heart of the Mexican worker was very good, very honorable, very honest," says Morgan. "I found that their work ethic was really strong. They didn't want to cheat on their work. If they came to work, they worked. They had good manual dexterity. They had generally very good intentions. We had very little theft. We had no vandalism. They were proud of what they did.

"A lot of times, young kids come and work. They'd be sixteen, seventeen, or eighteen, and they'd work until they got to the end of the year. Then they get certain mandatory bonuses and holiday pay—by law. They would go home and they would not come back. You know, maybe they have a friend who's in another factory—and all the factories have help wanted signs out. So it's a free labor pool. And you're free to walk across the street and go to another place. So now visualize yourself as an eighteen-year-old working in a factory and you want to take two weeks off. Well, you quit your job, you take two weeks off, you come back and you get another job. So that created what's called turnover. I think the turnover rates in some of the plants can run 10 or 15 percent per month. So if you had a hundred workers, you had fifteen jobs open at the end of the month, every month. So turnover, particularly in Tijuana, is big. The big sites for maquiladoras are Tijuana, of course, and just south of El Paso in Juárez—then to a lesser degree Nogales, Arizona, and there are five or six in Texas. More and more factories opened up over time and I think the wages became more and more competitive.

"When I started working at it, in order to bring workers in, we had to have a bus company. So we had two bus companies that were authorized to drive on the highways to pick up workers in the colonias and bring them back. We sponsored labor unions that were nationally recognized. We had food programs where everyone received food coupons so that they could buy basic necessities in their hometown. We provided some support for child care. We gave dietary instructions. We gave health care instructions. We were basically bootstrapping-up the people coming into work. And you have to realize at that time, many of the people that were coming into work at the factory, it was their first job. And many of them were living in colonias that really didn't have much in the way of services. So just learning sanitation and how to work and how to appear and how to be responsible, all those things had to be ingrained and taught."

The only form of civics that seems to endure does so through the prism of capitalism. The health care, the child care, the wraparound services, Morgan says, "it's all largely market driven. And I say that in the kindest light. It's kind of like wages alone won't solve problems. So the reality is when you bring people in that have very little skill and you want them to do something that involves some skill, you obviously have to do training. And when they have families and they have no care, these things all kind of build. I think we think of it in modern parlance as 'it takes a village to raise a child.' You really have a lot of things that go into making a society."

I ask Morgan, "How come we stopped making society domestically? Companies used to provide all these services to employees in the U.S."

"Look, I had an office in Detroit for many years. And when you go to the inner cities of the United States where you have high unemployment, you find that you have a potential workforce that's not trained, not skilled, not motivated. And I don't care what color or race they are, or what religion they are, if you have people that have limited education and very little world experience, they're going to take more time to develop into human beings that are useful. And so you've got to expend more there. And our society says no, we want to hire the best we can for the least amount we can. And when you go to that model, you're going to avoid the inner city. It's too expensive to provide all those services in the U.S."

Morgan emphasizes that when he got into the maquiladora business most of the jobs the U.S. exported to Mexico were "low-skill" positions. "They were the jobs that were boring and hard to fill," he says. "A lot of the jobs that were exported in Mexico were, if I may, they were like the buggy whip manufacturers. Last gasp for a dying product—send them down to Mexico. We'll sell some more buggy whips because we'll get them cheap enough. That was the U.S. approach."

While there have been plenty of repetitious, mindless industrialized jobs sent to maquiladoras, we shouldn't forget about all the Mexicans Morgan hired in managerial roles, the ones with advanced degrees, the ones who made him beam with pride when he mentioned that they've gone on to be "very rich men."

"Now what's interesting," he adds, "the Japanese approach was entirely different. They went high-tech. So if you went into the Sony plant in Tijuana back in the 1990s, you would see the futuristic manufacturing plant where you'd have a huge room of assembly going on. There'd be three guys in white coats walking around. Everything would be controlled, the temperature and humidity, and they'd be walking around with clipboards as the lines were going through automation and production. You didn't see that with the stuff the U.S. companies moved out. A little bit in automotive. I think in El Paso, some of the General Dynamics plants down there were pretty well automated. American companies tend to be a little bit more shortsighted than the Japanese. I had some dealings with Japanese who were manufacturing in Mexico. They didn't care if they made a profit. Didn't enter their mind. They plan in the extreme long-term. What they focus on is *market share*. If we're increasing our market share, eventually we'll win.

"I travel so much that what I noticed was how much Americans are behind the times," says Morgan. "You go to China and ride on the mainland at 200 kilometers an hour. Our most advanced cities are backwards, compared to the rest of the world. It's kind of the American backwardness that comes with complacency. A lot of people still think we're number one in everything. If you're number one, you don't really have to worry about it. I think we are pretty isolated here.

"Mexico, in my opinion, always has bad press in the U.S. And I think the problems that Mexico has with the cartels and the drug trade has had a tremendous impact on the psyche of Americans who had, for many years, a very positive attitude about Mexico and about Tijuana. Americans are afraid. They're just afraid. They're afraid of bombs. They're afraid of Muslims. They're afraid of drugs. I had my office in Detroit for almost twenty years and, for a long time, you could say that if Detroit was a country, Americans wouldn't be allowed to go there because of the murder rate and the theft rate and all that kind of stuff. But it's an American city. So for some reason we don't think about it."

A few years ago, Morgan decided to take a step back from operating maquiladoras. He's still involved in the business but mostly through his law work, representing maquiladora operators and the landlords who own the property where the facilities are built. He says the facilities he used to run are still going, still churning out buggy whips in the eastern stretches of Tijuana, just a few miles from the prototypes.

"Quite frankly," says Morgan, "whether we have a fence or not a fence, I think one of the things we should have done a long time ago and we never did is we never really grappled with immigration. We built our immigration laws on the idea that people are coming from Europe by boat. We don't do very well with people walking across the border and we never did.

"My own view is, at least initially, we should basically do a census. And if I were king—" King Morgan stops to smile, "—I would announce that we're coming out now with an international travel card and everyone is eligible to get one. And noncitizens have to have an international travel card or they're subject to deportation. And give six or eight months for people to come in and get an international travel card and then get a nonresident Social Security number. If they carry the card, they're not subject to arrest—they're not subject to deportation. And if you don't have the card, you will get deported. And we'll know who's here—we kind of started to do that with the Dreamers, so at least we know how many there are. And then what would happen," Morgan stops to smile, like he's getting to the good part, "you say to industry in America, 'Well, who wants these people?' And we'll say, 'Okay, Agriculture wants them. Okay, so if you work in Ag, you can go and work for two years and then you have to return home for a year. If you want to work in factories, you have to work for three years and you can return for a year. If you want to work in restaurants, you can work for five years and return for a year.' And you could regulate. And since they have nonresident Social Security numbers, you can deduct taxes from them. And you would normalize the situation. You could control it."

Isn't this the quintessential American approach to implementation of the ID card? This country would never agree to the use of such a card so that individuals can cross our borders to share culture or perspective, or to escape danger; the card is only tenable because it allows industry to access as many workers as possible. We do not need your bird songs; we need you to assemble Levolor blinds.

Within this market-driven approach, which often feels demoralizingly inescapable, there is something very practical and humane about an international ID card that recognizes the fact that workers compete globally, a card that allows for a world where people can traverse borders as freely as trucks full of hard window coverings.

CHAPTER 34

THE FACTORY ACTIVITY IN NEIGHBORHOODS like Barrio Logan has been shrinking in the decades since NAFTA was implemented. Industrial spaces in the neighborhood are, one by one, being converted for other uses like the Border X craft brewery and the store selling oatmeal and almond bath bombs. Barrio Logan is in that middle space, mixing art galleries and the old dulcería, the Don Diego VFW Post and Sew Loka: A Modern Sewing Studio. The coffee shop Por Vida remains central command. Inside, the Virgin Mary and Frida Kahlo commingle on the walls, and potted cacti line the service counter where regular and decaf are offered but get lost in the glare of headliners like Horchata Cold Brew and Mexican Mocha.

I find Victor Ochoa in the back, talking with just about everyone who passes. He recognizes most people and carefully eyeballs the unfamiliar. Victor has a photo book on the wooden table in front of him; it's a collection of every image he posted to Facebook over the last three years. Those who are in their sixties or seventies—people Victor's age—stop to admire the book for a moment; they flip through a few pages, maybe listen to a story or two; but most who are younger are politely amused, if not completely confused, by the printed pictures, the impetus to create such an object without irony. Victor points out images of his art, of his mother who died last March, of his father who died many years ago.

"I bought my car in Tijuana a long time ago, in Otay," he recalls, looking at one image, and I resist asking if Roque De La Fuente Sr. was the seller.

"One time," he says, "me and my dad were cruising downtown, Revolución, and we saw this wino in the gutter with a bottle and he had pissed on himself. My dad said, 'That's how you're going to end up.' His attitude about artists was that they liked to get loaded and they end up poor and they don't know how to manage money and all the negative stereotypes about artists. When you're from a poor family, you want your son to be able to survive society."

As he speaks, Victor becomes annoyed by the flimsiness of the wooden stool where he sits. "You hipsters all have skinny asses," he says. It *is* a flimsy stool *and* Victor has a formidable figure so it is a bad combination. We relocate outside and sit on a bench under a tree. A wooden arrow—pointing down the block to Chicano Park—is nailed into the trunk of the tree, which is painted bright like the Mexican flag with bands of green, white, and red. Victor watches the skinny-ass hipsters go by, and the scene doesn't seem to stop. New artists are always showing somewhere on the drag; there are regular night crawls with galleries staying open late, pouring wine, then pouring more wine, stopping only to mark asking prices with red dots.

Milo Lorenzana emerges from Por Vida to pay his respects to Victor. He is one of the few millennials with enough deference to give Victor more than thirty seconds with the photo book, but he also has a swagger of his own, a vibe of authority. Milo is one of the owners of Por Vida, clad in gray sweat pants that only the boss could pull off. He is otherwise hidden under a baseball cap, behind sunglasses and stubble. Victor says Milo is "the shit." He is part of the class of entrepreneurs transforming Barrio Logan. "Right now there is a renaissance in food in Tijuana," Victor says. "And a lot of that shit is coming up here now."

Milo points to El Carrito just a few doors down. It's an old diner that's been shuttered for years. Brown craft paper covers the windows and renovations are wrapping up inside. "We did as little work on it as possible," he says. "I wanted to preserve as much as possible."

Victor says decades ago everyone knew El Carrito not just for the chilaquiles and tortas but also for the community organizing, for the visions it fostered of concrete pillars as murals. I ask Milo if he's preserving that too—the sense of activism. Hearing my question, Victor reminds Milo that there is a meeting in the neighborhood at 5 p.m. to discuss how everyone might respond to the next Patriot Picnic.

"They're just trying to stir the pot," says Milo. Then he's hit with a sudden idea and claps, snaps, points at Victor and says, "You know what would really get them?" He pauses for moment then says, "Let them do their thing in an *empty* park. That'll show them!"

Victor doesn't look sold on the idea—a bit confused by it, in fact—but just as he starts to respond, Sergio García walks up to join the conversation and the moment immediately shifts.

Like Milo, Sergio is tucked under a baseball cap but his stubble is more sculpted than Milo's. Sergio is handsome, with tattooed arms and thick-rimmed glasses. His project—there are no more jobs, only projects— is Los Slydogz, which he describes as Chicano soul food. Sometimes he calls it campesino soul food. Sergio, who has a degree in International Business from the University of California at San Diego, is operating Los Slydogz out of a mobile cart, which he "sourced in Mexico" on an eight-state culinary road trip. "I don't really like to say Mexican food," he says, "because if you say that here then people are like, 'Where's my California burrito?'" Victor and Milo laugh. Sergio continues: "I'm trying to create a new space for the food I know and love, for the flavors I grew up with. It's peasant food, really."

Andrew Zimmern—food critic? expert eater?—featured Los Slydogz as one of his favorite "West Coast Eats" for the Travel Channel. These days, Sergio's cart gets booked all over town and he is contemplating bricks and mortar.

As Milo and Sergio say their goodbyes to Victor, he reminds them about the community meeting at 5 p.m. They both nod: "right on," they say, almost in unison, and each man promises to do his best to be there.

Victor watches them for a moment; their conversation about lease renewals trails off as they make their way down the block. "See the younger generation," he says, "like them, they're not so much into protesting. They're more focused on making some money and having a good life." Victor points to Milo's lowrider in the parking lot next to Por Vida. "I never really thought a lot about money. I know that sounds ridiculous but it's true. And I think it's true of a lot of people I was protesting with. I never really made art for money. It wasn't ever all that possible. What I cared about was making sure I could keep making art."

But now Victor sees a new focus in Barrio Logan, new faces. "It's changing a lot," he says, squinting into the setting sun. "Some people don't like it because so many white people are here now," he says, laughing.

I ask where the people are going once they get pushed out of the neighborhood. "Back to Tijuana," he says, "or doubling up with extended family."

CHAPTER 35

JUST ONE OF THE SIX companies building the prototypes is publicly traded, which means Sterling Construction of Texas is the only place for investors to park. The company's stock value has increased 65 percent since its design proposal was selected. The private equity firm BlackRock—one of Sterling's single biggest shareholders—increased its investment in the company by 195 percent after the winning bidders were announced.[1]

Nearly all the prototypes are finished; the boom trucks are leaving, so are the cranes, each 65 x 65 staging area is being cleared of its equipment. The KWR and W. G. Yates crews have a few more rivets to set. Eduardo Olmos and Ralph DeSio are in the viewing area with one last pool of reporters and photographers. Ralph is guessing all the work will be wrapped up within a few days. After that, he says, Border Patrol will "audition the quality of the prototypes." When pressed on what *audition* means, Ralph says, "They're supposed to have characteristics of anti-climbing, anti-scaling, anti-tunneling and be able to deter penetration. It's supposed to take you one hour to get through it if you had to—you know, to cut through the concrete."

As luck would have it, two men hopped the primary fence behind the prototypes earlier in the morning, just before The Media arrived. Eduardo shrugs off questions about the apprehensions, unruffled, as ever. "When someone jumps the fence," he says, "somebody on-site makes a call, Border Patrol handles the situation and allows everyone to continue work." Eduardo uses a singsong tone that makes the whole thing seem downright boring—the main point, he says, is that the prototypes will be finished in the one-month timeline that was promised when construction began.

Ralph provides a little more color, as is his wont: "We've had various construction projects along the border—infrastructure, repairs—and people jumping over the fence would take advantage of that situation because there is so much activity going on. If you're not paying attention they can just jump over, blend in, and wander off. They do it regularly at Border Field State Park when we have the Friendship Park pavilion open. You got to stay on your toes." Ralph laughs and it looks like he's done but then he adds one more point: "As a matter of fact," he says, "when we had a press conference a few days back, we had a guy jump the fence then!" Eduardo walks away from the conversation, looking as though he wants to save himself from the pain of overhearing it.

The migrants who jump the fence at the construction site continue to be asylum seekers, by and large. They do not run or try to blend in once they land on their feet; they look for an agent to whom they can surrender. They are eager to start the process, to find safety, work, maybe have a boxing coach like Edgar Sandoval in their lives. But they will not end up in National City at the Community Youth Athletic Center. They are all on their way to a detention facility.

CHAPTER 36

IMMIGRATION AND CUSTOMS ENFORCEMENT USES 630 detention facilities across the country[1]—at least one in every state. The exact number of migrants in detention constantly fluctuates but in 2015 there were 51,162 people in California immigrant detention centers, which was second only to Texas.[2] But even when migrants become detainees they remain migrants, moving between cities and states, from one facility to another. Two thirds stay in a private, for-profit facility like the one operated by CoreCivic three miles from the prototypes.[3] The company bought forty acres in Otay Mesa in 2010 for $10.3 million.[4]

Three years into operation, the Otay Mesa Detention Center is nearly at capacity with 1,500 detainees. CoreCivic would like to build more space but the state legislature recently passed a bill prohibiting any privately owned detention centers from expanding—a response to mounting documentation about detainees dying without adequate medical care in private prisons, including facilities run by CoreCivic.[5] The prohibition, however, will not apply to the company's Otay Mesa center; federal authorities lobbied state legislators to get exemptions for the facility. The winning argument was that CoreCivic *owns* the land where the Otay Mesa center is built and so the company reserves the right to expand as much as it wants on private property. CoreCivic has announced it will increase the number of beds in Otay by 30 percent in a year and, eventually, it hopes to double the number. Because of the facility's earning capacity, the county assessor now has CoreCivic's forty acres valued at $123 million,[6] more than twelve times what the company paid for it.

In Otay, there is a mix of asylum seekers and people convicted of crimes—some fall into both columns—and everyone is separated into different groups: blue jumpsuits indicate asylum seekers who entered at a legal port of entry, orange indicates those with nonviolent criminal convictions such as crossing the border illegally, red means watch out. In Otay, most of the migrants manage to stay away from confinement in a cell, getting housed in open space, common living areas—called "pods"—with beds, tables, and chairs.

The center also has immigration courtrooms custom-built within its facilities. There are five of them, all off a long, sterile hallway, and in one of the rooms there is a middle-aged white man, perched high, with perfectly parted, slicked-back hair. His blue button-down peeks out from beneath his judicial robe, as does the gold bracelet around his wrist. Centered on the blue wall behind him is the insignia for the Department of Justice.

The hard, wooden benches in the gallery are nearly full. There are about twenty-five people and I appear to be the only one who is not a migrant, a lawyer, or working for the court. The benches look and feel like pews; the migrants in the congregation wait to be called, each person anticipates the sound of their name, bouncing a knee up and down, vacillating between staring into the distance and squeezing their eyes shut.

The court is open for seven hours and each hour the judge is able to get through five or six hearings. Most of them last only a few minutes, often with much longer intervals between, when paperwork is passed around, procedures followed. Immigration court is where one goes for a final decision, a taste of stasis, but mostly it is a place for more shuffling. People are shuffled and so is paperwork, dates are shuffled and so are venues. The bureaucratic action mostly involves the court clerk, seated at the judge's side, and the lawyer for the federal government, and both of them move as though they could do this in their sleep. The lawyer for the government is the only lawyer who gets to stay in one place; all the others, representing migrants, are on the move, coming in from other courtrooms, or just arriving from another court building two hours away in Riverside County or Orange County. They are often a little out of breath, sometimes a bit disheveled, and always lugging overstuffed accordion file folders. The lawyer representing the federal government is settled in front of a desktop. Next to her computer she has her own stack of files, at least as tall as five reams of paper. Each time a hearing ends she chucks another file into a metal cart right next to her desk, with a satisfying flick of the wrist. There are moments when everyone is waiting on her, and the only sound in the room is her fingers racing across the keyboard. And there are other quiet moments when she is doing the waiting; while the judge reviews a file or a new migrant approaches the bar, more shuffling, and in these moments she slumps behind the stack of files, zoning out for a moment, biting her nails: she is comfortable here; her job is a series of predictable systems. Her comportment really only changes when she walks a piece of paper over to one of the migrants' lawyers: she always delivers it with the same tense smile.

The judge starts each hearing by stating, for the record, the defendant's name, nine-digit case number, and the nature of the hearing. There are several possibilities in immigration court: master calendar hearings when, at the beginning of the process, the judge and lawyers create a road map for a case, identifying next steps, setting future dates; bond hearings, which are about whether a migrant will be released from detention and, if so, the money it will require; merit hearings when asylum seekers present the specifics of their case; and of course there are reset master calendar hearings when everything starts over with more shuffling.

A recording of every hearing is captured by microphones at the bench, at the counsel tables—there are even microphones over the gallery, dangling from ceiling panels.

Often when the judge and lawyers speak it sounds as though they are reading from a script that bores them. Here is one recurring sequence:

Judge: "Do you have a fear of returning to ____." (Fill in the blank, I heard Nepal, Cameroon, China, Honduras, India, Somalia, Ghana, Mexico, Guatemala, Republic of the Congo, and the Democratic Republic of the Congo.)

Migrant (or lawyer if the migrant is lucky enough to have one): "Yes, your honor."

Judge: "Do you have an application for assignment?"

If the migrant says yes then a date is set for a merits hearing; if the migrant says no then a timeline is set for completing the application.

"On November 30, what are you supposed to bring to me?"the judge asks one migrant.

"My application."

"And what could happen if you don't bring that?"

"You could send me back to Mexico."

"I think you understand."

Each person who seeks asylum must write down the circumstances of their case in the most vivid detail possible, supplying supporting evidence: medical records, photographs, police reports. Each migrant must complete the application in English, and one of them tells the judge that he is having trouble because he does not know enough English.

"Are you telling me there is no one in this facility who speaks English and Spanish?" the judge asks him through an interpreter.

"No," he says.

The judge looks at him and purses his lips. "That's just not true," he says. His face is generally doughy with compassion but can harden in an instant. "I see lawyers who help fill out applications—other detainees can help."

"I am in G pod," the migrant says through an interpreter, "and there are people there who could help me but I don't know if they will write the correct answers."

"Why should I not find your application abandoned?" the judge asks, almost certainly knowing the man is not clear on what this means, knowing the man does not have a lawyer at his side to explain what it means. The migrant says nothing and the judge gives him two more weeks to complete the application; the migrant thanks him and leaves, no closer to obtaining the help needed to complete the application.

The judge works hard to maintain neutrality in his words and tone, though sometimes he slips, particularly if the migrant who crosses the bar is someone he's been dealing with for a long time. "I gave you three hearings to find an attorney," he says to one, "looks like you finally found one."

Often there is the voice of an interpreter trailing the judge, echoing his sentences in a second language. In these cases the migrant wears a headset so that the interpreter's voice is amplified. The interpreters too are shuffled in and out, according to the linguistic needs of any given hearing in one of the courtrooms. They sit at the judge's side and he seems to glare less at the ones who do their job quietly. When he is working with one of them, he slows down his speech and uses a soft register, like he's reading a book to children.

So few of the migrants have lawyers, and many ask for more time to find representation. One man says if he can have just two more weeks he can find a lawyer. One woman requests a change of venue because her husband and children are hundreds of miles away. "I've heard four hours of testimony," the judge tells her. "I don't think it would be judiciously efficient to grant a change of venue."

Most of what the judge says hinges on sophisticated phrases, *judiciously efficient*, which do nothing to wipe the uncertainty off the migrants' faces as they shuffle on—back to the gallery, back to the pod, or back out into the world with a GPS tracker on each ankle, one from the government, the other from the bond company.

When the judge does grant a bond it always comes with a warning: "If you do not return for your next court date you could be given an order for removal in your absence."

Some of the few moments that don't feel scripted are when the judge works out the next hearing date with the lawyers, poring over the calendar. "I have January 22, 25, and 27," says the judge. "Your choice."

"January 25 is great, your honor," says the migrant's lawyer.

Across the aisle, the lawyer for the federal government nods.

"It's yours," says the judge.

For a moment it almost feels like they're scheduling a lunch, a get-together, and everyone involved basks in the brief informality.

The barrel-chested bailiff wears a CoreCivic pullover and manages much of the courtroom shuffle, escorting migrants in and out in groups of two and three. He does not carry a firearm but the jumble of keys at his waist jingles with every step. When a migrant is called, the bailiff brings him from the gallery to the counsel's table, each time raising his foot at the bar to stop the short wooden gate from slamming behind him.

When one woman arrives at the counsel's table she says she has eight family members waiting to come into the gallery. The benches are still mostly full so the judge tells her she can have two people come in or she can wait until later in the day. She says she will wait and returns to the gallery.

The shine in the judge's hair fades as morning turns to afternoon. There is one hour for lunch when the judge retreats to his chambers and the bailiff gets off his feet, takes out his earpiece, and starts popping Skittles. When he finishes the bag of candies he gives a big yawn, which eventually devolves into a soft "oh fuck" under his breath. He looks at his watch to see how close he is to the end then stands abruptly at the sound of the judge's chamber door opening. He says, "All rise," and everyone else stands too; the judge, looking exhausted by the ceremony, tells everyone to sit back down.

One of the first cases after lunch involves a woman from Somalia, and after some back-and-forth between the clerk, the bailiff, and the judge, it is determined there is not a Somali interpreter at the court on this particular day and so one will need to be dialed in from a remote location. The process begins with the loud sound of a ringing phone, which fills the room in a way that indicates the call is about to get much louder. And indeed it does, as a woman's voice comes blaring into the room to announce that we've reached "Interpretalk." The judge introduces himself, confirms an access code, and requests a Somali interpreter. The operator places the judge on hold and piano fills the courtroom, the highest notes pinging bluntly against the ear.

Suddenly a man's voice comes over the speaker and he announces his name and an ID number. It sounds like he's a bit out of breath or finishing off morsels in his mouth, as if he's been caught in the middle of something and needs a minute to create professional order in his comportment.

The judge swears him in and the interpreter begins echoing everything he says. The volume of his voice so overpowers the speakers it sounds like he's yelling at everyone in the room.

"Charges dropped based on admissions and concessions," says the judge at one point before the interpreter repeats it in Somali. *Charges dropped based on admissions and concessions*—that's another recurring line in the script. Many migrants who are caught crossing the border illegally face an assortment of charges, most of which get dropped if they agree to return to their country of origin. When additional charges are *dropped based on admissions and concessions* it means the migrant might be granted a *voluntary departure*; this spares them the debt of the plane ticket and a "review of moral character," both of which come with an *order for removal*, which is less desirable than the already undesirable *voluntary departure*.

Through the Somali interpreter the judge asks the migrant if she has any questions about the difference between *voluntary departure* and *order for removal*. She says no. The judge always asks the migrants if they have any questions; most say no, and it's not easy to tell if this is because they do not have questions or they are afraid to ask the questions they need to ask.

Whenever someone does take the invitation to present a question, particularly late in the day, the judge, the bailiff, the clerk, and the government's lawyer all start to sag just a little bit more.

Another woman from Somalia, a Muslim with her head covered, is called before the court and tells the judge she was forced into an arranged marriage back home. She says that if she returns she will be killed. The judge tells her to save it for the merits hearing. "You need to write everything down so I can review it," he tells her without looking up from the note he is making. She nods, taken aback by his disconnect. She is shuffled out and a woman from Mexico is shuffled in.

The judge asks the woman from Mexico if she has a fear of returning home, she says yes. Through an interpreter she tells him that back home, when she tried to stand up for her sister who was raped, she was beaten and knifed. She raises her sleeve to show scars on her arm; she lowers her head to show scars on her scalp. "These are the reasons I left," she says in Spanish. The judge closes his eyes and raises his hand, ever so slightly, to stop the interpreter. He does not look up from the bench to see the scars but instructs the woman just as he did the other: "Write it down. I'll review it on the application."

Eventually the gallery has emptied and the judge tells the migrant with the eight guests it's her turn to approach the bar. She tells him that only three of her guests have remained, the others had to return to work, and the judge says the remaining three can come in. The bailiff steps out of the courtroom and returns with a man and two small children; the boy looks to be about five, the girl is maybe three. For several minutes the migrant, seated at counsel's table, does not look back at them. The boy and girl are giddy at the sight of the back of the woman's head. "Shhh," says the man trying to wrangle them and keep them from charging straight for the woman just the other side of the bar. Suddenly she does turn around, only for a brief moment while she can control the tremble spreading across her face. She waves and smiles but the smile breaks her control and she turns back to the judge, who misses all the action with his head lost in a paper shuffle. The woman, who has been in detention for 105 days, asks to be let out on bond. Her reasons are obvious—present. The judge declines the request.

The last case of the day is for an asylum seeker who is out on bond and has failed to show up for the hearing—a rarity, as 86 percent of immigrants comply with their court obligations.[7] The judge races through the script, sending the migrant back to Honduras, in absentia, by order of removal. This man will not actually return to Honduras until a warrant is served, which could take a few weeks, or until he is pulled over with a busted tail-light, which could take twenty years.

CHAPTER 37

THE U.S. GRANTS ASYLUM TO only about 35 percent of those who apply.[1] The federal government is working to drive the number down, issuing memorandums mandating stricter standards for evaluating testimony and evidence, memorandums instructing judges to get through more cases each day and bring up denial rates.[2] "The asylum system is being raped," Chris Harris says with some East Coast fire—that's his Border Patrol agent half, but then his union representative half takes over, and he raises his hand, as if to bring himself back down to a more diplomatic tone: "It's being *abused*," he says, leaning against his SUV, which is parked atop the Tijuana River canal just behind the Las Americas Outlets. "Twice now I've had media at the border and both times large groups of Indian males have come across. They're well dressed, really nicely dressed—these guys have matching shoes. I'm like, 'Dude, you shop together or what?' They all pretend they don't speak English even though English is one of their national languages. And I got a little annoyed and I was probably a little unprofessional but I said, 'I know one of you works in a call center. I know you're all lying. Somebody speaks English.' But they all claim they don't speak English. And they're all going to claim credible fear in India. It's a democratic country! But we're entertaining that as asylum.

"Don't get me wrong," Chris adds, "I don't ever want see the opportunity for asylum to go away. After my first wife died, I met a woman from Cambodia—we dated for a long time. Her family, they were peasants—literally, they had a dirt floor hut, water buffalo, rice paddies. She had no idea what her birthday was. Her mother didn't know. At first I thought that was funny. She told me when her family got to the U.S., her mother just picked out the same day, the same month for all her kids—just a different year for each. They were escaping the Khmer Rouge and Pol Pot and they crossed a river into Thailand. One of her brothers drowned.

"Anyway, they lived in a refugee camp in Thailand for a year, then they got to the Philippines and they were in a refugee camp there for a year, then they were sponsored by a church in Oklahoma and then she got her LPR status, Lawful Permanent Resident, asylum. That's *real* asylum. You don't want to ever see that go away. That's a beacon of this country."

I am struck by how specific Chris's ex-girlfriend is in his memory and just how abstracted the Indian men were for him. I would be interested to learn if the men were, for instance, Muslims—perhaps Muslims from the state of Gujarat, where English is not an official language, and where decades ago Narendra Modi demonstrated what so many American politicians already established, that a democratic nation can be so violently undemocratic.[3]

Chris and I stand at the top of the river canal, which looks just like all those Los Angeles viaducts in all those movies with angled concrete walls, 50 feet high, baking in the sun. The riverbed is cooled by a small flow of water, not more than fifteen feet wide, mostly sewage. At certain spots in the riverbed, tangled sod and garbage have created small islands just above the water level. These are the spots where deportados, the stateless migrants, build encampments. They have already shuffled through the U.S. immigration system and the Mexican immigration system and discovered that living right on top of the border is one of the few places they can avoid removal—most of the time. "If they're on the U.S. side a little bit," says Chris, "we're probably not going to do too much. If it gets a little too stupid, we'll push them back." For now he's not too worried about what he sees on this particular day. "They're on the Mexican side mostly," he says, shrugging.

"You'll see a lot of syringes on the ground here," he says, pointing at two needles within eyesight. He looks to the spot where the river bends into the U.S. and says, "There used to be tons of hooches—TJPD coming in and it would look like old Vietnam era footage, search and destroy. They would go in and torch everything. If you were on patrol and TJPD did a raid, you'd have forty, fifty people running at you," he says, shaking his head. "Most of them were just trying to get away from TJPD, but some would take advantage of it to get north. I was down here one time. I'm rolling around in this," he says, pointing down into the river water, "with syringes, broken bottles, feces. It got so physical, so ugly—tear gas and mace and whatnot. Afterward my partner says 'You don't look good.' And I said, 'I'm all right.' He goes, 'I'm calling the EMS.' I said, 'No, no.' But you know what? He was right because I ended up having a heart attack and quadruple bypass surgery," Chris says, laughing off the grave experience.

One reporter who's been connecting with deportados for years tells me that whenever the TJPD does a raid, many of the people living in the river canal will hastily cut themselves, "knowing the cops won't take anyone who is bleeding to jail."

"I used to go and talk to them," says Chris, "but I don't do that anymore with people because you could trigger somebody by going, 'Hey, how you doing my friend?' If somebody's emotionally disturbed, you have to be real careful. This is an area that can go bad real quick."

During this autumn of clogged immigration courts and prototypes of The Wall, the riverbed is lively. I see three separate encampments, each with six or seven tents. The encampments tend to stay about this size, staying small and spreading out; they're often strategically close to floodwater-control gates, which are tucked away in certain spots along the river. The gates are in little alcoves, carved into the canal walls, shaded spaces that provide the illusion of privacy for going to the bathroom, shooting up, sex. And the grating on the gates serves as shelving for everything from clothes to food to sets of works.

I have seen all the private acts of the deportados in the control gate alcoves; it's too easy to unintentionally catch the action while crossing over the river on one of the footbridges. Downers seem to be the prevailing choice: when the drug hits the bloodstream most people put their full weight back against the control gate, which is pitched at a subtle angle that almost satisfies the itch to immediately lie down in a dry spot—but not quite. A lot of people end up slowly bending their knees, sliding down the gate and settling for a wet seat in the sewer water, which at least keeps them in the shade with the gate to rest against. The raw, toxic smell of the water dominates in all directions—except to the immediate north, of course, where the mall maintains a formidable blockade of candles, perfumes, colognes, lotions, and oil diffusers.

"You've seen the heroin users before," Chris says, pointing at a man not far from us, staggering in the other direction at the top of the canal wall. We watch him for a moment, willing him another step or two away from the edge of the angled wall. It's not uncommon to see someone get high, lose their balance, and fall, rolling down to the concrete riverbed. "That looks like he's got the nod. I'm not going to screw with him."

We turn the other way, looking down at one encampment where a man has stepped out of his tent to urinate. "They defecate where they hang out," Chris says, pointing at him. "I don't get it."

I want to tell Chris that I think people generally defecate where they hang out when they have no other place to do so but just then a man approaches us, walking along the top of the canal. When Chris feels the man's presences over his shoulder, he turns toward him and puts his weight back, defensive: "¿Cómo está?" he says. "How you doing, my friend?"

"I want to tell you something," the man says in English. He is short and graying, fragile-looking and sweaty under his wool poncho.

Chris proceeds with just a dash of hesitation, keeping a few feet between him and the old man: "What's that?"

The old man points at a man across the river in a red T-shirt with a backpack, and he rats him out as a dealer. Chris thanks him for the information and adds, "You speak good English."

The old man shrugs and says he learns a lot of English in the canals.

"Well, thank you my friend," Chris says to him. "You take care of yourself, all right? Be safe. Vaya con Dios."

The old man puts out his hand for a little remuneration—he does so subtly, but still, it's there, open. He smiles at Chris, expectant. Chris shakes his head, apologetic yet firm, and starts back toward the driver's side of the SUV. The old man watches him for a moment, as if anticipating the moment Chris might turn around with a crisp $20 neatly folded between his fingers. But Chris does not turn and so the old man continues along the foul river.

Chris takes me for a ride into the Tijuana River Estuary, which starts just west of Las Americas Premium Outlets. Even though the landscape is managed as a wildlife refuge and nature reserve, official tests show that the water is overrun by several contaminants, including but not limited to mercury, chloroform, dichlorobenzene, copper, nickel, zinc, oil, ammonia, fecal coliform, enterococcus bacteria, and "suspended solids," whatever that might include.[4] The estuary is managed by thirty different agencies from every level of U.S. government as well as international bodies.

Chris takes me to Goat Canyon, where, in addition to the chemical brew, there's a steady flow of debris in the water. The small canyon is essentially two large concrete catch basins with orange trash booms doing their best to collect as much as they can, lots of plastic water bottles and tires and broken pieces of foam. And in this spot, the flow of tainted water is rerouted to a nearby wastewater sewage treatment center, though fragments of seed-laced waste do sometimes escape, evidenced by the occasional zucchini sprouting in the basin.

"After the center treats the water," says Chris, "it shoots its by-product three miles offshore into the ocean. Now, I truly believe that the government doesn't *really* want to know what's in this water, chemical-wise. I've seen pushback on doing testing and I get it's expensive, but I'll tell you why I think there's pushback. Again, these are only my own theories, but that's a *sewage* treatment plant," Chris says, pointing at the structure where the water is treated. "It's *not* a chemical reclamation plant. So, for instance, if the EPA ever found out that this water was chock-full of chemicals, can it legally keep permitting that plant to shoot out chemicals into the ocean? Or will they have to say, 'Holy crap! Now we have to build a half-a-billion-dollar chemical reclamation plant'?"

If the river floods in the winter, the storm water rushes past the trash booms on the way to the ocean. The deluge can also bring tons of sediment. In 2008, Border Patrol filled in a popular crossing spot near the estuary, Smuggler's Gulch, with nearly two million cubic yards of dirt. Several spots in and around the 2,500-acre estuary have been altered in order to transform it into a security zone.

Chris takes me to Stewart's Drain, a concrete canal under two fences that have been constructed across one of the river channels in the estuary. The drain is meant to allow rainwater from the south to continue its natural flow across the international line. The smell at the drain is so intense I tell Chris it feels like there is a chemical fire in my nose. He shrugs and says, "This is not a bad day." He sniffs at the air and says it again, "No, this is not a bad day at all, my friend."

Border Patrol maintains a series of grates on the U.S. side of Stewart's Drain so that no one can use the canal as a passage from one country to the other. Chris says that Border Patrol opens the grates whenever it rains—in accordance with domestic and international law, he emphasizes—so the storm water is unimpeded. "But," he adds, "no other water is supposed to come through the drain." I look up at the blue sky then back down at the bright green water at our feet. Chris shrugs.

"Rainwater is one thing," he says, "but this is continuous now—every day something's running across. Some days it smells more like sewage. Other days it's more like chemicals. Our guys are down in this stuff. One of my guys, I have his boots—they're falling apart. He was in the stuff, tracking a guy out—there's deportados living in there sometimes—and my agent went back to the station, showered, and his boots were already falling apart. The chemicals were dissolving them. They were dissolving!

"The National Border Patrol Council had a lawsuit against the government about seventeen years ago for hazardous duty. So, they tested the soil and everything. And we have this picture as an exhibit—you know, a picture tells a thousand words—and in this picture, you have in the background a tent set up by the military with medics and decontamination showers. And their guys are in full-on biohazard gear. And here's our guy just standing there in a uniform. I mean, the dichotomy between our agency and the military going, 'Oh yeah, you need to work in this environment in biohazard gear.' No shit!

"Don't forget, we eat here. We don't go out to a restaurant for lunch. And if it's a windy day, you'll have the grit and dirt in your mouth, ingesting it. It's in your nose. You're breathing it.

"And the government of Mexico will tell you, 'Well, it's illegal dumping,' which is true.[5] Let me tell you, there's muchos maquiladoras down there. These are American corporations and international corporations. They didn't go down there just for cheap labor. That's part of it. They went down there for nonexistent or lax environmental laws. So shame on the companies. These American corporations and international corporations, they're the ones down there dumping shit."

CHAPTER 38

THE ESTUARY EMPTIES INTO THE Pacific at Imperial Beach, where surfers enjoyed the breakers long before Tijuana mushroomed with industrialization. One of them was Serge Dedina, who moved to the town with his parents when he was seven. "They found a house for $120 a month in 1971," he says, "and I've been here ever since. Our first day, we drove down to the south end of our street where you can see Tijuana. There was no border fence back then. My parents thought we were millionaires growing up, living in Southern California on the beach," he says, laughing.

"When I was a little older, my friends and I would actually jump the cable at Border Field State Park. There was just some posts and a cable. We would ride our bikes around Playas, ride back and no one cared. That's how I grew up.

"When I was in high school and got my driver's license, I was surfing in Baja two to three times per week. We would go before school, after school. I will never forget bodysurfing into Tijuana. In the afternoon, families would come from the south and spend the day clamming and we would hang out with those folks."

The Border Patrol no longer allows bodysurfing between countries and everyone is formally discouraged from even swimming up to the borderline. There is a bright yellow sign on the beach that reads:

DANGER

SEWAGE

CONTAMINATED WATER

AVOID WATER CONTACT FROM THIS POINT SOUTH

TO THE

INTERNATIONAL BORDER

Even north of the warning risks persist. "A week ago Monday," Serge says, "my sons were out surfing mid-morning and a plume of sewage that had been dumped that night washed through the border and my son got really, really sick. He had diarrhea, blood in his stool, vomiting and had to go to urgent care to get antibiotics. That kind of stuff happens all the time. And there have been cases of encephalitis, orbital socket bacterial infections, hepatitis A."

Serge is sitting at a lifeguard station, looking across the ocean. Imperial Beach's signature pier is lively, per usual, with people fishing and texting and wandering, some drifting into the Tin Fish, where the fryers are always on and the speakers never quit, sending Top 40 music and order numbers echoing out across the Pacific. San Diego Bay is to the north of us, through the haze, and the Tijuana River Estuary is behind us. "My mom and dad just fell in love with the estuary," says Serge. "We would have picnics every weekend at the river mouth. In the 1980s is when we started having really bad pollution problems."

That's when Serge went away to college. He earned a PhD in geography and eventually founded a binational organization called Wildcoast, which, among other things, tries to pressure and cajole all thirty agencies that are in charge of cleaning up the international waters that flow into Imperial Beach.

"Anytime it rains," he says, "the storm water of Tijuana mixes with the sewage systems and then you get flows going into the Tijuana River, which crosses the border and comes out here. That's a problem. Then you've got cataclysmic rains that wash away the sewage infrastructure—pipes washed away. And during dry weather, the pump stations break down and make the sewage system malfunction to where it discharges on the beach. Then you get trucks that have toxic waste or they pump out septic tanks into a concrete channel and it discharges in the Tijuana River."

Whenever Serge tried to effect change with the big agencies—the Environmental Protection Agency, the International Boundary and Water Commission—he says the reply was always the same. "They'd just say, 'Everything is fine, don't worry your pretty little surfer head.' You've got this overarching federal, state, and local political infrastructure, but there is a huge vacuum where no one takes responsibility for anything. You're constantly having to push the people that should be in power to actually try to do something."

So Serge—with his perfect tan, natural highlights, and commitment to the land—ran for mayor of Imperial Beach in 2014 and won. "Do you know those World War II movies where the submarine starts leaking," he says, "spouting water and it's all hands on deck? That's where we're on right now. The whole system needs to go to the next level.

"In addition to having one of the most significant water pollution problems in all of North America, we also have some of the most horrendous air pollution from diesel trucks that are idling on the border. That has a huge impact on public health on both sides of the border.

"The fact that American companies place their assembly plants on the Mexican side is not because of the lack of environmental regulations, but the lack of *enforcement* of the regulations.

"As mayor, I work very closely with the Border Patrol. They have emerged as a really important ally for us. The Border Patrol has been significantly impacted by pollution. I say this with all respect; they come in contact daily with toxic pollution coming across the border. And, you know, I really believe, as an environmentalist, but also as mayor, that if you only work with environmentalists, you don't get environmental work done. We've really made a point of reaching out to nontraditional partners, military families, the Border Patrol union—that's been valuable in getting traction on this. And over the years, I've learned to always make sure that when I talk about the border, I talk about the Border Patrol, the military, *national security*. And hey, that works for me. Because you know what? Security of the border has multiple connotations. It means keeping bad guys on both sides of the border from hurting people. It means reducing air and water quality problems, and it means increasing the social, economic, and cultural ties we have on the border. You don't make borders more secure by dividing people. You make borders more secure by strengthening ties at all levels so people feel comfortable, secure, and safe. I'm talking about very strong civic, economic, cultural, and political ties, where people work with transparency and legal protection, where the rules are clear and people feel *secure* to invest, people feel *secure* to cross the border, people feel *secure* to shop on both sides of the border and have lives on both sides of the border. Even some of our city employees live across the border in Tijuana and cross every day.

"There is a functioning political, economic, ecological, and cultural ecosystem here. You're continually on both sides of the border to solve problems or create connections and make things happen—there is no barrier there. It's actually a force of attraction that pulls people together."

PART 3

DESTRUCTION

CHAPTER 39

IT IS EARLY NOVEMBER AND I'm sitting with Jill Holslin in a restaurant on an industrial drag in the Tijuana neighborhood of Otay. The prototypes have only been up for two weeks and Jill was part of the first group of artists to move in on them.

It was just a few days ago. She was with a crew of architects, documentarians, drivers, gaffers, and spotlight operators who quietly descended on Las Torres in the late afternoon and parked three trucks right up against the primary fence. The bed of each truck was covered with a plywood platform where they set up cameras, lights, computers. They went about it quickly, no interaction with Mexican law enforcement. "Obviously we didn't want to lose our equipment," Jill says. She wore a hoodie that night, and across the chest it read, "Aliens in the Hood."

The light graffiti show began at dusk, under a pink and orange sky. The first bright yellow image was a lucha libre wrestler projected onto the W. G. Yates design.

After a minute, the masked face vanished and suddenly there was text instead:

Build Bridges
Not Borders
#RefugeesWelcomeHere
#NoOneIsIllegal

And after another minute the text went away and the wrestler was back, then a stick figure climbing a wall, then the Statue of Liberty, then a long, skinny ladder up to the very top of the prototype—and the images rotated again and again, in quick succession.

"I really wanted the ladder," Jill says. "And I thought about having it say, 'No border wall' but you know what? I thought, I want the icon of the ladder without words on it because it is such an icon, it doesn't need words. Ladders have been used in a lot of border art projects so it was mostly a nod to that." In particular, Jill mentions her affection for Andrew Sturm's short film *31FootLadders*, which features an enterprising man who sees a 30-foot wall as opportunity to start a company that specializes in 31-foot ladders. What could possibly be more American?

"And the group I was doing the project with, they said, 'We want it to be funny too.' And I said, 'Yeah I guess you're right.' " She laughs. "It's important. I always forget. I get overanalytical. I just get worried because you don't want to reduce this to some kind of ludicrous cat-and-mouse game. What I'm not really keen on is this idea that we're breaking the law by creating this art. It was important to me that this happen from Mexico and not be about us trespassing onto the prototype site itself—that's a completely different context. I didn't want us to equate ourselves with the coyotes or cartels who are against the Border Patrol. It's not that simple. I didn't want the messages to be reduced to that level.

"The message I wanted to project was not that we're breaking the law. The message I wanted to project is that the United States is breaking the law by not allowing refugees to enter and apply for asylum—and that American values are being betrayed by these walls."

CHAPTER 40

NOW THAT CONSTRUCTION IS COMPLETE and media requests have thinned out, Eduardo Olmos finds himself attending to other duties. He is one of three agents charged with opening the giant mesh gate for "Door of Hope," the ceremony organized by Enrique Morones of Border Angels. As Eduardo holds his position, one foot is in the U.S., the country he protects, and one is in Mexico, the country of his birth. Or, if one considers another map—and we should consider other maps—if one considers topography or climate or roads, anything other than political lines, then we can simply say Eduardo Olmos is standing with both feet firmly in the Southwest.

The Door of Hope event gives a dozen groups three minutes each to step forward and embrace loved ones on the far side of the international line. Enrique is the one who selects candidates for the event—passing their names on to Border Patrol in advance for vetting—and he stands just a few feet away for all the reunions in his bright purple T-shirt, captured as background during many of the tearful moments.

This event usually produces very meaningful experiences and today is no exception: grandparents hold a grandchild for the first time; a man hugs his mother after more than a decade apart. But the final embrace upstages all others: arriving from the south, Evelia Reyes approaches the open gate in a white dress while Brian Houston approaches from the north in a gray tuxedo. With help from a Tijuana judge, they use their three minutes to get married. The bride's daughter, in her own gown and tiara, runs into Houston's arms the moment she sees him. He squeezes her tight but puts her down immediately so vows can commence. Everyone is taken aback, including the agents. Eduardo shifts on his feet, looking to his fellow agents, who have no answers. Even Enrique seems caught off guard and will later tell one reporter, "I thought it was just a proposal." Apparently the couple hatched the plan in advance on the phone and everyone on location goes along. Vows are exchanged and, thanks to Enrique, there are plenty of paparazzi. Images of the ceremony are sent out across the world via the likes of the AP and Reuters.

CHAPTER 41

IT WAS AS IF THE moment of the improvised wedding created a clamor that the prototypes have yet to achieve. The protesters did not arrive, a revival of Standing Rock was not mounted, and now the prototypes are complete. Equipment has been cleared away and the 4,000-gallon water deliveries have come to an end. Law enforcement has largely retreated—though various agencies remain on the scene. A few Border Patrol agents are routinely camped out in the shade of the scrub oak to the north, and there are eyes on the maze of fencing in the desert.

The cold that Gaudencio had warned about when I first arrived, the chill in the air he foretold during the unkind heat of summer, has finally arrived in Las Torres. Early evening fires crackle outside the plywood and cinder block homes. After four weeks of construction, eight models of The Wall stand at the edge of the colonia. As Ralph DeSio put it, they await their auditions. But everyone in Las Torres is bored with them already. Locals go about the business of cooking dinner and finishing car repairs by flashlight, agnostic to the monoliths that tower over their neighborhood. There is a distinct lack of audience.

This is something that caught the attention of Jeff Schwilk, a retired Marine who organized a "Build the Wall" rally shortly after the government announced the completion of the prototypes. Jeff says the idea was to give The Wall "a boost."

The Sheriff's Department put attendance for the event at sixty but a local reporter gave Jeff credit for a hundred and noted that at least one person came from as far as Arizona.

Jeff has had better showings. He is the founder of San Diegans for Secure Borders, which has a mailing list of a thousand, and some of the group's events do draw hundreds of people. Jeff became interested in the border when he moved to San Diego County nearly two decades ago. "I had just retired from the Marine Corps," he says, "and I thought, okay, I'm done serving my country. America's not going to have another 9/11. And then I'm seeing all these vulnerabilities in the system. I didn't know squat."

The *vulnerabilities* were large groups of migrants, twenty or thirty at a time, crossing in the desert after Operation Gatekeeper pushed them into East County. Jeff started doing border watches with a group that eventually became the San Diego Minutemen. "I just felt like my twenty-one years doing Marine Corps Intelligence was kind of suited to this kind of work. But," he adds, "we only did that for a couple years."

I remember Bob Maupin's mention of the San Diego Minutemen, how he put together Maupin's Marauders after determining the Minutemen were "really weird" and "did not know how to handle themselves." Gently I float his name: "So you must know Bob Maupin," I say.

"Oh, yeah," Jeff says, looking a bit cautious, "I know Bob. He has his little fence."

The word *little* jumps out. I ask Jeff if they're in touch.

"I haven't talked to him for a while," he says.

Citizen patrols of the southern border go back nearly two centuries. They are the point of origin for U.S. Border Patrol, and the mythology involves everything from Stephen Austin protecting the white settlers in Texas from Mexicans, to the first border watchman hired by the U.S. Department of Commerce and Labor in 1904. Much of the energy then was about enforcing the 1882 Chinese Exclusion Act, keeping Chinese workers from crossing into the country.

Over the past twelve years there has been a patchwork of citizen patrols—sometimes collaborating, sometimes clashing—all along the border but particularly in San Diego County, from Jim Wood financing the Border Project in the Campo desert with small donations made by people like Alice in Brooklyn, to Jeff Schwilk and Bob Maupin leading two different patrols in the same desert.

I ask Jeff why the San Diego Minutemen stopped doing their patrols.

"We really realized," he says, "that it wasn't worth it, having people drive an hour and a half down to the Campo. We didn't have sensors. We didn't have night vision that was real good. We didn't have all the communications Border Patrol has. So we're kind of winging it and it just really wasn't a very effective use of time and resources."

Jeff does note that Border Patrol started doing more hiring after the Minutemen patrols in California and Arizona gained notoriety. "Border Patrol just about doubled in size," he says, "in part due to our political pressure back then. So we felt like we'd kind of accomplished a lot of our mission by getting many more agents out there."

CHAPTER 42

JEFF MORPHED THE SAN DIEGO Minutemen into San Diegans for Secure Borders, which is much more focused on political activism—not unlike the "Build the Wall" rally. Notwithstanding the modest turnout for the event, Jeff delivered a formidable lineup of speakers including Border Patrol agent and disgruntled Republican Chris Harris, as well as Duncan Hunter, the U.S. congressman who represents California's 50th District, which includes much of East County.

The name Duncan Hunter is synonymous with building The Wall, in part because so far there have been *two* Duncan Hunters making the case for it. The current congressman, Duncan *Duane* Hunter, was preceded by his father, Duncan *Lee* Hunter, who served in Congress for three decades. In the early 1990s, unable to drum up enough support among his congressional colleagues for much wall funding, Duncan's father began pulling together resources to put up the primary fence. "He essentially got the fence done for free," his son tells me, and it sounds like an inherited talking point but he says it emphatically, with genuine pride.

Once again I find myself in the crowded world of San Diego County craft breweries—this time at Stone Brewing in the city of Escondido. The congressman is sitting across from me with a pint of beer on the table; he stops what he's saying to take a hit off the vaping pen tucked into his palm. While his lungs are full he ekes out a detail—"There were landing mats sitting on a military base not being used"—then he lets out a vapor plume that dissipates across the patio where we sit on a sunny afternoon. "They used the National Guard to put it up. It didn't even cost anything. Until then, you had people driving Mack trucks over. You had banzai charges—a thousand illegal aliens charged toward the border. The Border Patrol guys would catch some of them and the rest would get away and that was that."

Duncan's father was so well known for championing The Wall, he was so determined to jury-rig it out of recycled materials, that it eventually led to personal consequences. "He had death threats," says Duncan. "It happened when he talked about securing the border and building a border fence."

"Have you spent a lot of time on the other side of the border?"

"I used to surf at Imperial Beach all the time, surf the slews, which is a great break that's still right there at the border. Yeah, I went to Tijuana a few times. We got a little bullwhip and a sombrero when I was a kid," he says, smiling. "But after the death threats we stopped going. I haven't been back since."

"Do you remember, as a kid, the border being a conversation in your family?" I ask. "At the dinner table, around the house?"

"It's something that we discussed. My dad took me down there by the outlet mall right by the border off of 5 and we were at a food truck, shrimp, and we were just kind of looking around in awe that the mall could be there. It's a more secure place now. They would have been overwhelmed instantaneously without the fence. We talked about that quite a bit. We still talk about that."

When Duncan's father made a presidential run in 2007 he gave up his congressional seat and Duncan won it in the next election, becoming Congress's first combat veteran from the wars in Iraq and Afghanistan.

He had enlisted as a Marine in the wake of 9/11 and was still a reservist in 2007. Duncan was called back to service during his congressional campaign. He won the June primary from an outpost in Afghanistan with 72 percent of the vote.

Duncan joined the Marines to help fight the War on Terror, the war that unshackled all wars from the battlefield and militarized our airports and stadiums, our concerts and police departments. And Duncan brings this approach to his family's quest to build The Wall. The border as a militarized zone is a foregone conclusion; the question is how best to do it. "It's like anything in the Marine Corps," he says, "you have to have a wall, you always have a physical barrier—but it's not going to stop people who are dedicated to attacking you or getting in, it slows them down long enough to respond to them. That's what an obstacle plan is. You don't put concertina wire out and then say all the sentries can go to sleep now because we have concertina wire outside of our base camp. You still have to have guys on watch." For Duncan the border is not a complicated community or region; it is a front, facing the enemy and the line must be fortified.

"The fence doesn't work without a high-speed road either. Otherwise guys will bring 20-foot ladders for a 19-foot fence and there is no Border Patrol there, or they're not able to get there in time, and the guy goes on his jolly way. You've *got* to have a road. It's a major force multiplier. You have one guy that watches two or three miles, but he can get to a spot at the fence within two minutes on a quad.

"The last thing is electricity. If you're going to have sensors, you have to have power. It's different here in San Diego than it's going to be in Imperial Valley or Arizona or Texas where there is no power. The best idea I've seen so far for those places is put solar banks every twenty feet and that's able to power the different sensors.

"But the wall, to me, is absolutely necessary. I'm down with the wall or a fence or whatever you want to call it so long as the Border Patrol can see through it. Without that, the rest of the stuff doesn't matter because things will happen too quickly.

"They say you can't build a wall on rough terrain and that's baloney. I've looked at lots of people who have built walls or dam structures, barricades or barriers in really tough terrain. It's not *impossible*. You also don't need to build a wall on the side of the Grand Canyon because people aren't going to walk sideways against gravity across the side of the Grand Canyon, so you're not going to have a fence everywhere, just most places."

I do not mention that the Grand Canyon is well north of the Mexico-U.S. border, or that I have not yet encountered a topography that migrants won't try to cross, but I do ask, "How much will all of that cost?"

Unfazed he says, "It's going to be billions and billions of dollars."

War is expensive.

I ask Duncan to clarify the people beyond the enemy line, to tell me how he sees them. "Illegal immigrants who have committed crimes or are seedy characters," he says. "We have to go throughout the U.S., find out where there are the bad actors, where they're getting across and try to get them out of the country. Then make sure they can't come back across."

I ask about the migrants who aren't *bad actors* who are coming for work or safety or both.

He jumps on the question: "Hey, but by coming across the border illegally, you're breaking the law. You're committing a criminal act by doing it. If I sneak across the border into Germany or any other country in the world and I do it sneakily, I'm breaking the law. I'm there illegally. And if they find me, I'm going to get in trouble.

"The rule of law, the system we have, is not working right now and these people are getting into the country outside of the rule of law. They're breaking the law. They're bringing the lawlessness that they're running from, you're bringing those same problems that you're escaping. You're letting them in.

"We haven't talked about the OTMs, the Other Than Mexican people: China, Pakistan, Iraq, Syria, India—whatever, name your place, former Soviet satellite state stuff. You have a free-for-all with them knowing the way to get to the U.S. is just walking across the border. And that's what we have here in San Diego. It's that easy. Anybody from anywhere for any purpose could just go to Mexico or go to any South or Central American country, work their way north, rent a car at Budget rental in Mexico City, drive north, go to a place where you don't see anybody and hop across the border. Why would we want that? You've got to prioritize what kind of people get access to the country."

"What kind of people should have access to the country?"

"It should be who loves America! If you like America and bring your knowledge and make our country a richer place, come on over. Oh, you have a nuclear chemistry degree too?—okay, you're really coming over. We'd love to have you. Thank you. But if you've committed three crimes in Venezuela though, and you're trying to come over here to work, then, no, you don't get in.

"We want *good* people coming. And I think that's a major challenge. I don't know how you vet someone's heart and soul, make sure they're not going to jump in a truck and mow people down, do whatever, join a gang. I don't think we should give the benefit of the doubt to people who are breaking the law originally by coming into the country illegally. The burden's on you as an immigrant, to prove that you want to be an American, that you want to blend in and do our thing here. I think the burden should be on the immigrant to show they're not a criminal. They want to just have a normal life and work hard and commit to the American Dream."

After an hour, Duncan wants to leave while I still have questions. He drinks the last of his beer and we both stand to shake hands. He turns to go and I notice something in the chair where he was sitting. I lean down and see that it is Duncan's vaping pen. I grab it and call after him. He turns around and I walk over to return it.

"Oh Jesus, thanks," he says with relief, probably imagining that moment on the freeway when he might have reached into his empty pocket.

In June of 2016 the State of California passed a measure outlawing use of electronic cigarettes in public spaces such as restaurants and bars, and in March of 2017 it was reported that Duncan and his wife are under FBI investigation for private use of campaign funds.[1] I mentioned both of these things not to point out that Duncan might have committed as many as sixty crimes or that California's statewide prohibition on electronic cigarettes needs to be more stringently enforced by Stone Brewing, per se. The point is, as Duncan would put it, *the rule of law*, and the fact that those who push to enforce it without exceptions tend to live their lives as though they are exceptions.

CHAPTER 43

TESTING OF THE PROTOTYPES HAS begun, and Las Torres is the place to be. A few doors down from Aurelia and Gaudencio, a young man is standing outside his house, making tea over an open fire. His name is Alexis and he lives on the road with his girlfriend, Rosa, who stands next to him, trying to keep her bandaged thumb slightly above her heart. Blood is soaking through the gauze, slowly, which will need to be replaced soon. She accidentally cut herself with a kitchen knife. Alexis has made her tea from salvia leaves, which, he tells me, is not only helping Rosa heal but is also providing her with hallucinations. Alexis sips on his own cup. He stirs what remains in a handle-less pot, keeping it warm. Then he steps up to the primary fence to watch the action on the other side. I join him.

This afternoon there are about twenty men on location. Only one is in a clearly marked Border Patrol uniform, though it does appear he's been pulled off a desk because his short sleeve shirt is too nicely pressed and there is no firearm—not even a notepad—hanging from his belt. His hands remain comfortably in his pockets as he supervises the scene.

Most of the men are likely from BORTAC, the SWAT-style special response unit of Border Patrol, dressed for the climbing occasion: cargo pants, T-shirts stretched over muscles, baseball hats and sunglasses working in tandem to keep the sun away. The days can still be plenty warm even though the nights bite with cold. BORTAC agents move from one prototype to another as a pack. They are trailed by two men in collared shirts, who keep several feet of space for themselves; they carry clipboards and wear hard hats, which they continually adjust atop their heads, looking for a more comfortable fit that just isn't there.

There is only one other man, working on his own to measure off a perimeter for each prototype—even the prototypes get their own borders, which are marked with wood stakes and yellow CAUTION tape.

Officials explained they needed to wait a month to begin testing the prototypes because some concrete required more time to dry. Now all the contestants are ready and three fundamental questions remain: Can they be climbed? Can they be dug under? Can they withstand cutting tools? Border Patrol estimates that the testing could take "up to two months."

The agency doesn't have much of a presence on the scene outside the personnel doing the testing. Every half hour or so an agent zips by on an ATV. And at one point four agents in cowboy hats trot by on horses because it wouldn't be a border without cowboy hats and horses.

The testing moves to the Fisher Sand & Gravel model, which is, perhaps, the simplest of the eight: three 30-foot-high concrete panels, all the same color of the Otay granite. One of the men reaches up to feel the seam between two of the beige panels, trying to feed his fingers as deep as possible into the crevasse. After a while, he hammers a peg into the seam and tests it to see if it will support his weight. All the others watch.

The group has been going down the line, from one prototype to the next, feeling surfaces, hitches, seams, seeking out any texture that might be leveraged.

Eventually the men arrive at the KWR Construction model, one of only two designs made mostly of steel and, perhaps more importantly, one of only two designs that use bollards, allowing agents to see through to the other side—something they all emphasize is essential.

While everyone stands together, looking up at the prototype, one of the two men with clipboards finds a folding chair, which he positions at the edge of the model so he can prop his feet up against the steel bollard on the end. One BORTAC agent runs up to the model, jumps on and latches to one of the bollards with his hands. He shimmies up a few feet, pushing off with one leg then the other, crab-walking toward the sun. It takes him about a minute to get halfway up the bollard—and the bollards only run two thirds of the way to the top of the prototype. The last third of the barrier is flat sheets of metal topped off by a hollow tube with a diameter of at least four feet.

On the far side of the KWR model, two men ascend in a boom lift, eventually coming up over the top of the prototype. They lower rope while all the men who had been clustered at the base spread out to suit up with harnesses, ropes, gloves, helmets. Black mats, a bit thicker than wrestling mats, are spread out at the base of the prototype.

Everyone stands back as one man approaches the prototype and grabs the rope lowered from the boom, running it through the belay device at his waist. He stands directly in front of the structure and claps his hands, sending a plume of chalk into the air. Then he wraps his hands around a bollard and lifts one foot onto each of the bollards on either side of his hands. He begins to inch his way up, his legs powering his arms, a clump of carabiners jingling at his belt all the way.

It takes him thirty seconds or so to get to the top of the bollards, where they meet the flat sheets of metal. He hangs there for a moment.

Alexis, still sipping the tea, calls out to him: "Hello sir. Hello!"

The man climbing the prototype can likely hear Alexis, as can all the men on the scene but no one reacts. Alexis laughs and tells me "these guys are nothing" compared to the crew he saw the day before.

"What was going on yesterday?" I ask.

"Same as today," he says, "but they looked like really tough guys—like they were *Marines*." The way he says Marines it seems to mean the apex of tough.

The man at the top of the bollards looks down at the man who holds the other end of the rope secured to his harness. He nods and the rope is loosened as he begins rappelling back toward the ground.

A few minutes later another man climbs the KWR model, taking a slightly different approach, spread out a bit more across four bollards— one for each hand and one for each foot. He makes it up to the steel panels too, but now the rope goes taut, as the man holding the other end assumes the climber's body weight, allowing him to dangle freely. He rummages around in the spot where the bollards meets the panel, feeling blindly with his hand, looking for a spot to grab. After several minutes he too rappels back down to the ground.

Alexis continues to yell at all the men: "Hey, c'mon—faster! Faster!" Still no one reacts and I'm guessing it's because he's smiling through it all and Alexis's smile is too charming, too goofy, to take the heckling too seriously. Each time another man dangles at the top of the bollards, Rosa stares up from her seat by the fire; her mouth is open, as if she's lost in the scene of a movie.

She and Alexis are in their early twenties. He works odd jobs, some construction; like Aurelia and Gaudencio, like most of the people on this drag of Las Torres, Alexis scrapes together work and shelter and sustenance and hygiene. He and his neighbors pay negligible rents, or squat; the landowners are mostly away, uninterested until the neighborhood capitalization potential improves.

Alexis has been in Las Torres for a couple of years. The cinder block home behind him is one room, about ten feet by fifteen feet, most of which is taken up by a bed, standing fan, and small recliner. He puts his empty teacup on a rock beside the fire, opens a forty, and returns to the primary fence, shouting, "Who the hell is they expecting to come across the border? Some invaders? They make it look like war!" He sips from his beer, pointing at the men as, one after another, they each scale the KWR model then rappel down.

CHAPTER 44

IT IS JANUARY 2018 AND Enrique Morones is all over the news. He raised the necessary $15,000 to pay for materials and permits for Sal Barajas's new mural in Chicano Park—one that tells the story of Border Angels. The new work is, in some ways, an addendum to Barajas's last work. Enrique raised money for that mural too—$10,000—and it features an iron fist labeled "ICE," squeezing the neck of a migrant. *The San Diego Union-Tribune* published an article claiming there were a lot of "detractors" who were "upset at the mural's message," though the reporting was thin, based on comments by two private citizens who hadn't yet seen the murals in person, so it's hard to decipher just how many detractors there were, but my sense is that they probably did not outnumber the patriots who showed up for the picnic. This time around, Enrique and Barajas are staying away from any directly violent images. The new mural will feature the Virgin of Guadalupe carrying a jug of water into the desert. Barajas is hoping to finish before the next Chicano Park Day[1] in the spring.

But the press isn't all good for Enrique these days—the story of the impromptu wedding at the Door of Hope event has become more complicated in recent weeks. As it turns out, the groom, Brian Houston, could not travel to Tijuana to marry his girlfriend because he was out on bail. He had been arrested earlier in the year after he was caught crossing into the U.S. with forty-seven pounds of meth, forty-three pounds of cocaine, and forty-three pounds of heroin stuffed into the spare tire and paneling of his Volkswagen Jetta.[2] By the time he married Evelia Reyes at Friendship Park, with cameras rolling, Houston had already pled guilty to three counts of drug smuggling and was awaiting sentencing.

"Turns out we provided armed security for a cartel wedding," a CBP spokesperson told *The San Diego Union-Tribune.* Houston's lawyers told the same reporter that their client was a "drug mule" who did not know he was transporting the contraband.[3]

Border Patrol officials and Enrique Morones have been passing blame back and forth. Enrique says he knew Houston "had some legal troubles" but didn't know about his criminal charges and plea bargain. Enrique also points out that Border Angels is only responsible for submitting the names of dozens of applicants. From there, Border Patrol officials are responsible for vetting the applications and settling on a final list of participants.

No one from the agency seems to know how Houston made it past the vetting process but everyone is sure they are mad at Enrique. "It's all about Enrique and the Enrique road show," Chris Harris tells me. "He screwed up. I mean, c'mon, this guy Houston was a U.S. citizen, marrying a girl on the Southside. And they asked him why don't you go down there? 'Oh, personal reasons.' Well, the personal reasons turned out he's on pre-sentencing release facing twenty years in prison! The cartel does not tell a first-time smuggler, 'Hey, here's 120 pounds of different drugs.' He's cartel! Our guys are standing there, they were basically armed security at a cartel wedding. Enrique swears he didn't know. Enrique goes, 'No, Border Patrol's fault.' You can blame whoever you want, Enrique. You just caused our new chief to say that gate is not opening again. That's done."

The new chief for the San Diego sector, Rodney Scott, released a statement confirming the Door of Hope will not open this year. The Door of Hope, he said, is actually a maintenance gate, and "moving forward, the maintenance gate will be used for maintenance purposes only." Scott also reminded the public that if they want to connect with loved ones they can do so at any of the 328 official ports of entry administered by the federal government, and he emphasized that "many of those ports of entry are open 24 hours a day, 365 days a year."

CHAPTER 45

IT WAS AT A PORT of entry, in San Ysidro, where Brian Houston was caught with 133 pounds of drugs. It was *not* a Border Patrol agent who nabbed him but a customs officer.

Deep inside the stacking doll that is the Department of Homeland Security, Border Patrol is nestled inside a larger agency known as U.S. Customs and Border Protection, which also includes customs officers. The customs officers wear navy blue uniforms and conduct inspections at ports of entry like the one in San Ysidro; Border Patrol agents, in olive green, protect the border between the ports. There is a distinct line between the two arms of the agency. Angelica DeCima, an officer at the San Ysidro Port, tells me, "Sometimes the media will call us customs *agents*. And I'll say, 'No, those are Border Patrol *agents*, but here at the ports of entry, we're customs *officers*.' I correct them when I can," she says with a polite smile.

Angelica is a chief officer, a boss, but her authority is quiet. She has a calm demeanor and controls everything down to her tightly gathered ponytail. She's been with U.S. Customs for twenty years and is originally from San Diego. She loves working in her hometown. "I won't go anywhere else permanently," she says without hesitation.

Over the course of Angelica's time at the San Ysidro port, it has undergone a major expansion. Work continues on more lanes for cars but pedestrians already have two separate bridges, PedEast and PedWest, separated by about a mile.

PedEast is the older crossing, with several strip malls in the surrounding area: motels, clothing shops, restaurants. The approach to PedEast is just past the trolley station where the South Bay's blue line terminates—the sound of bells always lingers. There is a McDonald's, there are currency exchange booths, convenience stores, street vendors selling hats, plastic toys wrapped in more plastic, fresh-cut mangos. Squirrels and birds feast on the pulverized crackers and bottle caps full of water left behind for them. The walk along PedEast feels informal and alive.

PedWest, the newer crossing, is directly across from Las Americas Outlets and it feels more like a very long jet bridge closed off from the outside world—more portal than port.

Sixty of the 328 ports of entry maintained by Customs and Border Protection are between Mexico and the U.S.—these include eight rail lines, two dams, two ferries, and various bridges. Angelica works at the busiest of all these ports. She says at San Ysidro they seize 60 percent of the country's methamphetamine. "Ten years ago," she says, "we were seeing predominantly marijuana in the trunks. But it's very big, bulky stuff. Over the years, we started seeing the harder narcotics, smaller packaging and deeper concealments. Then we started seeing mixed loads where you would have a couple packages of meth, a couple packages of cocaine, now fentanyl also."

At least two thirds of the criminal activity stopped at the Mexico-U.S. border is stopped at ports of entry by customs officers, not *between* the ports of entry by Border Patrol agents. And if you take away the misdemeanor of crossing an international line without permission, and other minor violations, then more like 80 to 90 percent of crime is interdicted at ports of entry and not between them.[1]

Angelica walks me through the large hall where pedestrians wait in long, snaking lines to see an officer. It is a new facility with high ceilings and natural light—it could be an immigration line in any modernized, international airport. The expansion of the port, which began in 2014, has not only added the new processing hall, but there also are a couple floors of offices, secondary interview rooms, secondary vehicle inspection areas, parking lots, and holding facilities—it is a massive complex. Nowhere is the border more *unlike* a straight line on the map than at a port of entry.

The facilities all feel mint-condition with one exception: a two-story, small Spanish Colonial building from 1937, yellow stucco accented by bright blue tiles. It served as the original customs building and is protected by landmark status. "So we can't knock it down," says Angelica. "The facade has to remain the same."

Angelica and I stand outside the old building, and we turn to look at what might be considered the epicenter of the port: a twenty-five-lane traffic jam where hundreds of cars look like they're parked with idling engines but in reality all of them are crawling toward the primary inspection booths, one inch at a time. It's anxiety inducing, staring out across the frustration and restlessness. The border is the place where travel patterns are disrupted. The wait might be twenty minutes, or it might be three hours. There is a fast-pass system, SENTRI, but even those dedicated lanes back up. Port wait times are a part of the usual traffic updates across radio stations.

We stand just short of the first lanes of clogged traffic, and Angelica points at our feet. "Do you see that sign?" she asks. I look down at a plaque that reads:

INTERNATIONAL BOUNDARY OF THE
UNITED STATES AND MEXICO

"It goes along a diagonal line," she says. There is an angled buffer area between the officially marked international line and the spot where the U.S. government has placed customs booths. "Between the booth and the actual international boundary," Angelica says, "it could be maybe fifty yards depending on where you are, so we have all this area to roam." She waves her arm out across a large swath of the traffic jam and then, in a moment, proceeds in that direction, cutting across the first lane then the second. Angelica steps in front of one car after another without hesitating; I stay as close as possible, as the drivers all around me fight for every inch. There are other officers circulating around vehicles, making preliminary inspections with various instruments: dogs, mirrors, flashlights, sensors for everything from heat to radiation levels. Some wear kneepads and get down on the ground to look at a vehicle's undercarriage.

"We have our officers who are part of the antiterrorism enforcement team," Angelica says. "They're out here looking for that needle in the haystack. They might be tapping tanks, tapping the corner panel of the vehicle. You'll see some guys out there with a density meter. They're checking for density in the spare tires, the corner panels."

These preliminary inspections are all happening before each vehicle arrives at a booth with a customs officer who will conduct another inspection, checking plates and identification against law enforcement databases. From there, most vehicles are let into the country (with the possibility of encountering an interior Border Patrol checkpoint, of course) while others are sent to another inspection area, which is called secondary inspection, even though it's a third layer, after the antiterrorism foot patrols and the inspection booths. This is where vehicles get emptied out and X-rayed.

Matching an identification or license plate number in a law enforcement database isn't the only thing that might earn X-rays and hours in an interview room. "We can rely on the computer but the computer is not going to tell us if this person is lying," says Angelica. "Your training and your instincts, that's what it's all about. One of the things we learn when we go to the academy is interviewing techniques. That's huge for us. We learn behavior analysis. We learn to determine if someone is nervous and we use all those skills during that inspection to determine if there is something wrong or they might be lying to us. That's when we send them to secondary and the officer can work on that case longer and more in-depth."

At this point Angelica and I are standing in the center lane, looking out at the cars approaching the inspection booths. And while she describes looking for unsteady hands and shifty eyes, I feel overwhelmed by the slow-moving rush of angst and pollution. Angelica remains unfazed. Standing in the thick haze of car exhaust, she tells me about all the famous port stories: "There's the one we call 'Seat Man.' It was a guy sewn into the seat of a van. There are two Seat Men, actually. The more recent one is the velour seat, the first one was the leather seat.

"Sometimes people are put into a corner panel of a vehicle or the dashboard or the engine compartment. There was a case at the Tecate port of entry, they put a little girl in a piñata."

Angelica says they get a lot of runners, too—people who blow past the inspection booths in their cars, trying to speed away. "They rarely get away here," she says, "because we have the runner suppression system. Each lane has a red button and if somebody tries to run the port either from primary or they don't want to go to secondary and they try to take off, we press that button and the tire shredders come up, arms come down, lights come on and it shuts down the port.

"Since we put that in place we've been getting fewer runners. But sometimes they still try to do it from the southbound lanes—they'll start going northbound in the southbound lanes. For anybody who does get through our runner suppression, we have pursuit vehicles and officers will go after them. We'll call the local San Diego PD and Border Patrol to assist us with that."

Sometimes there are grim discoveries: someone who overheated in a trunk or was burned by an engine block. Angelica once discovered that an eighty-year-old woman with a walker had drugs strapped to her waist— "that went viral," she says.

I look to the right and just beyond all the traffic there are a bunch of empty lanes leading to empty booths. I ask Angelica why they aren't in use. "Those aren't quite done yet," she says. "They should be open soon. That's going to be our outbound inspection area. There are going to be ten southbound lanes going into Mexico. Don't forget we have the authority to do southbound inspections; stop and search people going outbound. We fight child abductions. We're on the lookout for wanted people trying to head out of here who maybe committed a murder or various violations. But weapons and money are what we really look for; the illicit proceeds from narcotics smuggling and all kinds of guns."

Not only does the U.S. supply the market for drug consumption but we also supply the firepower for the violence. Guns are much more difficult to buy in Mexico than in the U.S. There is one legal gun seller in Mexico: the Directorate of Arms and Munitions Sales, located on a heavily fortified military base in Mexico City. Those who wish to apply sit in a fluorescently lit waiting area that looks a lot like any bureaucratic office in the U.S. The permit process takes months, involving six documents and a rigorous background check.

Seventy percent of the guns recovered in Mexico come from the U.S.[2] Cartels work with buyers in the U.S. who can run the guns across the border,[3] or they send a reliable man up to a city like Dallas where there are gun shows throughout the year. And in a state like Texas an undocumented migrant cannot get a driver's license but he can buy firearms at a gun show. Rifles hide well in large appliances—stoves, refrigerators—and are taken across every port, from San Ysidro to Brownsville. Public executions by criminals in Mexico are often carried out with semiautomatic AR-15s, a spray of hundreds of bullets for each victim from a famous American export.

CHAPTER 46

"NOW DON'T FORGET," SAYS LANCE LeNoir, "if a cartel's got a successful tunnel it means there's one entrance in Mexico and one in the U.S.—you've got to have people working on both sides."

Lance is in charge of the San Diego Sector Confined Space Entry Team but he prefers the term Tunnel Rats. "It's an homage back to the old Vietnam Tunnel Rats," he says, "Marines, Australian sappers who went through the Vietcong tunnel systems over there." Lance isn't sure if *Tunnel Rat* is a term of endearment or disdain but he likes it and considers it a salute to the very few in the world who have become experts on the matter of underground, confined spaces.

The phrase itself, *Tunnel Rats*—and the notion to use it as homage—somehow perfectly captures Lance's complex blend of flippant humor and respectfulness, a laid-back, Mayberry kind of feel, which probably charmed a lot of teachers in Broken Arrow, Oklahoma, where he grew up. He has straight, floppy hair and gum in his mouth. When I ask how old he is he says, "The wrong side of forty." He was a police officer in Tulsa before he joined Border Patrol nearly two decades ago and fell into the assignment of learning about tunnels.

We sit in a press briefing room at sector headquarters in the South Bay city of Chula Vista. The space is adorned with trophies that the Tunnel Rats have recovered on raids, including a jury-rigged elevator that looks like a rusted cage and a section of railroad tracks wide enough for a flatbed dolly cart.

"See, it all comes down to intel," he says. "You've got to have source intel—wherever it may come from. That's pretty much the driving force that gets us these tunnel discoveries. You've got to know your area. If you don't know what's in your area, how can you develop any type of plan to combat or circumvent that? You're just blind. You're reacting to everything. So we'll go to all these buildings in these tunnel threat areas, which is easy to know: you've got infrastructure immediately to the south and almost immediately to the north—buildings to hide away your entrances on both sides, that's a tunnel threat.

"Who is in that building? What are they particularly doing? What are they selling? How long have they been there? Developing a rapport with them. Providing them with information and getting information in return, basically creating a de facto intel network of sorts. It's not secret squirrel, CIA type stuff in there—we're part of the community. We're reaching out to them and they're reaching out to us."

"Is there ever resistance in the community? Any resentment about the surveillance?"

"No," he says. "I think they realize that they want to put on a solid, positive front because anything otherwise is suspicious, and they know that. But we're also not just knuckleheads on a street corner, we sense the suspicious stuff. That's what we're in tune with as law enforcement officers. The longer you've been in it, the more you start picking up on it, whether you like it or not. It's a hard thing to explain, how somebody develops instincts or how to pick up on suspicious behavior. Can you describe what he's doing? Probably not. You've just got a feeling. That's it. I just got a feeling.

"I have had poor reads on people that I just completely missed. I'm embarrassed about it to this day. You become a little harder and a little colder, a little more unfeeling sometimes, a little more doubtful, suspicious . . ." He stops for a moment, as if he's caught himself off guard thinking about it. Then he adds, "There are a lot of negative things there to be honest with you."

I ask Lance what happens once his sources lead him to a new tunnel. "How do you go about getting in?"

"We collaborate and consult with our partners on the Southside. They send whatever low-level military unit, or the guy who got the short straw—who knows—but he goes in and basically walks the tunnel out and makes sure there's nobody in there, which is good, that means we don't have to do it. That's something that we prefer to avoid. There is no place to hide inside most tunnels.

"After it's cleared, we'll go in and assess the thing. We check the air, that's the first thing we do. That's the biggest killer in any confined space, running out of oxygen. Or any noxious or toxic atmosphere in there, we have to mitigate that before we go in. And we like to have two points of exit because it guarantees ventilation of air. And it gives us another avenue to escape if something bad should happen. There is a threat of danger in there—I don't like throwing that out there, but there is.

"Every now and then, somebody will miscommunicate or drop the ball, more often than not in Mexico, and they'll come in and pour dirt into the exit, basically sealing it up. They've done that to us three times now and when we're in the tunnel, your air becomes a vacuum at that point because it's only coming in one way. The air comes in through the one opening and hits the high-pressure zone in there—it can't go any further because it's being pushed—and it goes right back out. That happened to us once and we went from 20.3 percent oxygen down to 14 percent in ten feet. We were right on the edge of that and our air meters just went crazy. It was like running a half marathon. I've been in so many tunnels, my lungs are sensitized to different changes in the oxygen level. It's just weird. I can tell when the air is getting kind of thin. I can't tell you exactly, but I could come within a couple of points.

"I'm constantly amazed by the fact that somebody can subsist underground in a confined space in limited oxygen. You know, the people who are digging these tunnels, they're only ventilating these things with leaf blowers and floor dryers—you know, the things you use when your house floods. And the bounce house blowers too, which is very ingenious by the way, very ingenious. We actually seize bounce house blowers and use them for our own ventilation as necessary. They're that good. The funny thing about them is that they look goofy, but they're only about $40 and they put out ten times more air pressure than the $800 confined space ram fans that we have. I don't even use those anymore. I just keep stockpiling the bounce house blowers. If one goes bad, I throw it away and bring in another one. It's like a hair dryer on steroids!"

After Lance has control of the airflow, he inspects the geology and, as he puts it, "there's good dirt and there's bad dirt." The dry stuff held together with big stones is bad. "Those tunnels are prone to collapse," he says. "It may take days, weeks, months, but they're on borrowed time."

Lance is always hoping for high moisture levels in the dirt. Wet dirt is good dirt—it acts like a glue and holds the tunnel together. "It's just like at the beach," Lance says. "Near the surf the sand is nice and compact—you can hold it, it keeps its shape—but further away, it's dry and just goes right through your fingers."

Lance also inspects the wiring. "All these tunnels, when they construct them, have to have electricity, and it's usually powered from the Southside and it's usually done in a very crappy way. If they short and you touch them, it's bad. It's worse than being tased."

After checking the airflow and the dirt and the wiring, Lance can finally start looking for evidence. The Tunnel Rats mostly find marijuana. "It's a bulk item," he says. "You need a lot of it to make any type of profit, you have to get a lot of it over. It is also a perishable item. It has to be moved relatively quickly or it will go bad." One recent tunnel discovery in Otay Mesa yielded over two hundred 25-pound bundles of marijuana in a cramped room not big enough to allow anyone to stand up straight. "Try to picture in your head," he says, "muscling up 25-pound bundles in a three-foot by three-foot space. It's like a miniature T-Rex in there. You use muscles you never thought you had.

"If anything is to be admired in our adversary, or these tunnels, it's persistence and audacity."

Lance tells me about a tunnel with thirty-four tons of marijuana. There were multiple levels to the structure, which was thirty feet deep. "They actually dug an underground bunker. It was accessible by an elevator. There was actually a tile floor on top of the elevator so when it went down, it was mixed in with the floor. They just threw a rug over it and you'd never know there was an elevator there.

"Once I found a tunnel with forty-eight pairs of soccer cleats. I was like, what in the hell? Did they abduct a couple of soccer teams? Well, when we were pushing the evidence north on a cart that had a dead battery, it came to me really quick: our boots were sinking in the sand. We couldn't move! They were using the soccer cleats! I looked at all of them and they were worn down to the nub.

"The tunnels over here tend to be deep and considerably long. I think the longest one in the Tucson sector was 700 feet. Ours was 3,000. It's not a competitive thing, it's just the nature of the regions. I think San Diego is up to sixty-three tunnels now, total, and almost thirty of those are the sophisticated ones, the super-long ones that require a rail system. Seems like there are always a couple of them in play."

One of the deepest tunnels found in San Diego County was ninety feet deep. Each wall prototype has footing six feet deep, which is something but not nearly enough to disrupt the underground flow of products into the U.S.

CHAPTER 47

EDUARDO OLMOS CONFIRMS THAT TESTING of the prototypes is continuing but he's being stingy with details. Even Ralph DeSio is being unusually tight-lipped about the whole matter. In fact, the agency is not even conducting all of the testing out in the open. While the climbing and rappelling has been taking place on the 30-foot prototypes at the border, subjected to Alexis's heckling, efforts to breach the barriers with power tools have been conducted at a *second* location on a *second* set of structures.

Just north of the prototypes, there is a dirt road wedged between Brown Field Municipal Airport and an auto junkyard; it leads to fenced-off federal land. It is at this secondary site where Border Patrol is seeing if it can breach each design. Instead of working on the full-size 30-foot prototypes at the construction site, they are drilling and cutting into 10-foot-high mock-ups—prototypes of the prototypes. It's happening out of sight so that bandits don't get any ideas about methods or tools.

Agents are trying to break through each of the 10-foot mock-ups using over sixty different tools, from plasma cutters to quick saws. The request for proposals required that each design be able to prevent a physical breach larger than 12 inches in diameter.

And it is quite possible that Lance LeNoir might pass under both testing locations, the 30-foot prototypes and the 10-foot mock-ups, as he checks the oxygen levels and the quality of the dirt in a newly discovered tunnel, dozens of feet below the surface of the earth. He'll check for two exits, of course, because, as any Tunnel Rat knows, every viable smuggling operation is a binational effort.

CHAPTER 48

"SOME LOCALS WERE PART OF the problem—smuggling," says Donna Tisdale. She's showing me some of the hot spots along the dirt roads around her ranch in East County. "My daughter used to baby-sit for a family who lived right on the border like us and a few years later, when the boys were teenagers, they got enticed into smuggling drugs. Something happened and the boys and their mother were beaten up terribly. They left town immediately.

"It changes the dynamics of the neighborhood because all of a sudden, there are all these unknowns and you don't know who to trust and who not to trust. Also they brought in agents from other areas who don't know the locals, so all of a sudden, we were all suspects.

"This pig farm up here," Donna says, pointing at a small house, rotting with trees and vines and tall grass all closing in on it, "we used to sell hay to him. He would pay my husband in one-hundred-dollar bills. I said, 'I don't think pig farming is that prosperous. Something is going on.' It turned out that he had tunnels. Pigs were his cover. He was smuggling aliens and drugs in and shipping guns back. He also had a long-distance trucking business.

"So locals are part of the problem too. It isn't just people coming from out of the area. Money talks. And you begin to wonder who you can trust in your own neighborhood."

CHAPTER 49

"**THIS OPIOID THING IS A** really good example of a problem that originated from within," says Ed. He's a special agent with ICE and his boss will only let me use his first name. "It got completely out of control. These places like Ohio and West Virginia, all these other places where it was pill milling, it was so rampant and totally out of control. That's *us*. Nobody else is doing that to us."

We keep meeting early in the morning, and it always seems like he's coming off a long night: cigarettes and sixteen-ounce cans of Monster energy drinks are routinely involved. "I don't sleep as much as I should," he admits, scratching at his thinning hair.

His days often become unpredictable by 10 a.m. so I find him wherever and whenever he can spare time early. Today it's downtown San Diego at the federal courthouse.

Though Ed's business card says Immigration and Customs Enforcement, he actively avoids using the acronym ICE. He's much more likely to refer to Homeland Security Investigations, or HSI—another doll nested in the Department of Homeland Security—and he emphasizes that ICE stands for Immigration and *Customs* Enforcement.

"We have a tough balance," he says, "because all of us have the immigration enforcement authority. But it's not just immigration-centric. People get caught up in the fervor, the stigma of the name and how it's presented. *ICE* and *Border Patrol*: they're represented like thugs. It's funny when you listen to this movement to abolish ICE. People don't take into consideration that it's very diversified, all the things that we have to look at: you can deal with firearms, antiquities—some guys love the commercial fraud aspect: handbags, shoes, clothing. As mundane as those things sound, they are massive drivers for the U.S. economy. Some of these companies, like Gucci, you're talking about millions of dollars' worth of fraud. And on the immigration side you might be part of investigations about war crimes and human rights violations around the world, human trafficking. A lot of that is this cultish brainwashing thing with young girls, mostly for sex trafficking. It's like if the Super Bowl is in Denver, there are going to be pimps and traveling road shows of girls, getting hotels. It's fascinating. These huge events like Comic-Con bring people in. It's horrible. People don't see it as part of the underbelly."

Ed was born in the Bronx but has fully embraced Southern California, despite having to tell people at barbecues that, yes, he is a special agent for ICE. "Socially," he says, "it becomes kind of tough. I can't really go to parties or dinner parties or anything because—oh, my gosh!—I get attacked. We lost the civility of how you communicate within society. Some people just like to place blame. No matter who the president is, there is always going to be someone who is mad. We've had anarchists since the beginning of this country, practically—that's the beauty of America, the diversity aspect, but boy, it sure does create polarization."

Ed jumps from task force to task force but his specialty is narcotics. "I have steered into the fentanyl problem," he says. "The problem now is that a lot of drugs are morphing from organic to nonorganic. So we have fentanyl, right, which is a synthetic opioid, a replacement for heroin. With organics there are droughts, floods, war zones, and things that can affect the grow cycle, the harvest, the interdiction. With a synthetic, none of that comes into play. You can just keep producing. And the DEA can get a new synthetic emergency classed—they recently banned four versions—but within ten days, a chemist can change one molecule to make a derivative and it's not banned. That's the problem with synthetics.

"But I do not go with the 'don't do drugs' philosophy. You can tell people not to do it, but that could be futile to the masses. I'm not going to pitch that line. There will always be people who are so unsatisfied with their normal life or for a thrill or a slew of other issues, they are going to resort to using drugs.

"Here in San Diego we have more manpower than you have in almost any other sector. And Tijuana has been a historic smuggling route for decades, not just drugs; you're talking about people and goods. We have the largest amount of narcotics come through here that go through to the rest of the country. I call San Diego a transient county. There is criminal activity here to process things further into the interior.

"We have this huge concentration of juvenile smugglers. They strap two kilos of meth or fentanyl on their body and come through the port. They're U.S. citizens who live in Tijuana. They're sixteen and seventeen years old, crossing the border on their way to high school; people are exploiting minors and taking advantage of the fact that they come from poor conditions. They can make $300 or $400 and to them and their family, that would be a huge benefit because their mom is struggling. They get caught, then the entire cycle is tying up the court system.

"No drug organization believes that 100 percent of their product is going to make it. It's like a retail business, they call it 'shrink,' product loss from shoplifting. It's the same thing. If I have 100 kilos, would I love to see 100 kilos make it through? Absolutely. But I'm still going to break it down into six or seven types of vehicles because two might get intercepted, but I'll be making such a large profit on the remainder that gets through. That's a calculable loss. What did I lose? Someone who was down on their luck who drove the car and took the risk? I was only going to pay them $1,000. The car that I bought at an auction and gave them to drive? That was nothing. It's just all written into the profit margin. It's fascinating to look at because they are really these large businesses and it's always interesting to see how they run their operation. They've been doing it a long time and they have a success rate.

"The biggest problem with fentanyl is that these guys have cut it into everything. There is a recent case where some guys had come from New Orleans, these businessmen, and they were just going down to Tijuana for a bachelor party. They bought a bag of coke and it was laced with fentanyl. There were two deaths in that group.

"Look, I think I do a lot of good for people. Stopping child exploitation is very powerful work and it's very hard work. Human trafficking, intercepting fentanyl.

"I get that immigration is a hot-button thing. People get very caught in the fervor of those arguments. I tell people that we *are* a land of immigrants, but you have to look at the history of immigration. And look at the country today. America, in 2018, has a way of life. There are expectations. I'm not talking about unusual things, I'm talking about the infrastructure. Where we're at now is nothing like where we were when people flooded

Ellis Island. Those people came because this country was in a building process, but they were offered nothing when they got here. There was no infrastructure yet. The Irish were coming off and being spit on. They threw lime on you to delouse you. That's how it worked. And essentially, half the dudes would get off and there was the guy from the Army sitting there, signing you up. That's what it was: 'You're here, you made it to America, now you're technically becoming an indentured servant to the United States to serve in its military.' If you did that today, people would be freaking screaming. But that is what existed during that time.

"It has morphed because we have become a very wealthy and successful country that has a lot to offer, the entitlement systems and these services that have been put into place over decades. And when you start talking about the immigration side, it begins to put strains on the structure.

"How many people could you take in one location? People say, 'Well, the United States is a big place.' But the infrastructure only moves as it is built and you know how that goes: it's passing bond measures, raising taxes, expanding streets. When you begin to flood those infrastructures, how much can they possibly take?

"The economy in the United States is thriving and robust right now. Which means that you would be less prone to take a menial job when you have the ability to get a less labor-intensive job at better pay. It's human nature to do that. But is there still a need for low-wage workers? Absolutely. People want strawberries, but they'll shit their pants if that strawberry quart was $17 because you've got to pay a union guy to go pick it. In reality, it all happens on slave labor—it's all fucking slave labor. And we don't move as a society to address that reality. Like, how do we fill those roles? Because to fill those roles, it's not black and white. You can't just plug the need with a person who raises their hand and walks 2,000 miles or 6,000 miles to get here. That person has all kinds of issues when they get here.

"Look back to when public housing came into play in the middle part of the last century, these massive concrete monstrosities in cities. They huddled the masses. They got all the low-income people in there and centralized them in one area. Then that area becomes decrepit and crime-ridden. The government's answer was to just get them in housing and get them off the streets. But there is a whole slew of things that have to go along with that. There should be worker's compensation insurance. There should be tax and health care. Do they have children who are going to go into the school system? All these things add up, but no one will ever talk about that. No one wants to hear the dirty details. Should there be something for immigrants? Yeah. But this comes back to what can you bear? What can a state bear? Why is it on me as a property owner to pay into taxes to give immigrants affordable housing?

"Look, I don't see immigration as an invasion like a lot of the extreme right would say because that's a term that should be used for much different things. I would say that on the left, it becomes nuts when you realize that there is no pause to understand the capacity to deal with this. They get caught up in the fervor of people beating war drums and saying this isn't a humane thing to do, but how many people is our infrastructure designed to take?"

CHAPTER 50

THE TESTING OF EACH PROTOTYPE was designed to answer the most critical questions: Can it be climbed? Can it be dug under? Can it withstand cutting tools? News reports have announced that each design passed all the tests, so the president is on his way to see them—it's a time for those who championed The Wall to celebrate.

However, it should be noted that the reporting of these test results has been propped up by quotes from agents—not actual data. What, exactly, "passed" might mean remains unclear: testing methodology and specified results are not available, says Border Patrol, the only available information is that the prototypes are a smashing success.

It is early morning, March 13, 2018, and the region is feeling fraught even before the president lands at the naval base. For the first few months of the year, it's felt like everything has been tightening in slow motion. The rules at Friendship Park, for instance, were changed in the wake of the Door of Hope, cross-border wedding. Border Patrol will now impose a limit of ten visitors at a time in the pavilion area, the visits will be limited to thirty minutes, and the binational garden—where there is no wire mesh, only bollards—is now off-limits. It is unclear if John Fanestil and Guillermo Navarrete will be able to continue their Sunday services in the long term. Enrique Morones's face, recurring across news platforms, has been bright-red-angry for weeks. Add to that, Roger Ogden organized a second Patriot Picnic in Chicano Park, with similar results: hundreds of protesters forcing a handful of patriots to leave under police protection, taunts, and cameras all around.

And a few days ago, a woman was dragged into a Border Patrol SUV in National City as her daughters stood on the street corner screaming, confused about where to go from there as the vehicle pulled away.

In addition to the usual Border Patrol presence across the county, there have also been several ICE raids over the past few days. The raids—which ICE never calls raids but EROs, or Enforcement and Removal Operations—have been ubiquitous across California and some have targeted high-profile employers like 7-Eleven. Until now, most of the action has been in Northern California and Los Angeles County, not so much in the San Diego region. But that changed just ahead of the president's visit with over one hundred arrests in the county in just three days.

By the time the president's helicopter touches down at Brown Field airport, just a few miles from the prototypes, everything has been in place for hours:

On the U.S. side of the border, land is sealed off for miles in all directions. About a dozen tractor-trailers are parked, mostly in a single-file row, just south of the prototypes, blocking the sight lines from Las Torres. The morning has been wet, the whole winter has been, the cracked earth turned to swampy mud. It is particularly messy in Las Torres, where the foot traffic was heavy at sunrise but has been cleared out now that the president is getting close. The chalk paintings and posters on the south-facing side of the primary fence are hearts and hands and smiles, and they are all that remain of the activists who were on the scene earlier in the morning. The Mexican authorities would not let them torch a piñata as planned, so they took it with them.

Reporters have crowded onto a few rooftops with choice angles, which law enforcement seems to be tolerating. It looks like there is U.S. law enforcement in Las Torres too, probably Secret Service: white men with earpieces and stern faces.

The presidential procession begins with seven agents, arriving on horseback. Then an armed, olive-green Humvee rolls onto the scene, leading a convoy of black SUVs, the last of which has its back doors open and two armed men riding with their legs dangling out of the vehicle. Sharpshooters are in position atop the tractor-trailers, scanning the Southside with binoculars.

The president's SUV comes to a stop and he gets out. From the rooftops of Las Torres, the only real trace of him is his feet, just below the tractor-trailers, as he moves between prototypes. His steps always initiate a small stampede from the pool of White House reporters, running ahead of him to secure the right spot for photographs, video, asking unanswered questions.

Ultimately the best view of the president is on television, per usual, streamed to a screen in the comfort of your own home. That's where you can see him so clearly, flanked by his chief of staff, John Kelly, and the secretary of the Department of Homeland Security, Kirstjen Nielsen—Duncan Hunter is tagging along, just a few feet behind the trio. Border Patrol personnel flip through a three-ring binder with the president, perhaps taking a look at those test results we've heard so much about.

"I do have a preference," the president says to the home audience when asked if he has a favorite. "The problem is, you have to have see-through," he says, "you have to know what's on the other side of the wall." His statement must disappoint six of the eight contestants, all of whom have solid concrete bases. He admits he's partial to the ELTA design—everyone seems seduced by the royal blue steel—but he says it won't do because of its solid base. "You could be two feet from a criminal cartel and you don't even know they're there."

After a while John Kelly and Kirstjen Nielsen peel off from the prototype viewing. The president spends about half an hour taking a look around. At one point, while talking to the cameras, he pulls over Rodney Scott, the chief Border Patrol agent for the sector, to say something about the importance of a bollard style barrier. Scott emphasizes the binational cooperation that the bollard style enables. "We have great partners in Mexico with the law enforcement on that side," he says. "I can call them for assistance. I don't have the opportunity to get ahead of the threat if I can't see it approaching."

The line about *great partners* looks like it takes a moment or two to land with the president but when it does he cuts in and swings the conversation back around: "If we don't have a wall system we're not going to have a country," he says. "There's a lot of problems in Mexico. They got a lot of problems over there."

The "Free Speech Zone," a few miles over, near Enrico Fermi Drive, has around a dozen or so people holding signs expressing their affection for the president and The Wall. The Dreamers are downtown, talking DACA;

other immigration activists are at the San Ysidro port, welcoming pedestrians as they enter the country.

Jeff Schwilk has arranged a rally for the president, though not in the Free Speech Zone—"not enough parking there," he says. Instead, San Diegans for Secure Borders gather in an empty lot between Brown Field airport and the prototypes. A few hundred turn out for the rally and a dozen of them drive to the entrance of the airport when they hear that the president is leaving so he can make it up to Los Angeles in time for an evening fundraiser.

After the president's motorcade speeds past the ecstatic supporters outside the airport, Jeff says, "We were hoping he would maybe come out and shake hands." Some on the scene say they saw the president's window down as he passed by. A few thought they might have seen him waving but no one could be certain.

CHAPTER 51

THE PRESIDENT SAYS HE'S CONTEMPLATING what the final version of The Wall will look like and, in the meantime, he's sending the National Guard to join the Border Patrol agents, customs officers, Department of Homeland Security officials, sheriff's deputies, and local police officers who are already at the border.

It's been reported that the decision was in response to a group of 1,300 migrants, almost all of them from Central America, who have spent weeks marching north through Mexico. This happens every year and it's usually called the Viacrucis Migrante, though the president has more recently dubbed it a "Caravan."

The Viacrucis is an ancient idea—a re-creation of Christ on his way to crucifixion—but *this* iteration of it in Mexico has been around for about a decade: a group of radical leftists and liberation theology priests decided to make it a protest march against decisions by the Mexican government to tighten deportation policies for Central Americans. One person who participated in the Viacrucis told me, "It's important to keep it religious. In Mexico, foreigners aren't allowed to participate in protests. So the only way you can have these Central Americans doing this protest march is to call it a religious march. Otherwise the military would break it up." Many of the migrants carry handheld wooden crosses, and every now and then someone drags a full-size cross for a mile or so.

While the religious aspects of the march have given it legal standing, the sheer size of the march is what makes it successful: there is not much that three or six or twelve law enforcement officials can do at an immigration checkpoint if a thousand people approach it en masse.

The march has evolved over the years but originally it came to an end at a well-known migrant shelter in the Mexican town of Ixtepec, in the state of Oaxaca. Then some migrants started going all the way to Mexico City so they could protest outside the National Human Rights Commission of Mexico. Each year it was a different issue, Mexico's federal immigration policies or the kidnapping of migrants, and after the protests, the marchers dispersed. Some continued north to cross into the U.S. or to get jobs in the maquiladoras along the border; some stayed in the Mexican capital and applied for asylum.

But in 2014, the Viacrucis became much more politically pointed. That year Mexican president Enrique Peña Nieto initiated Programa Frontera Sur, or the Southern Border Program, which is primarily designed to reduce the flow of Central Americans across Mexico's 750-mile southern border with Guatemala and Belize. In the first year of the program, the U.S. Department of Defense provided training to Mexican troops patrolling the border, as well as surveillance tips, and the State Department gave over $10 million for equipment at security checkpoints.[1]

As the Southern Border Program was fully realized, organizers of the march decided to confront the Mexican government more directly. In 2014, the Mexico City protests were larger than they had ever been, and that year a bigger faction of marchers decided to go all the way to the U.S. border to apply for asylum. The tension has been building since then. "I have instructed the Secretary of Homeland Security," the president recently tweeted, "not to let these large Caravans of people into our country."

CHAPTER 52

ON THE MEXICAN SIDE OF the San Ysidro Port of Entry, the migrants have gathered in a plaza, just in front of a switchback staircase that leads to the long PedWest pedestrian bridge into the U.S. There are roughly two hundred people in an encampment, all of them coming off more than a month of traveling by foot.

It is a wet morning, still misty. Women are wrapping their hair into loose buns. About half the people in the encampment look to be children—some teenagers but even more small kids and toddlers. I see a young girl around eight years old; she's carrying a baby in one arm and a jug of drinking water in the other. Some of the kids are still asleep in tents and under tarps tied to the metal crowd control barriers that form a perimeter around the encampment. One of the kids, who I have yet to locate, has the remote control for the red Lamborghini that is so skillfully maneuvering around all the feet and sleeping bags. The car has attracted the attention of more than one stray dog.

Even though no one from the encampment has entered the U.S. yet, so many people are already wearing at least one emblem of the country: American Eagle hoodies, Captain America pajamas, Dodgers shirts, Yankees hats, Nike sneakers, Jordache denim, most of it ill-fitting donations, which keep coming all morning. Each time more trash bags are delivered, bursting with clothes, three or four men from the encampment come forward to carry them away. I watched seven bags get unloaded in a matter of minutes, mostly shoes and jeans and sweaters. It's spring but feels like Southern California winter: gray, cold, a threat of rain. Every now and again the sun breaks through, making everything suddenly hot and muggy, but when the clouds return so does the chill.

About a dozen reporting crews have set up cameras on the far side of the metal barriers around the encampment. I use the word "crews" loosely here, as it certainly applies to, say, CNN and Univision, but does not apply to some of the local and online outfits that could only send one person—a reporter who must first secure the camera to the tripod and confirm that the focus is just right before jumping into the shot. There are often four or five reporters inside the encampment at any given time, and a couple of camera operators, scouring the crowd for expressive faces; some are willing to come out of tents for on-camera interviews, where narratives are crudely translated, scars and burn marks revealed.

Direct access to the encampment, inside the metal barriers, is intermittent, and is mostly controlled by volunteers for Pueblo Sin Fronteras, who preserve space for the migrants to periodically eat, sleep, and breathe. Most of the volunteers participated in some or all of the march through Mexico, and Pueblo Sin Fronteras has a big presence at the encampment— the volunteers are easy to spot in red and white baseball caps with the organization's name. One of them often has the megaphone and is making an announcement about food distribution, sleeping arrangements, communication with U.S. Customs, all matters of survival at the San Ysidro Port of Entry.

The director of Pueblo Sin Fronteras, Irineo Mujica, wears a bright purple pullover and the bed head of a sleep-deprived man. He gives interviews in Spanish and English, working a double to make the same points to different audiences. The violence in Guatemala and Honduras and El Salvador—"small countries," Irineo emphasizes—should be the main priority for all of the countries throughout the Americas. "You can handle the poverty," says Irineo, "but you can't handle someone trying to kill you."

A reporter asks if Irineo shares the concerns expressed by others that families might be split up if they do get into the United States. "That is definitely a big concern," he says, "but it is a temporary separation. If they go back home the separation will be final because a lot of them will die." There is a blunt nature to Irineo's statements that tends to chase away follow-up questions. "The law in the United States," he says, "the law says they have the right to apply for asylum. This is the *law*. And we have to obey the law."

The migrants are *in* the proverbial line. It may not be single-file as at Ellis Island but they are definitely in line, doing just what Duncan Hunter asked of them, waiting their turn to enter legally. And as they wait, they maintain order: the plaza ground is swept in the morning and at night by members of the encampment, and trash is collected after each meal. When food arrives, anxiousness and hunger do not disrupt the process of serving one person at a time. There is oatmeal for breakfast and tacos in fresh tortillas with beans and rice for lunch; coffee in the morning, horchata in the afternoon and drinking water throughout the day—enough plastic bottles to break an environmentalist's heart.

One mother tries to get her daughter to eat her plate of food but the little girl is perfectly happy munching away at the Mexican pan dulce in one fist while staring at the doll in her other fist—a Barbie in a hard hat and reflective vest.

A young woman named Stefano looks entirely beleaguered by weeks of travel but, nonetheless, committed to making a statement in pink flip-flops and a striped miniskirt over fishnets. What's more, she has accents: a cream-colored scarf and aviator sunglasses. Her commitment to her look, to herself, adds a bolt of energy to the midday mood, as she meanders the encampment saying hello to others. When I ask Stefano if she joined the caravan alone, she says she left her family behind in Honduras. "I want to be on my own," she says, hiding behind the aviators.

As we talk, I'm struck by her stoicism, the sobriety in her voice that contradicts her flamboyance. She is twenty-three and so much of her story is unclear to me but the only point she seems to want to clarify, again and again, is "es mi culpa." *It's my fault.*

"But right now there are three of us," she adds. "I'm getting a lot of support. With the care of the people, I've been able to go forward."

A circle of kids forms around a soccer ball and another helicopter circles overhead. A man makes the rounds, quietly, just outside the metal barriers of the encampment with a small box, asking for spare change. It's not just The Media sharing the plaza with the encampment but thousands of pedestrians throughout the day, coming and going, many of whom linger for a while. There is occasional honking coming from an adjacent overpass, and it's hard to tell if it's support for the migrants or traffic jam angst.

Local Mexican radio stations swing by in vans painted in loud colors with even louder DJs inside. They emerge to hand out chocolates and cup-cakes and branded T-shirts, and they stay awhile to broadcast live. One station brings a big red picture frame that has "Todos Somos Inmigrantes" written on it, and kids line up to take their picture. Another station brings a couple of piñatas. Each DJ infuses the scene with a burst of energy for a half hour or so then leaves and everyone feels the stillness for a minute.

Evening arrives and I take the pedestrian bridge back to the U.S. At the end of the bridge there is yet another spiral staircase and at the base of that staircase there are about twenty people resting on the ground, just before a gate turnstile. The Mexican authorities let them through to walk across the bridge but they can't get past the private security guards stationed at the turnstile leading to U.S. Customs. This is where the asylum request would be made if there were a U.S. official present to hear it. But the security guards are under no legal obligation to listen, and they have told those encamped at the turnstile that the port is at capacity.

I present my passport and the security guards let me through. I walk into the customs hall with a capacity of 120 and it's empty, as are most of the processing offices behind the initial inspection counters. Three officers sit idle and they all wave me over to their respective counters, simultaneously, as if competing for relief from the boredom.

After a couple of days all the reporters have discovered the WiFi signal at the coffee shop across the street from the plaza. Stefano and a posse of twenty-somethings have known about it from the beginning; their spot is behind the shop, smoking, far from everyone but still in range of the signal.

The encampment is feeling more entrenched, more settled: a man stands alone, clipping his nails; a girl loses herself in an Etch A Sketch, slumped against one of the metal barriers. More tents and tarps are up now, most of them anchored in place by one-gallon jugs of water. In addition to the food tables and radio station visits, doctors and nurses have set up tents for basic care. After more than a month of walking, there are lingering complications from malnutrition and dehydration, viruses and bacteria, busted feet and lack of sleep. One of the Pueblo Sin Fronteras volunteers makes an announcement through the megaphone in Spanish: "Will the children who have not yet seen the doctor please go into the doctor's office," he says, repeating it again and again.

The man who was collecting spare change in a box yesterday is doing so again but a woman confronts him and says he shouldn't do something like that without the consent of the group. During an afternoon administrative meeting, he seeks and gets permission to collect small donations on behalf of everyone in the encampment.

More provisions are dropped off: tampons, toiletries, large boxes of diapers, lots of Cup Noodles. There are coloring books and mazes but a bunch of the kids dive after travel-size shampoo and soap instead.

More locals are showing up to stay and serve a meal or drop pesos in the box; some strum guitars, others just stop to talk. A teenage boy shows up with a deck of cards and does magic tricks for a crowded circle of smaller kids for an hour or so. I imagine they are all the tricks that his family is sick of seeing because he looks so very alive and thrilled to be surrounded by such an engaged audience, all these bright eyes and dropped jaws.

Near the edge of the encampment one of the migrants leans against the metal barrier, talking to a local guy who is flipping through messages on his phone. The migrant wears a brown leather jacket and camouflage hat. "Yesterday we were having some coffee," he says in Spanish, "and we met a guy who told us 'before, I used to cross swimming, I was a wetback.' He also said they crossed in a field and it only took them a few minutes."

The local nods.

"He said crossing used to be much easier."

The local nods again.

"Now they put the wall."

The local is still nodding, still looking at his phone, and says, "I remember when I crossed, I was twenty-nine. It took me literally five minutes and then I brought all of my family." Then he pops up from his phone with a sudden question, "Wait, where do you go to the toilet?"

"We go over there," says the migrant, motioning to a building across the street, "but we have to pay 10 pesos every time you use it. So a woman complained because she said they were taking advantage, and they threatened to put it on the internet."

The local guy asks the man in the encampment if he's contemplating staying in Mexico. There are good jobs he tells him. "A lot of people stay here working in the mines," he says. "There are so many Haitians who stay here and work in the mines."

"We'll see."

The two men shake hands and the local says, "I hope everything turns out fine."

"God willing," says the migrant. "He's the only one with power, *he* migrated and erased borders."

After a week, the mood at the encampment has changed: less resolve, more restlessness.

There is more Mexican law enforcement at the plaza: municipal and federal police, special units in military fatigues, Grupos Beta. A siren comes through the megaphone to indicate an announcement is on the way, but it has bad timing and collides with a siren from a police car.

A gray-haired man lifts a dustpan full of trash, and as he lets it slide down into a plastic bag I see bits of busted plastic from a crashed remote-control Lamborghini.

There is another siren through the megaphone and an announcement. This time the news is that twenty-two people have been let into the port to apply for asylum and a burst of energy runs through the encampment. Never mind the denial rates that await them, either side of 80 percent, for now there is victory in exercising the right to apply.

It is during this fleeting jubilation that Millie Weaver arrives. She is reporting for InfoWars, along with a camera operator and a producer—two nearly indistinguishable white men in gray sweatshirts and gray hats.

There is one more member of the InfoWars team: Louie, a local with a well-trimmed mustache and slicked-back, thinning hair. He was around yesterday, offering his services as a translator to all the white reporters. He had no takers but today Louie found Millie. Standing at her side, Louie wears a brown poncho but underneath he's got on a black-collared shirt, black shoes, and black pants, like he's booked for a catering gig later in the day.

Millie shuffles through the crowd, hunched and squinting, looking cold and all turned around in an unfamiliar supermarket. Eventually she makes eye contact with a middle-aged man who is sipping coffee. She straightens herself and asks him, "Do you know where all these people are from?"

Louie says the question in Spanish—I miss his exact wording, regrettably, because I'm curious about how he handled *these people*. Whatever he says gets across to the man, who says, "Honduras."

"Honduras," says Louie.

"Y Guatemala," says the migrant.

"Guatemala," says Louie.

"Y El Salvador, Nicaragua," says the migrant.

And Louie says, "El Salvador, Nicaragua," really earning it.

Then Millie does a recap, looking into the camera: "So everyone here is from Honduras, Guatemala, El Salvador, Nicaragua."

Nearly every time she approaches someone, Millie begins by asking, "What country are you from?" And she asks in English, despite the fact that she has a Spanish-language translator in a poncho following her, and despite the fact that there are very few English-speaking migrants in the camp. Her approach confuses most people, even with Louie's efforts to smooth things over.

At one point Millie looks into the camera and says, "We're passing out food now, we're passing out chocolates." She reaches into a plastic bag held by her producer and pulls out a fistful of candy—Tootsie Rolls, Starbursts, Jolly Ranchers. She releases the candy underhand, like she's bowling, scattering it everywhere. A bunch of kids have been trailing her but only a few of them go for the sugar. They all just had a big lunch and most of the kids look a bit uneasy about getting anywhere near Millie or owing her anything. So they stare instead. Millie looks superimposed on the scene; she stands out with that big, branded microphone, long blond hair, and loud, over-pronounced English—she has a tendency to speak at a volume that indicates a helicopter is landing behind her.

"Obviously if these kids were hungry," she says into the camera, "They would be taking the food. Clearly they are being well fed here in Mexico—they are very well received." Louie, meanwhile, manages to score a few Starbursts and slips them into a pocket under his poncho.

Millie spots Stefano—in a dark red skirt today—and almost breaks into a run on her way to ask for an interview. Stefano agrees to it and when she starts speaking about the violence back home Millie cuts in: "Is it because you're trans? Transgendered?"

Stefano nods.

"And there are more of you coming?"

Stefano doesn't hear the question because she and Louie are haggling over Louie's interpreting. Stefano asks Louie to clarify that there are people back in Honduras who love her but the possibility of violence is too great to stay.

Millie sees the opening and jumps in: "So there are people back in his hometown who like him?"

Stefano and Louie nod but they both look confused, perhaps because Millie seems to have missed the point Stefano was making—the violence, the necessity of leaving. If Stefano has people who love her back home, Millie asks her viewers, if she's well fed in Mexico, then why does she need to go to the U.S.?

All of Millie's interviews are sculpted to arrive at this point, to demonstrate that the act of migration is an act of choice, no matter how many times Millie must look past the essence of what her interviewees are saying, no matter the surrender to distortion required. Millie tells her viewers that twenty-two migrants got into the country today. "They pled refugee status and have been given asylum into the United States," she says, despite the fact that no one was granted asylum today. Twenty-two people had their right to apply for asylum unobstructed today, and, statistically speaking, all but two or three of them will be rejected and deported, but none of these details fit into the story Millie has come to tell. "There is hope and encouragement among those here," she says. "And we'll have to see if this leads to more people coming here to get into the United States."

Once this point is made, Millie and her crew call it quits. Louie stands around with them while the cameraman packs away his equipment. The producer says to Millie, "How much do you want to give him?" He says this as if Louie weren't standing next to him, as if Louie hadn't been translating into English for the past hour. Millie shrugs. The producer takes a wad of cash from his pocket, turns his back to Louie, contemplates two $20s but grabs a $20 and a $10 instead and hands over $30. Louie takes it, thumbs it, and rolls his eyes. "Thanks, buddy," says the producer. Louie loiters for a moment then stuffs the cash into his pocket, pops a Starburst, and leaves.

Other reporters remain on the scene, and one asks Irineo Mujica about the choice to stay at the plaza: "Some of the shelters have said they had empty beds last night. Are you advising everyone to sleep on the plaza? Is there a certain strategy here?"

"We told people," says Irineo in Spanish, "that whoever wished to sleep in a shelter because they had their sick children were more than welcome to go to a shelter. They decide whether they want to stay here or not, we respect everyone's decision because it is their right." Irineo seems earnest when he talks about the personal sovereignty; but still, there is a clear preference for people to stay together in a large group. "I'm still worried about kidnappings," he says. Every night he sends volunteers to shelters to check on the migrants, trying to deter criminals from moving in on them.

A light rain begins to fall when I finally catch Nicole Ramos between conversations. She is a pro bono immigration lawyer so someone is always tapping her on the shoulder. "Not only have there been kidnappings," she says, "but we know that Mexican immigration and law enforcement has been detaining and deporting Central Americans. Last week they took away a Guatemalan family in handcuffs. That's one of the main reasons the caravan has been traveling in a group, doing this with high visibility. Otherwise there is a danger of them being taken away."

Nicole has been working with migrants in Tijuana since 2015. She's from New Jersey and comfortable with confrontation. A few years ago, when migrants began finding out she was a lawyer they asked her to accompany them to the port so they could make an asylum claim. "I thought it was so strange," she says, "and I would tell them the law is so short in this regard: you just walk up to a customs officer and you tell them. And they would say, 'No, that doesn't work.' And it was true, they were turning people away. These people are trying to *submit to the inspection* of the U.S. government. So I've been kind of a crazy lady since about December of 2015, screaming at Customs and Border Patrol, making insane Facebook Live videos."

"What happens today for the people who got through?"

"Honestly, for the first two to seven days we don't have any knowledge of what's going on for each person. CBP does a basic intake and transfers them to ICE for detention. That's what they're supposed to do but we have proof that some people have expressed fear for their lives and were deported to Central America by CBP, so who knows.

"They won't even put them in any kind of online detainee locator for the first several days while they're still in CBP custody. And people don't have the right to consult with an attorney while they're there. So it's really like sending them into a black hole. We don't know if they're separating families."

Nicole has been at the encampment every day, listening to as many stories as she can. "Even the few who do have a good shot at a successful claim in the U.S.," she says, "some of them are starting to choose not to go for it after hearing about the horrors of the detention system, the kidnapping of children, children dying in detention, pregnant women losing their babies in detention—I know two women who have miscarried because they didn't get adequate medical care.

"And there have been changes instituted on how asylum officers are supposed to conduct the interview and what questions to ask. They're supposed to look at migrants with more suspicion. The bar seems to be getting higher and higher. 'Well, they're all liars'—that's the talking point.

"The other policy, which hasn't been implemented but is being bandied about, is that CBP officers—not asylum officers—might actually become the ones to do the initial interviews where migrants outline the circumstances that brought them to the U.S. But asylum officers receive training on how to deal with trauma survivors. CBP officers do not have any of that training. They are a law enforcement agency. Many of them come from a military background and they've worked in theaters of combat—that's not a good combination to deal with a highly traumatized population."

Activists have been talking about the possibility that another march might soon be starting in southern Mexico—they might not wait until next year, might not wait for Easter and the cover of religion. I ask Nicole, "Do you think this will happen again in a few months?"

"I don't know," she says, looking out over the encampment. "I think that now people in Mexico are suffering from caravan fatigue. I think there are more towns in southern Mexico that were previously more hospitable that are not. I also think that's a reflection of the values that are being communicated to society by authorities. When authorities were processing people for humanitarian visas and treating people more humanely, the response they received along the journey was more humane. But that's changing.

"Now we just need more people to not be exhausted," she says, sighing. "We have this thing amongst ourselves called Tijuana magic; when you need something, it will happen."

CHAPTER 53

IT'S THE FIRST WEEK OF June, just a few days before California's 2018 primary. Roque De La Fuente is one of thirty-two candidates on the ballot for Dianne Feinstein's Senate seat. He's also on primary ballots in several other states—all in the name of building his profile for a national campaign against the president. He's been impossible to track down for a couple of months now but three days before voting in California he calls me.

"Did you see the hit piece?" he asks, all flustered.

"Hit piece?"

"This reporter from the *L.A. Times*, Mariel Garza. Did you see her article?"

"No." I pull it up and start scanning it while Roque continues.

"I've got to respond." He stops speaking, to give me time to find the story, but that only lasts for a few seconds before he starts up again: "Did you see it yet?—the hit piece she wrote about me?"

The article doesn't take much reading because the headline gives it all away: "Hey California, Don't Vote for the Guy Running for Senate in Five States."

Ms. Garza is one of the first to catch on to the fact that Roque is running for a U.S. Senate seat in several states. Her discovery was prompted, at least in part, by Roque's surprise second-place finish in a recent poll for the California primary.

"I think she got scared of me," Roque says. "I think that's why she decided to go after me—she's scared. And she doesn't understand how the state election laws work."

Roque isn't entering the primaries to win them; his only objective is to build name recognition, build a brand across the country, wherever he can, making preparations for his next presidential run.

Not since bankruptcy court has Roque gained mastery over a system the way he's gained mastery of state election laws across the country. For him, each effort to get on a primary ballot costs a few thousand dollars: pay the state some fees, pay some folks to collect signatures, et voilà. And if he were to actually win any of the contests, the only requirement to remain a qualifying candidate would be to establish residency before Election Day in the state where he's on the ballot.

"This reporter," Roque says, "what's her name? Garza. She didn't even speak to me. If she had I would have told her that she missed the point about the election. Now what I need to do is sit down and do a piece, and hopefully I can force them to print it by Monday or Tuesday."

Roque goes silent for a moment while I read the last of the story. Then I hear him say, "I wish you could help me in trying to get this thing written."

I stop reading. It's time for me to say something but I'm suddenly terrified. "Roque, I wish I could be helpful but—"

"—Let me email you what I have—"

"—Roque—"

"—How busy are you today?"

"I'm busy. I mean, I can't—I'm sorry."

"All right, fine, I'll get my daughter to help me. But listen: I might need to bring you in on this."

I say, "Thanks," not really sure why—probably because I can tell from Roque's tone of voice that whenever he says "I might need to bring you in on this" it's supposed to come across as an honor. "Sounds good, Roque."

He hangs up, just as anxious as he was when he called. Some part of me feels bad, and I spend the rest of the day fearful that his name will show up on my screen, but he goes silent again. I track the paper for his op-ed but nothing materializes. Three days later he finishes eighth in the field of thirty-two with 135,279 votes.

CHAPTER 54

IT IS AUGUST OF 2018 and the 30-foot prototypes have hovered over the old primary fence for ten months. But now the ineffectual corrugated metal is being removed from Las Torres. Across from Aurelia and Gaudencio, a new primary fence is under construction. This has been expected for some time. What might come as a surprise to the six builders so patiently awaiting an announcement is that none of their designs have been selected for the new primary fence. The prototypes stand awkwardly close by, still hovering, as cranes pivot with prefabricated panels of a familiar fence: the same steel bollard design from Friendship Park.

This steel bollard design—about 20 feet high with flat metal sheets at the top—has been in use for several years now, a product of the Obama administration; there are stretches out near Bob Maupin and Donna Tisdale, where the last 14 miles of open desert in San Diego County are, piece by piece, getting cut in half by sections of new fencing.

Once the new primary fence is finished in Las Torres the secondary fence will also be replaced—and extended farther east, if the government can seal up negotiations with Roque for the acquisition of more land. Border Patrol has confirmed that the new secondary fence will also be a steel bollard design and not any of the eight prototypes.

CHAPTER 55

THE FLOW OF MIGRANTS CONTINUES to bottleneck in Tijuana, testing the city's capacity. It is November of 2018 and a new group of marchers has set up an encampment on the south side of the San Ysidro port.

Every day it's a different number of people allowed to apply for asylum. Nicole Ramos is at the encampment regularly, just as she was in the spring; she says that sometimes seventy people get through and sometimes no one does. "The average is probably around twenty a day," she tells me.

We're standing in the plaza and Nicole draws my attention to two Grupos Beta agents sitting under a red tent on the edge of the encampment. Both of them wear a puffy jacket the color of the agency's trademark bright orange. "They control the list," she says, rolling her eyes at them from a safe distance. Grupos Beta agents make up part of Mexico's federal immigration enforcement authority—they are the ones that the pollero Ernesto described as the "real dogs."

It's 7 a.m. and there are around thirty migrants waiting in line to give their names to the agents. Each name is handwritten in a spiral notebook and the agents usually stop taking names around 9:30 or 10:00. In the afternoon, they make an announcement about how many people—and which people—get to cross over, apply for asylum, and enter the U.S. immigration detention system.

But each day more names are added to the notebook than are crossed out. The pages are filling up and there is a greater sense of urgency in the encampment. People are looking for more ways to turn themselves in to a U.S. Border Patrol agent or customs officer. The U.S. military just moved 1,800 troops to California, most of them in San Diego County, along with armored vehicles and enough cement barricades and knotted razor wire to block off the possibility of pedestrians storming the inspection booths at the San Ysidro port.

A couple of days ago there were scores of people who tried to get into the U.S. by walking across the Tijuana River canal. Many of those who took the risk of descending the angled concrete walls of the canal were women clutching children. The U.S. military used tear gas to push everyone back into Zona Norte.

The families that do manage to find a way into the U.S. have been separated. This practice goes back more than a year[1] but only recently did it become policy, described as a deterrent, defended with the book of Romans by U.S. Attorney General Jeff Sessions: "obey the laws of government because God ordained the government for his purposes."[2]

A majority of the public wants the practice stopped, so do the courts—a judge ordered that families be reunited and the separations ended. An executive order was issued to cancel the practice but it continues with impunity.

Shelters in Tijuana that closed after the influx of Haitians in 2016 are opening again—and filling up.

I walk about a mile from the encampment to a shelter called Desayunador Salesiano Padre Chava to meet a woman named Paulina Olvera. On the way I pass a couple of other open shelters in Zona Norte with the zona de tolerancia anchored by Hong Kong Gentlemen's Club. "Those are the shelters I'm most worried about," says Paulina when I reach her. She has seen all of Tijuana's migrant shelters—thirty-eight, by her own count—as a founding member of Espacio Migrante, a youth activist group that helped coordinate a citywide response to the arrival of 20,000 Haitians in 2016. "That changed everything in Tijuana."

There are roughly twenty-five people lined up outside the shelter. A few of them seem unstable, a few are coming down from something, but mostly there are tired-looking families. Groups of four and five are let inside every few minutes to get breakfast: eggs and toast, oatmeal and coffee. Kids cut the line with everyone's blessing.

When each person reaches the crowded inside, their first stop is to see the little girl with the economy-size bottle of Dial. She gives everyone a squirt of soap on their way to a sink. And after each person washes their hands, there is a young boy dispersing and retrieving three hand towels, making sure no one steals them. The action takes place under the watch of Jesus, who hovers as a sculpture suspended from the ceiling at the center of the room. He is on a cross but somehow liberated from it; his arms are outstretched, summoning everyone to breakfast.

"It's very dangerous that there's migrants staying at the shelters in Zona Norte," Paulina says. "We know that there's a lot of bad activity going on around there and people do see migrants as prey. They can be taken advantage of.

"I would say that there's three types of shelters in Tijuana. Some have been doing the work for, like, thirty years—like this one. And then there's other shelters that maybe have been around for seven or ten years and they're the ones in Zona Norte, so very dangerous. And then the new ones that opened for the Haitians.

"A lot of the Haitians have residency now because in Tijuana, there's a lot of work opportunities," says Paulina. "It's not very well paid but there's also a lot of people that live off of those wages—that's the thing, right? And the business owners and maquiladora owners, they're like, 'Yeah, great! Keep coming!' They even call or write us and ask, 'Do you know any Haitians or Central Americans who want to work? We need deportees.'"

Many of the Central Americans who are currently waiting to apply for asylum in the U.S. are granted temporary humanitarian visas, but Paulina says they confront obstacles that others before them didn't face. "The municipal police," she says, "they have to meet a quota for regular arrests. That's how they measure success, which doesn't make the city feel any safer. They target the Central Americans because they know they can. It's easy for them to just arrest migrants around the shelters. They take their money and they put them in jail for twenty-four hours and they let them go and then they harass them more. It's a different experience than the Haitians.

"Why do you think that is?"

"I've talked to a lot of the Haitians about this: why?" she says. "And I think it's easier to accept somebody that's from far away and they're different. But then, our next-door neighbors and it's like, 'No!' Central Americans have been coming since forever. The feeling of Tijuana residents toward Haitians is like, oh, they're good hardworking people. But then with Central Americans, they are more negative. They repeat the same narrative of the U.S. government, and the Mexican government, something like, 'Oh, they might be gang members,' or 'they're not educated'—it's the same rhetoric."

The volunteers at Desayunador Salesiano serve the food in equal portions; they collect trash and move everyone through as warmly and quickly as possible. Most of those on the way out disappear up the street past the gas station. A few find shade somewhere on the block and talk for a while, still nowhere to go, staring up at the freeway overpass set against the sky. One man carries a guitar and shows the marks of a long night in his sagging face and mostly unbuttoned shirt. Another man is sitting on the curb, slumped over, crying with a banana in his hand.

Around eleven, the line outside the building starts dying down. An Astro van shows up, packed with donations of clothes and food, all of which are brought inside one shopping cart at a time. Each time the cart is loaded someone shouts, "¡Foto! ¡Foto!" and a picture is snapped of the bags of pasta and beans and rice, the cans of vegetables and soup, the jars of peanut butter, the cartons of milk: lunch is right around the corner.

One last group finishes their breakfast at a long table, seated in dented folding chairs. It feels like a fellowship hall at a church, and, in so many ways, the place reminds me of the Christ Ministry Center. The way Bill Jenkins turned a dying congregation into a crowded facility made to multitask for the migrants in Normal Heights, Desayunador Salesiano is operating at maximum capacity in Zona Centro. There are beds, of course, and a doctor on-site; there are computer stations and classes for navigating immigration and English. The two shelters are just eighteen miles from each other but they operate in asymmetrical landscapes: there are at least thirty-eight migrant shelters in Tijuana and only Christ Ministry Center and Bill Jenkins in San Diego.

CHAPTER 56

I GET ANOTHER TEXT FROM Civile Ephedouard:

Hi Gibson, how are you today? I
write you to let you know now
I'm ready for work because get
my work permit. Now you could
help me find some job

It's been four months since I last saw him. I write back with congratulations for the work permit and tell Civile I'm heading over for a visit.

The loft at Christ Ministry Center is once again at the legal maximum capacity—or, as Bill Jenkins would put it: plenty of room left.

Civile reminds me that he's been at the shelter for nearly two years. He is the sole remaining vestige of the 2016 arrivals, the elder statesman, filled with equal parts gratitude and restlessness. "I am losing time," is how he puts it. "I know I am losing time." He is sitting at his desktop trying to download the *Cambridge English Dictionary*. But it's going slowly because it's still the same old 100 GB machine.

Civile is still "going through the process," still waiting for his merits hearing, which is currently scheduled for the middle of next year but, as he knows, these things sometimes get shuffled around. He still doesn't have any legal representation. "I looked for a lawyer," he says, "but I could not find one. But now I want to start working so I can *pay* a lawyer," and he punches the word *pay* with a hint of empowerment because of the work permit. "Fixing the houses," he says, "that's what I'm looking for. Electricity and plumbing." He opens a large brown envelope taken from beneath his pillow and pulls out certificates for his professional training in both trades back in Haiti. He has the skills; it's the network he lacks: "I need somebody to show me the work," he says, "because up until now, I cannot find it."

He has an application in at every place in the neighborhood that's willing to take one, from 7-Eleven to Pancho Villa, the local supermarket. "They don't call me yet," he says. "None of them."

A friend put him in touch with a hotel manager who might need someone in housekeeping. Civile is supposed to take the bus over to meet the man soon. "I don't want to go," he says, nodding as though cleansed by saying it aloud. "It's minimum wage. I don't want to go but I am going."

He takes his professional certificates back from me and returns them to the envelope.

He tells me he's noticed job opportunities that require a driver's license; so he made an appointment to take a test at the DMV. "I'm sure I will get a job," he says. "That's why I stay. I stay even though I'm losing a little time.

"I'm going to the hotel where they get $11 an hour. If I can't find another thing, then I'm doing it. But I think I can get something better. I know, I am losing the time, I'm losing time. But I'm sure," he says, before stopping: "I *think* it will be okay."

As I leave the loft, I hear people gathering in the courtyard below. A service is about to begin, one of the fourteen congregations that use the sanctuary. There is the Eritrean Church, the Hispanic/Latino Ministry Church, the Marshallese Church—the exact theology and language rotate throughout the week. Exodus United Methodist Church has the Sunday 10:30 a.m. slot.

The parishioners are filing in and I slip past them to see Bill Jenkins in his office. He is at his desk, surrounded by images of his foster child, as ever, but there are new images of Harry—Bill updates them regularly. There is the image of Bill speaking into a microphone with Harry in his arms; there is the studio shot of Harry hugging Bill's neck as fiercely as he can.

But when I arrive, the expression on Bill's face is out of sync with the smiles all around him. Recently he found out that he and his wife will not be allowed to adopt Harry. "Sadly for us," he says, pushing his glasses up the bridge of his nose, "Harry's mother and the child welfare court could not work things out. So it appears Harry will be returned to his father, who's in Brazil now. His mother will likely get deported too. At least the family will be reunited." He says he'll have the "achy-breaky heart syndrome for a while. Harry blessed our home for two years with laughter and love. We are better folks because he came into our lives.

"You know, I had some students who came here and they asked me, 'Why do you do what you're doing?' I said, 'Because I give a damn about poor people, because Jesus did, and because I was born poor. I know what it means to be poor.'

"I was born in 1948 and I grew up in Mississippi so I had a front-row seat to the civil rights movement. I can tell you things that happened within forty or fifty miles of my little town called Yazoo City. You may not have ever heard of Yazoo City, but you've heard of Philadelphia, Mississippi, where three civil rights workers were killed, and you've heard of Money, Mississippi, where Emmett Till got killed, and Medgar Evers getting shot in his front yard in Jackson—all of that was within a fifty-mile radius of my house. James Meredith integrating the University of Mississippi, 1962—I'll never forget that night.

"I grew up during that era, in a society I didn't create, I didn't understand. Our next-door neighbors were black. We went over to their house and their kids came over to ours and spent the night. We didn't think anything of it, but when we went to town on Saturday nights, there were these signs that said, *whites only* or the water fountain for *colored*. I didn't understand it.

"But I got my teaching degree and went to teach at Rosedale High School and it changed my life. It was a 100 percent black school in the heart of the Mississippi Delta. This was 1969, one year after Martin Luther King had been assassinated a hundred miles up the road in Memphis. The schools in Mississippi were still segregated even though the courts had ordered desegregation. They hadn't really started doing it. I was hoping to go back to my high school and do my student teaching—stay with my mother, eat her food, let her wash my clothes," he says, laughing. "But that wasn't in God's plans. I got assigned to Rosedale instead. And it was there that I really began to see how *ingrained* racism is in this country, and how—just simply by the color of my skin—I was privileged, particularly being a white male. Even though I was poor, I was light-years ahead of a black male—and especially a black female.

"And there was this common misperception that all of the black kids in Mississippi wanted to go to the white high schools, but the black high schools had their own system set up. They had their own football team and their own mascot and their own traditions. And they were not really happy to see me walk on campus. That gave me the perspective of being in the minority, but it was more than that. It was hearing from these students, having my eyes opened to what they were going through. Even though I was teaching social studies, it would always get back to the practicality of the environment they were living in and I was living in.

"I didn't invent racism in Mississippi; I *grew up* in that society. But it came to the point where I said to myself, 'Okay, you didn't invent it, but what are you going to do to *change* it?'"

CHAPTER 57

JILL HOLSLIN IS STILL FEELING energized by the light graffiti experience and wants to do it again. She has ideas for other images to project—perhaps a section of the crumbling Berlin Wall? She's getting excited just thinking about it. "I want to do another one," she says. "But I don't even know if they're going to leave the prototypes there. They might not. Because they're not even using them for the new fences and they're talking about putting another crossing right there."

She says this not long after we pass the construction site, bouncing east along the primary fence in Las Torres. Soon we reach Nido de las Águilas, one of the last colonias, up against the open desert where all the barriers end and a canyon stretches across two countries.

The two men who own the half of the canyon that's in Mexico are Reginaldo Márquez Ávalos and Manuel Ochoa Hernández. They are good friends and both of their families own shares of the land. Jill has only met Reginaldo, who goes by Regis. That was six weeks ago, and when Jill called to schedule a time to see him she couldn't tell how well he remembered her. They met while she was making a video project in the place where the primary fence ends; he gave his number to her and, six weeks later, Jill is returning to ask for his help with a new project.

The small complex of plywood homes where the men live is perched high in the canyon and you can see all the colonias and the city in the distance below, even through the smog. Both men are in red shirts and faded jeans. Manuel, seventy-one, has messy hair, dusty jeans, and dustier boots; Regis, sixty-five, has neatly parted hair and wears loafers and a shiny belt buckle. They invite us to sit in green plastic Adirondack chairs under the shade of a tree. A few pairs of pants are drying on a nearby clothesline. We are about fifty feet from the primary fence, which looms over us, higher still in the canyon.

"When was the last time you came?" Regis asks Jill in Spanish.

"About six weeks ago. We were here at six in the morning with the drone."

"Oh yeah, you came with the drone." Then Regis looks at me: "Not him."

"Not him," says Jill. "No, no, no. It was another friend."

Everything, of course, is taking place in Spanish, which means I am feeling particularly dim-witted on this bright, beautiful morning.

"It's your first time here, right?" Regis says to me.

I nod.

Jill says, "Yes, yes, yes. Him, yes, it's his first time. He speaks Spanish too, just more slowly."

I nod again.

Jill takes out a pad and begins sketching a map. "Here is where the wall ends," she says. "And here is the canyon. Well, I have an idea, and I don't know if you'd find it interesting, but I'd like to experiment with this space." Jill taps on the map in the spot where the primary fence ends. "I want to rent one square meter of land from you, here, and one square meter on the U.S. side, here, from Roque De La Fuente, and I want to plant a tree right in the middle, on the line."

"Right on the line," Manuel repeats.

"Yes, yes, yes," she says. Manuel and Regis look at each other. Jill continues, "I know it's fucking stupid." She laughs at herself, waiting for their response.

Regis brushes his hand over his face and says, "What tree are you going to plant?"

"Sorry?" Jill looks a bit taken aback by the question, and rightly so. She arrived moments ago, unsure if she would be remembered, unsure how the unusual request would play out and Regis goes right to the particulars.

He repeats the question: "What tree are you going to plant?"

"I don't know. I'm thinking about that."

"But a tree requires care," Regis adds.

"Yes," Jill says, "so I'm thinking—"

"Or it dries up. The tree will die if you don't take care of it."

"Well, yes," says Jill, "that's the problem."

"And that would make me sad."

Regis and Manuel know their trees. "When we arrived here," says Regis, "there wasn't anything. Not a single tree." They bought land forty years ago, planting ever since, and so the property is peppered with walnut trees and guamúchil trees and pomegranate trees—anything that can survive in the arid environment with the rudimentary irrigation the men have run up into the canyon.

"I want a tree that's more or less symbolic," says Jill, "but I also want a tree that won't die because I know it's very far and there aren't any hoses."

"An artificial tree only," Regis says, shrugging.

"Well, no," Jill says, unwilling to accept defeat. She winces at the idea; we all wince at the idea, and then she says, "I'm thinking of an olive tree."

"An olive tree?" says Regis. "Ah."

"It's a symbol of peace. And they aren't exactly native, but it will thrive."

"The olive tree is native to Israel," Regis says, half declaring, half asking. "From Israel, right?"

"Yes, yes, yes," says Jill, "that part of the world, but there are lots of olive trees here too."

Then Manuel cuts in: "But why only one tree? It's the same work having to water more. Why not plant more?"

"What?" asks Jill.

"Why not plant more? Maybe you could plant one tree for each letter of the word 'love'? In English 'love' is," Manuel counts on his fingers, "five—five trees."

"Yeah, yeah, yeah," says Jill, mulling over it.

"Or 'peace,' " says Regis. "Peace is three in Spanish, paz."

Jill is intrigued, "Yes," but tries to bring the men back to a more simple image. "What I want to do is put a tree on the line to cancel it out. The line is an imposition of the government."

"Exactly!" says Manuel.

"And it's an imposition, more than anything, on nature—"

"—Exactly!—"

"—and what I want to do is to reintroduce nature in this space."

"But wouldn't it also be better," says Manuel, "to plant the five?"

"She only wants one," says Regis.

"So just one?" Manuel asks of Jill.

In that moment, as the conversation takes on hues of Beckett, Jill soft-ens a bit. "But you're thinking five trees?"

Manuel smiles. "Uh-huh," he says. Then stretching out his calloused hands in front of him, "It would symbolize 'love.' Or 'peace,' like he said," motioning to Regis.

"It could be," says Jill. "But, it seems like a lot of trees to me. Five."

"No," Manuel says, brushing aside the concern, "it wouldn't be."

Regis takes it even further: "We could help you take care of them."

And his friend jumps in: "Agreed."

"Really?" says Jill.

"Look," says Regis, "if you propose it and you include us in your pro-gram as your assistants, you're the one with the credit, but we support you. A human is born free and *is* free. Borders were created by countries, by politicians, so we support you. Like he said, you can put in a word *love* or *peace* or whatever you want to transmit. We are ready to help wherever and whenever you need us. We'll support you."

"Be expressive," says Manuel, "because just one alone—"

"—Yes," says Jill, "just one alone—"

"—One alone, well—"

"—I was thinking that one is a lot and no one is going to allow me to do it," Jill says, laughing. "But then you guys came along," she says, still laughing, and the men join in. "But no, this is great. I like these ideas a lot. And an olive tree, an olive tree—"

"An olive tree would endure a drought a lot," says Regis. "And we have a system of irrigation where we put a gallon and we poke it and it drips. We add nutrients and let it drip. It lasts a week. And every week, we give the gallon jugs a refill."

"Oh, this is great," says Jill. "How exciting."

"Are you going to invite people to help you complete the project?" asks Regis.

"Well, yes, I—"

"You're going to bring friends?"

"Oh yeah! I have friends who do gardening in San Diego and they're perfectionists and do everything with organic soil and all that. And I have a friend who has a pickup truck and we can bring the trees."

"And they'll help you finish planting and bringing good soil? And—"

"—Oh, yeah, yeah—"

"—all of that?"

"Yeah."

"Okay," says Regis. "And invite your family so they can come see."

"Oh, yeah!" says Jill. "I have my family—well, it's my son. I have a son who lives in New York and my other son lives in Egypt."

"They're really close by," says Regis, laughing.

Manuel laughs too and adds, "My family is here in Tijuana, we're seventy—"

"—Oh, wow—"

"—My children, my children-in-law, and my grandchildren."

"We'll invite them to participate in the project," Regis says to his friend. Then turning to Jill, "Right?"

"Yes, of course," says Jill.

"Wherever you want to plant the trees," says Regis, "the family will line up like this—" He grabs my hand and Manuel's, "—hand in hand."

"How cool," says Jill, beaming with joy, as if, in some ways, she has already accomplished more than she hoped.

"Imagine *that* project," says Regis.

"There's a Mexican saying, right?" says Manuel. "'He who is born to serve is useful. And he who isn't, is a good-for-nothing—why was he born?'"

The two men suggest we hike up into the canyon, and pick the perfect spot for the project. Regis grabs his slingshot in case we come across rattlesnakes. We walk along a road for a few minutes before stepping down into the rocky canyon. The landscape is dotted with cacti and debris. Manuel picks up what remains of a well-worn sweater. He raises the fabric to eye level and says, "This thread means that migrants are coming through here. And they rest and maybe they left those threads behind."

"They rest here," says Regis, "to wait to cross over when immigration is not there."

The canyon becomes quite shaded down near the bottom, thanks to the trees that have matured over the last four decades. Under a guamúchil tree there is a foam bedroll that looks to be semipermanently in place. And a few feet beyond that there is a big walnut tree, perhaps the biggest tree in the canyon, and it shades a small watering hole.

"Many migrants come here to bathe," says Regis. "They sleep and then cross over. And local families come on Saturday and Sunday to wash clothes in this water."

"Really?" Jill says, a bit incredulous, seeing the layer of bright green algae that covers the water.

Manuel, who is using a long stick to skim the algae off the top of the water, confirms what Regis said, "Uh-huh." He fishes out the algae in big clumps.

"They wash clothes here?" asks Jill.

"Yes. And they come to make swings for their kids," says Regis, who is leaning against a tire swing that hangs from the walnut tree, right next to the watering hole.

"Many, many migrants," says Manuel. "And I pity them. They don't have water and everything—to bathe. And they come here, they bathe, they wash their clothes."

Regis adds, "They come here to drink water but there are rattlesnakes."

"Oh, really?" says Jill.

"Oh, yeah. I've seen rabbits, snakes."

Manuel nods.

"And look," Regis says, pointing to carvings up and down the tree trunk, "many, many migrants write their names."

We walk north, climbing back up in the canyon. Jill and I follow the switchback path established by Manuel and Regis, and eventually we stand at the spot where the primary fence ends and the border is left unmarked. One can walk nearly a mile and a half to the east without coming upon another barrier. But that is beyond what we can see. In front of us there is only the new primary fence yielding to the open desert where Jill might soon plant a tree, or three trees, or five trees—whatever the exact number: the line will be canceled out.

CHAPTER 58

I HAVE BEEN CHARGED WITH the task of making an introduction between Jill and Roque De La Fuente. When I call him to see if he'll meet with me he says, "Come to my ex-wife's party."

I need to see him but an invite to the party of his ex-wife makes me hesitate. "Roque," I say, "I don't think—"

"Come! Eight o'clock tonight."

"It's so last minute, Roque," I say. "I don't want to crash. Your wife's not going to like it if you're adding people at the last minute."

"*Ex*-wife. Look," he says, "we've already invited 150 people. So you'll be 151. No big deal."

This sounds like a put-down but somehow still convinces me to go, the size of the party makes it feel approachable, big enough to hide in. Also I don't know if I'm capable of pitching the tree-planting idea over the phone.

I park on the road below Roque's house, which is high up on a hill. I did attempt to ascend the driveway, but was met at the top by a valet who offered to park for me. I felt uncomfortable with the formalities and drove back down. Now I'm looking up at the purple lights hitting the arched entrance of Roque's villa. Something about it reminds me of Disneyland and I'm wondering if this is a good idea. I don't like the look and sound of things up at his villa, or his ex-wife's villa, or their villa—whatever the case, it's definitely a *villa*, a suburban villa in the heart of the city of Rancho Santa Fe: a tall Carrara marble fountain anchors the driveway. Music bleeds out of two speakers, surely deafening everyone dancing between them, and the dance floor is surrounded by thousands of bright white watts on tall tripods that make it seem like the whole scene is getting blasted by searchlights.

I haven't talked to Roque since the week of the primary, since he asked me to help with his rebuttal to the "hit piece" in the *Los Angeles Times*. In the end, Roque made it onto primary ballots in nine states, earning votes from Wyoming to Rhode Island. He won nearly 10 percent of the vote in Hawaii and over 11 percent in Florida where he got 187,209 votes. So everything's going according to Roque's plan, despite the losses, and I'm eager to hear what comes next. How does 10 percent become 20? And 20 become 40? I convince myself to get out of the car and start walking up the long, steep driveway, tucking in my shirt along the way.

Red carpet marks the approach to the front doors, as one might expect. The entrance is crowded with bodies and I slip between a couple of shoulders. I find a corner and try to orient myself, which isn't easy because it is even louder inside where the music is trapped and conversations collide. There is Spanish everywhere and it occurs to me that I am probably the only person in the room who would prefer English. Everyone is shouting, talking over the music, talking over each other, and I see no way in—I can't even eavesdrop well.

I scan the room for Roque but he's not so easy to find. The domed ceiling of the room has Monet-esque drawings of famous French sites: the Eiffel Tower, the Arc de Triomphe, the Seine. The pastel motifs continue part of the way down the walls and somewhere not too far from the Left Bank I spot Roque. I walk over to tap him on the shoulder and just as I do, the buffet opens up, which causes a surge in that direction. It gets louder so we head outside where everyone has abandoned the dance floor.

We sit under a cabana, facing the fountain.

"I designed it personally," Roque tells me, pointing out each feature, three levels of ornate water basins, all overflowing into a large circular pool at the base. "I was in Carrara and I said the plate there," he points at the grand base of the fountain, "that needs to be as big as it can be and still fit in a shipping container. So it traveled here diagonally in a container. And I had to get it approved for the neighborhood. See, this is a private association and they're assholes. They wanted me to put it right in the middle of the circle. And I said, 'No, no, no—it's going to be very difficult to be a turnaround.' And they said, 'but that's where it belongs.'

"So when I submitted the plans I submitted them with a bunch of other plans for the house and I put everything in square feet—except for the fountain," he says, smiling the way he smiled the first time he described bankruptcy court to me. "And at the very back of the plans I put a small footnote that said everything in the plans is accurate in feet but the fountain was purchased in Italy so the fountain measurements are in meters." He laughs. "They said, 'That's not what we approved!' And I said, 'Yes, you did. Did you read the footnote?'"

As Roque stares at his design he is absolutely beaming. Under the searchlights, the fountain's cascading sprays of water glisten from every angle. Roque likes to do things big. He once told me he built the biggest U.S. flag—and that was his word, *built*. He said, "It was the tallest U.S. flag ever built, twenty stories high—I'm talking 2,400 square feet of flag."

Regardless of whether Roque has the biggest flag, or accurate numbers, his point remains: everything in this country can be measured in terms of real estate.

Roque is still burning about the hit piece in the *Los Angeles Times*. His op-ed never came to fruition. "Can you believe she tried to say I was a carpetbagger?" Roque says, shaking his head. "Lady, I may be a carpetbagger in other places but I'm not a carpetbagger here!"

Roque gives Texas as an example. He might be a carpetbagger in a place like Texas where he owns two hundred apartments in Victoria, a town he's never visited, "but," he says, "I've done more business in the State of California than anybody on that ballot. I own property in twenty-five cities in this state. What more do you want from me?"

For a moment, Roque reminisces about the days when he and David Wick were putting in "twenty offers a day" on bankruptcy court and auction block properties across the state. "Whenever someone would call us and say, 'Congratulations, you're the winning bidder!' we'd look at each other and say, 'Shit! What'd we buy?'"

Roque tells me he's about to finally close a deal with the government to sell America one more mile of Otay Mesa desert. If the deal goes through, Roque will have a cool $1.6 million and the Border Patrol will be closer to building a barrier across the canyon where migrants are crossing into the U.S. from Regis and Manuel's land. Again Roque is beaming, and it occurs to me that it is not a good time to bring up Jill and the idea of planting a tree in the open canyon.

Someone calls for Roque's attention and we both stand, but before he goes he says, "You know, people always ask me, 'Roque, what business are you in? Are you in the auto business?' And I say, 'No. I have car dealerships to pay for my daughter's wedding.' 'Well, aren't you in the real estate business out in Otay Mesa?' And I tell them, 'No, I make money there so I can travel in Europe.'" Then Roque pauses for a moment, his eyes narrow, fixed on me, and he says, "Now, you. Ask me what business I'm in?"

So I ask, "What business are you in, Roque?"

He leans forward, grits his teeth, and says, "I'm in the business of *making money.*"

The deal for a mile of desert will not only put more money in Roque's pocket and allow Border Patrol to close in on the canyon but both parties will also benefit from the transformation of Otay Mesa that will come with the county's third border crossing—or, as Roque likes to remind me, only the second *commercial* crossing. "The wall," he has said on more than one occasion, "is a crazy-stupid idea. We need more crossings."

CHAPTER 59

IT IS FEBRUARY 2019, THAT time of year when rain and flooding are possible, and the beginning of this year has been particularly wet. The prototype site is bustling with crews but they don't move as quickly in the mud as they did during the dry months. The secondary fence is gone now and construction of its steel bollard replacement will render the prototypes passed over for a second time. Not only have all eight models been rejected but now they're also in the way: thanks to the deal with Roque, the new secondary fences can extend farther east. The old secondary fence terminated at the staging area but the new one will cut right through it.

The Media was told that demolition would begin at ten o'clock in the morning but an unexplained urgency intervenes, driving the action to start at eight. Perhaps the urgency is driven by a fear of a last-minute graffiti project. Perhaps the urgency is driven by a sense of failure. And I don't mean failure in any personally judgmental way but with regard to the test results that were finally released to the public. Notwithstanding headlines from last year such as "Border Wall Prototypes Pass Tests,"[1] every design was breached with cutting tools that were applied to the 10-foot mockups—and some were breached in more ways than one.

Details regarding which techniques successfully breached which designs are redacted from the version of the test results released to the public, but even the redacted report shows that not all the testing could *be completed* because some of the designs risked collapsing.[2]

And now an excavator is on the scene to tear everything down. The big yellow construction vehicle labors through the mud on its way to the first target. The rain ended last night, leaving behind clouds and humidity, but the sun breaks through around the time the excavator extends its angled arm for the first time. There is a hydraulic jackhammer on the end and it pokes a concrete panel, knocking it down with a couple of quick jabs.

On some designs, each panel falls by itself when it gets poked; in some cases, a few 30-foot panels go together even though just one gets poked. A plume of concrete dust rises each time the panels hit the ground, and the plume is immediately doused with a fire hose hooked up to a tanker truck. Even in their destruction, the prototypes dig deeper into the desert for more water, 4,000 gallons at a time. The cost to build each model ranged from $320,000 to $486,411 but we will never have a measure of all the resources that were required to produce this show.

Mexican federal police drive up and down the road in Las Torres, slowly, in pickups with armed officers standing in the back, watching over the spectators who have gathered. Most of the people are wedged into the new see-through spaces between the bollards of the redesigned primary fence. Dozens of cameras film the scene, as seven of the prototypes are leveled in just a few hours. The jackhammer doesn't quite get to the KWR prototype—a stubborn model that takes several extra hours to take down completely. Perhaps that makes sense, as it was the most expensive to build. Eventually all of the prototypes are reduced to heaps of concrete rubble, twisted steel, and tangled balls of rebar.

As the design from W. G. Yates & Sons falls to the ground, an owl flies out of the hollow steel cylinder up top. Everyone who sees it gasps and watches the bird glide south.

CHAPTER 60

ON SEPTEMBER 18, THE PRESIDENT returned to Otay Mesa for one more visit. The fourteen miles of replacement primary fencing had been finished a few weeks earlier at a total cost of $147 million. At the time, a Border Patrol agent showing off the barrier to a television crew said, "It was funded and approved, and it was built under his administration. This is Trump's wall."[1] Now, the president stood in front of even more television cameras, surrounded by agents in OG-107s, crews in hard hats, and political appointees in suits. He looked directly into millions of living rooms to extol the new barriers, pointing out how the sheets of metal at the top of the bollards were not just structural but a security feature too: the flat surface is hard to scale and designed to absorb heat. Or, as the president put it: "You can fry an egg on that wall." His final act before departing was to autograph one of the steel bollards with a fat, black Sharpie.

I wasn't there that day. My last trip to the desert had been a few months earlier, not too long after the prototypes were disappeared. Jill and I were in Las Torres looking for Aurelia and Gaudencio. Through the bollards we saw that nothing was left of the construction site on the U.S. side of the border. Heaping piles of granite rocks were placed where the models once stood, and work on the replacement secondary fence had not yet begun.

It was late afternoon, when the road is usually buzzing with people coming home from schools and maquiladoras and pool halls, when Aurelia and her uncle are usually sorting through their haul for the day, and Melanie is running all the family dogs in circles. But on that day their house was closed and quiet; the road felt empty. The new primary fence stood twice as tall as the last, casting longer shadows over the colonia.

There was the sound of a radio, just a few doors down from Aurelia's. It was coming from the cinder block home where Alexis lives. I hadn't seen him since he had been yelling up at the BORTAC teams rappelling down the prototypes. He invited Jill and me over to the small dirt lot in front of his house, where he was sipping a forty, no salvia tea in the pot on that night, but he was hungry and thinking about heating up some soup.

I asked what he thought of the new fences.

"Yesterday," he said, "I saw eight people cross. They have, like, a stairs, like como—" He looked around and pointed at a ladder.

"A ladder," I said. "And then on the other side? They just fall?"

"Yes."

Alexis invited us into his home but Jill and I only stuck our heads in. Our shoes were covered in mud. "It's like gum," Alexis said, pointing at the ground, "You start stepping and it all comes together and then you can't even walk properly."

The conversation drifted in and out of Spanish, as Alexis worked hard to accommodate me in English. He told us he had been painting the house all week, showing us the white spots across his hands. And he had a new tarp over the roof.

"Does it keep the rain out?" I asked.

"Yes," he said, "they're super expensive though. This is what I spent my savings on."

"How much?"

"Like 600 pesos—what? Thirty dollars?—and that's a small one. I used to have another, but it's all worn out so I had to buy this one. They last nothing anyway, because of the sun. They dry out and then when you fold them, they break, but it's okay for a while, I guess."

"And Aurelia?" said Jill. "The family down the road—"

"Yes, of course—"

"Have you seen them lately? I haven't—"

"They got kicked out," said Alexis.

"What?"

"Look at their house, there is no door open, no windows, nada. They left. Some people came here to measure the land and they sort of hinted how they were going to pay us because they're going to take away our homes. But they didn't pay us anything. They came here to measure and they've kicked a lot of people out."

"They are going to put a new crossing here, no?" Jill said.

"That's what they say," Alexis said before chugging his forty. He didn't know where Aurelia's family was living. "God knows where they were going to send them," he said, "but people are disappearing."

The family's presence did remain by way of the strays that refused to go. A couple of them moved in with Alexis. Seeing how they lounged across his bed with their muddy paws, it was hard to imagine there was any room left on the bed for Alexis.

A young voice suddenly blasted across the colonia through a megaphone: "Bolillos. Pan y boleeeeeyos . . ."

We stepped out onto the road and a rickety, baby-blue Toyota Corolla came around the corner. A woman got out and called to us: "Bolillos." She was with a boy in a bright red jumpsuit, probably around ten, and he was the one with the megaphone.

The three of us walked over and the woman popped open her trunk to reveal piles of fresh breads and rolls. She said everything just came out of the oven and we were hit with doughy warmth when we leaned toward the trunk.

Alexis recognized the woman and the boy; they live in Las Torres and had just started selling regularly out of the car. *Selling* might not be the right word. The woman did take a few pesos from Jill and me but not from everyone. More than a dozen people who heard the call through the megaphone—"Bolillos!"—came out to collect something from the trunk, but not everyone had money. Still, the woman obliged each person, and her son kept calling out to those within earshot. Standing right at the fence, between two bollards, he flashed a smile before turning to blast the announcement through the megaphone, across the border to the north: "Boleeeeeyos!"

There were no takers. I could see a Border Patrol agent on an ATV under the scrub oak but he remained unmoving. The workers who were grating a new road did not react either. Their progress was wrapped in fencing, of course, and on that fencing there was an advertisement:

OTAY CROSSINGS COMMERCE PARK
311 ACRES
FINISHED LOTS SUMMER 2019
2–25 ACRE LOT SALES
BUILT-TO-SUITS

In the place where eight designs of The Wall once stood, there was now work on an approach road for a second commercial crossing, which would provide one more possible route for all the eighteen-wheelers moving products in an ever-expanding market.

ACKNOWLEDGMENTS

Thanks goes to:

Everyone who agreed to be interviewed for this book, giving their time and perspective. I am particularly grateful to those who went above and beyond: Jill Holslin, John Fanestil, Eduardo Olmos, David Wick, Christian Ramirez, Pedro Rios, Chris Harris, and Ricardo Favela.

The insightful reporters who taught me so much about the San Diego–Tijuana region: Sandra Dibble, Jean Guerrero, and Maya Srikrishnan.

Carl Shipek, Martha and Stan Rodriguez, and everyone at the Kumeyaay Community College.

Kenneth Madsen for his excellent mapping.

Francisco Trejo Morales for helping to get the Spanish just right.

Everyone who helped with translations and transcription: Sofia Cerda Campero, Lori Lawton, Pam Stevens, Mayra Cruz, Julissa Treviño, and Eva Fortes.

Levi Vonk, John Tucker, and Rich Benjamin for reading early pages and offering editorial input that made the book better.

Lisa Brennan-Jobs, Joseph O'Neill, Francisco Goldman, Mark Krotov, Amitava Kumar, Hanan Elstein, Rien Kuntari, Allison Amend, Carol Frederick and Ross Willows, Becky Teitel, Nayana and Tarik Currimbhoy, Elizabeth Grefath and Joshua Furst, Bodine and Alexis Boling, and Colin Robinson for friendship and encouragement.

Celeste Phillips for sage advice, legal and otherwise.

Sean Manning for trusting me to go into the desert and come out with a story, and to Jonathan Karp for publishing it.

Chris Parris-Lamb for patiently helping me figure this book out in the beginning and for always being such a good collaborator—it means the world to me.

Francis Greenburger, Ruth Adams, and all my colleagues at Art Omi for years of support and encouragement.

My friends at WNYC who have encouraged my work: Melissa Eagan, Karen Frillmann, Kai Wright, Rebecca Carroll, and Jim O'Grady.

My family—most of all Shug, Mark, and Julie.

Arshia Sattar, who inspires me in every way, particularly when it comes to seeing the world beyond my own perspective.

Sanjay Iyer and Terry Guerin—I miss both of you every day.

And, of course, Tasha and Gigi, my two greatest gifts.

A NOTE ON METHODOLOGY

The conversations and events in this book occurred between 2017 and 2019; not all are arranged in chronological order. Most of the action I experienced firsthand during regular visits to San Diego County and Tijuana during this time frame; in the cases where I could not be present I relied on written records and my interviews with eyewitnesses.

NOTES

CHAPTER 1

1 "San Ysidro LPOE Project Facts," General Services Administration, July 17, 2019, https://www.gsa.gov/about-us/regions/welcome-to-the-pacific-rim-region-9/land-ports-of-entry/san-ysidro-land-port-of-entry/san-ysidro-lpoe-project-facts.

2 Kristina Davis, "San Diego Settles Its Oldest Lawsuit," *San Diego Union-Tribune*, November 17, 2015, https://www.sandiegouniontribune.com/sdut-de-la-fuente-lawsuit-settled-otay-mesa-2015nov17-story.html. Alan Abrahamson, "County Loses Costly Lawsuit Over Jail Site," *Los Angeles Times*, September 29, 1990, https://www.latimes.com/archives/la-xpm-1990-09-29-me-871-story.html.

3 J. David Goodman, "San Diego Mogul, Seeking Residence for Mayor's Race, Says He Finds Bias," *New York Times*, April 13, 2017, https://www.nytimes.com/2017/04/13/nyregion/san-diego-mogul-seeking-residence-for-mayors-race-says-he-finds-bias.html.

4 Comptroller General of the United States, ""FINANCIAL AUDIT: Resolution Trust Corporation's 1995 and 1994 Financial Statements," United States General Accounting Office Report to Congress, July 1996, https://www.gao.gov/archive/1996/ai96123.pdf.

5 Timothy Curry and Lynn Shibut, "The Cost of the Savings and Loan Crisis: Truth and Consequences," FDIC Banking Review 13:2 (2000): 26–35.

6 Comptroller General of the United States, "FINANCIAL AUDIT: Resolution Trust Corporation's 1995 and 1994 Financial Statements."

7 General Services Administration, "Otay Mesa Land Port of Entry Fact Sheet: Reconfiguration and Modernization of the Existing Port of Entry," July 2013, https://www.gsa.gov/cdnstatic/Otay_Mesa_LPOE_Project_Fact_Sheet_-_Jun2013.pdf.

8   Natalie Kitroeff, "From Mexico to the U.S., a Nafta Tale of Two Truckers," *New York Times*, January 6, 2018, https://www.nytimes.com/2018/01/06/business/economy/nafta-border-truckers.html.

9   Sandra L. Shippey and Patrick W. Martin, "Legal and Practical Issues Involved with Maquiladora Financing," *Law and Business Review of the Americas* 8, no. 1 (2002): 273–77.

CHAPTER 2

1   Alicia A. Caldwell, "U.S. Warns Border Wall Construction Could Spark Large-Scale Protests," *Wall Street Journal*, September 12, 2017, https://www.wsj.com/articles/u-s-warns-border-wall-construction-could-spark-large-scale-protests-1505263853.

2   Greg Moran, "Trump's Border Wall Prototypes Triggered 10,000 OT Hours for 356 Employees of the San Diego Sheriff," *San Diego Union-Tribune*, February 3, 2018, https://www.sandiegouniontribune.com/news/watchdog/sd-me-sheriff-ot-20180203-story.html.

3   "Indian Reservations in San Diego County," University of San Diego, Legal Research Center, https://www.sandiego.edu/native-american/reservations.php.

4   "Background Information on the Campo Kumeyaay Nation," Smithsonian National Museum of the American Indian, https://americanindian.si.edu/Environment/pdf/07_01_Teacher_Background_Campo.pdf.

CHAPTER 3

1   There are various spellings for the name of the traditional gathering. I've used the one provided to me by Michael Connolly Miskwish.

CHAPTER 4

1   Phillip Molnar, "Trump Border Wall Misses Start Date," *San Diego Union-Tribune*, June 23, 2017, https://www.sandiegouniontribune.com/news/border-baja-california/sd-fi-border-wall-lawsuit-20170623-story.html.

2   Samantha Sharf, "America's Most Expensive Zip Codes 2017," *Forbes*, November 28, 2017, https://www.forbes.com/sites/samanthasharf/2017/11/28/full-list-americas-most-expensive-zip-codes-2017/#6c48c98d5d19.

CHAPTER 5

1 It is a widely held misconception that law enforcement cannot arrest undocumented migrants living in churches. Federal law permits it: https://uscode
.house.gov/view.xhtml?req=granuleid%3AUSC-prelim-title8-section1226
&num=0&edition=prelim#0-0-0-242.

2 Kalmala Kelkar, "When Labor Laws Left Farm Workers Behind—And
Vulnerable to Abuse," *PBS NewsHour*, September 18, 2016, https://www
.pbs.org/newshour/nation/labor-laws-left-farm-workers-behind-vulnerable
-abuse.

3 Daniel Costa and Jennifer Rosenbaum, "Temporary Foreign Workers by
the Numbers," Economic Policy Institute, March 7, 2017, https://www.epi
.org/publication/temporary-foreign-workers-by-the-numbers-new-estimates
-by-visa-classification/.

CHAPTER 6

1 "United States Border Patrol, Border Patrol Agent Nationwide Staffing by
Fiscal Year," March 8, 2019, https://www.cbp.gov/sites/default/files/assets
/documents/2019-Mar/Staffing%20FY1992-FY2018.pdf.

2 Jennifer G. Hickley, "The Real Cesar Chavez Has Been Lost to the Open
Borders Myth Makers," *Immigration Reform.com*, March 29, 2018, https://
www.immigrationreform.com/2018/03/29/real-cesar-chavez-lost-open
-borders-myth-makers/.

3 Ann E. Wray, "The Transcript of a Public Hearing with Cesar Chavez, Director, United Farm Workers Organizing Committee, AFLO-CIO and Members
of His Staff," The National Campaign for Agricultural Democracy, October 1,
1969, https://libraries.ucsd.edu/farmworkermovement/media/oral_history
/Cesar%20Chavez%20Asks_001.pdf.

4 Peter Waldman and Kartikay Mehrotra, "America's Worst Graveyard Shift
Is Grinding Up Workers," *Bloomberg Businessweek*, December 29, 2017,
https://www.bloomberg.com/news/features/2017-12-29/america-s-worst
-graveyard-shift-is-grinding-up-workers.

5 Don Bauder, "Qualcomm Engineers Get Axed, Then Train Foreign Replacements," *San Diego Reader*, March 30, 2016, https://www.sandiegoreader
.com/news/2016/mar/30/citylights-engineers-axed-train-replacements/#.

6 Firsthand accounts of workers training their own replacements—replacements
who are foreign nationals working in the U.S. under a visa—are well documented. I interviewed several individuals who had this experience for *Not*

Working: People Talk About Losing a Job and Finding Their Way in Today's Economy, and I included the account of Dale Harris in Hazelwood, Missouri.

CHAPTER 8

1   "John Edgar Wideman's Story of America, and Himself," WNYC, March 23, 2018, https://www.wnyc.org/story/john-edgar-wideman-making-american-history-personal/.

CHAPTER 9

1   Patricia Kirk, "Apartments, High-End Retail Spurring Redevelopment of Tijuana's Historic Downtown," *Urbanland*, March 18, 2017, https://urbanland.uli.org/development-business/apartments-high-end-retail-spurring-redevelopment-tijuanas-historic-downtown/.
2   Andrew Keatts, "How San Diego's Housing Shortage Became So Dire," *Voice of San Diego*, September 3, 2019, https://www.voiceofsandiego.org/topics/land-use/how-san-diegos-housing-shortage-became-so-dire/.
3   "Mortgage Burden Exceeds Historic Levels in 10 of the Largest U.S. Markets," Zillow, September 6, 2018, http://zillow.mediaroom.com/2018-09-06-Mortgage-Burden-Exceeds-Historic-Levels-in-10-of-the-Largest-U-S-Markets.
4   Brenda Garcia Millan, "Contemporary Displacement Patterns and Responses: Haitians at the U.S.-Mexico Border," Graduate School of the University of Oregon, June 2018, p. 5, https://scholarsbank.uoregon.edu/xmlui/bitstream/handle/1794/23708/GarciaMillan_oregon_0171N_12124.pdf?sequence=1&isAllowed=y.
5   Ibid., p. 36.

CHAPTER 10

1   Kirk Semple, "U.S. to Step Up Deportations of Haitians Amid Surge at Border," *New York Times*, September 22, 2016, https://www.nytimes.com/2016/09/23/world/americas/haiti-migrants-earthquake.html.
2   James Young, "How Brazilian Soccer Came to Haiti and Haitian Soccer Came to Brazil," *Vice*, January 12, 2019, https://www.vice.com/en_us/article/pgne5b/how-brazilian-soccer-came-to-haiti-and-haitian-soccer-came-to-brazil.
3   Office of Immigration Statistics, "Annual Flow Report," Department of Homeland Security, March 2019, https://www.dhs.gov/sites/default/files/publications/Refugees_Asylees_2017.pdf.

4 "Immigration Judge Reports—Asylum," TRAC Immigration, Newhouse School of Public Communications and the Whitman School of Management at Syracuse University, 2018, https://trac.syr.edu/immigration/reports/judgereports/.

5 Manuel Madrid, "Law Professors Denounce Sessions's Push for Case Quotas for Immigration Judges," *The American Prospect*, August 16, 2018, https://prospect.org/justice/law-professors-denounce-sessions-s-push-case-quotas-immigration-judges/.

6 Miriam Jordan, "A Refugee Caravan Is Hoping for Asylum in the U.S.; How Are These Cases Decided?," *New York Times*, April 30, 2018, https://www.nytimes.com/2018/04/30/us/migrant-caravan-asylum.html.

7 Ingrid Eagly, Esq., and Steven Shafer, Esq., "Access to Counsel in Immigration Court," American Immigration Council, September 28, 2016, https://www.americanimmigrationcouncil.org/research/access-counsel-immigration-court.

8 Karen DeYoung and Nick Miroff, "Trump Administration to End Provisional Residency Protection for 60,000 Haitians," *Washington Post*, November 21, 2017, https://www.washingtonpost.com/world/national-security/trump-administration-to-end-provisional-residency-protection-for-50000-haitians/2017/11/20/fa3fdd86-ce4a-11e7-9d3a-bcbe2af58c3a_story.html.

CHAPTER 11

1 "San Diego Sector Border Patrol Highlights Fiscal Year 2019 Accomplishments," U.S. Customs and Border Protection, November 1, 2019, https://www.cbp.gov/newsroom/local-media-release/san-diego-sector-border-patrol-highlights-fiscal-year-2019.

2 "ACLU: Know Your Rights with Border Patrol," American Civil Liberties Union of Arizona, https://www.acluaz.org/sites/default/files/field_documents/aclu_border_rights.pdf.

3 "Checkpoint America: Monitoring the Constitution-Free Zone," Cato Institute, https://www.cato.org/checkpoint-america.

4 Francisco Cantú, *The Line Becomes a River* (New York: Riverhead Books, 2018), 59–60.

CHAPTER 12

1 The writer and cultural critic José E. Limón noticed the ubiquity of *bandit* in *Dancing with the Devil: Society and Cultural Poetics in Mexican-American South Texas*, and he wrote that it was the word for "indigenous guerillas everywhere."

CHAPTER 14

1   Agence France-Presse, "U.S.-Mexico Border Migrant Deaths Rose in 2017 Even as Crossings Fell, U.N. Says," *Guardian*, February 6, 2018, https://www.theguardian.com/us-news/2018/feb/06/us-mexico-border-migrant-deaths-rose-2017.

2   "Southwest Border Sectors: Total Illegal Alien Apprehensions by Fiscal Year," United States Border Patrol, March 5, 2019, https://www.cbp.gov/sites/default/files/assets/documents/2019-Mar/bp-southwest-border-sector-apps-fy1960-fy2018.pdf.

3   The exact quote seems to be: "Be polite, be professional, but have a plan to kill everybody you meet," per *Armed Forces Journal*, August 1, 2006, http://armedforcesjournal.com/fiasco/.

CHAPTER 16

1   Office of Public Affairs, "Caddell Construction Co. Commits to Pay $2 Million Penalty in Agreement to Resolve Criminal Fraud Violations," Department of Justice Press Release, December 27, 2012, https://www.justice.gov/opa/pr/caddell-construction-co-commits-pay-2-million-penalty-agreement-resolve-criminal-fraud.

2   Office of Public Affairs, "North Dakota Executive Sentenced to Prison for Tax Fraud," Department of Justice Press Release, December 14, 2009, https://www.justice.gov/opa/pr/north-dakota-executive-sentenced-prison-tax-fraud.

3   Associated Press, "Former Dickinson Man Admits Child Porn Charge," *Bismarck Tribune*, April 3, 2005, https://bismarcktribune.com/news/local/former-dickinson-man-admits-child-porn-charge/article_868af336-da57-5ba7-b20b-78dba2fade9e.html.

4   Nick Miroff and Josh Dawsey, "'He Always Brings Them Up': Trump Tries to Steer Border Wall Deal to North Dakota Firm," *Washington Post*, May 23, 2019, https://www.washingtonpost.com/immigration/he-always-brings-them-up-trump-tries-to-steer-border-wall-deal-to-north-dakota-firm/2019/05/23/92d3858c-7b30-11e9-8bb7-0fc796cf2ec0_story.html. C. S. Hagen, "The Dark Side of Trump's Wall," *High Plains Reader*, January 31, 2018, https://hpr1.com/index.php/feature/news/the-dark-side-of-trumps-wall.

CHAPTER 17

1   Eric Bartl, "Five White Men Walk into Chicano Park . . . ," *San Diego Reader*, November 19, 2017, https://www.sandiegoreader.com/news/2017/nov/19/ stringers-five-white-men-walk-chicano-park/.

2   Roger Ogden lays out his views about Chicano Park on a website that he maintains: https://patriot-fire.net/2018/06/11/patriots-tour-of-chicano-park/.

3   Videos are scattered across various websites; the most comprehensive are posted on YouTube: https://www.youtube.com/watch?v=XsD2W39lDJg; https://www.youtube.com/watch?v=RHovNO_ktNI.

4   Kitty Calavita, *Inside the State: The Bracero Program, Immigration, and the I.N.S.* (New York: Quid Pro, 2010), 1.

5   Mary Bauer and Meredith Stewart, "Close to Slavery: Guestworker Programs in the United States," Southern Poverty Law Center, 2013, https://www .splcenter.org/sites/default/files/d6_legacy_files/downloads/publication /SPLC-Close-to-Slavery-2013.pdf.

CHAPTER 18

1   Michael Dear, "Monuments, Manifest Destiny, and Mexico, Part 2," *Prologue Magazine* 37, no. 2 (Summer 2005), https://www.archives.gov/publications /prologue/2005/summer/mexico-2.html.

2   Geri Spieler, "Look Who Was at the Gate? Pat Nixon and the US/Mexico Border," *HuffPost*, July 8, 2010, https://www.huffpost.com/entry/look-who -was-at-the-gate_b_638932.

3   While the Real ID Act of 2005 was chiefly focused on overhauling the issuance and authentication standards for identification documents in the wake of 9/11, it also allowed for far-reaching federal powers, including those pertaining to necessary waivers for border barrier construction. https://www .dhs.gov/real-id.

CHAPTER 19

1   As noted by Homi K. Bhabha in his introduction to Frantz Fanon's *The Wretched of the Earth*, "the Americans take their role as the barons of international capitalism very seriously." Homi K Bhabha. Foreword, in Frantz Fanon, *The Wretched of the Earth*, trans. Richard Philcox (New York: Grave Press, 2004).

CHAPTER 20

1 "San Diego Gains Reputation as Alien Center," San Diego *Evening Tribune*, December 7, 1977.
2 "Klan's Plans to Patrol Border Bother Officials," San Diego *Evening Tribune*, October 18, 1977.

CHAPTER 21

1 Alan Abrahamson, "County Loses Costly Lawsuit Over Jail Site," *Los Angeles Times*, September 29, 1990, https://www.latimes.com/archives/la-xpm -1990-09-29-me-871-story.html.

CHAPTER 22

1 Baldwin, James. *The Fire Next Time* (New York: Random House, 1963).

CHAPTER 24

1 Kumar, Amitava. *Immigrant, Montana*. New York: Knopf, 2018.

CHAPTER 25

1 Harold H. Marquis, *Fallbrook: Yesterday and Today, California* (Fallbrook Historical Society, 1977), 28–29.
2 Elizabeth Marie Himchak, "Rancho Bernardo Cross Undergoes Repairs," *San Diego Union-Tribune*, June 8, 2016, https://www.sandiegouniontribune .com/pomerado-news/sdpn-rancho-bernardo-cross-undergoes-repairs -2016jun09-story.html.
3 Ibid.
4 It should be noted that more recent scholarship has indicated that the Battle of San Pasqual might have taken place a bit farther north.

CHAPTER 28

1 DACA: Deferred Action for Childhood Arrivals is a U.S. immigration policy, established by the Obama Administration, that allowed some undocumented immigrants who were brought into the country as small children to register with the government in order to defer deportation and gain a work permit.

CHAPTER 30

1 U.S. Code, Title 8, Section 1225.
2 1951 Convention relating to the Status of Refugees.

CHAPTER 31

1 Adam Isacson, Maureen Meyer, and Hannah Smith, "Increased Enforcement at Mexico's Southern Border," WOLA, November 2015, https://www.wola.org/files/WOLA_Increased_Enforcement_at_Mexico's_Southern_Border_Nov2015.pdf; "Mexico Migrants Face Human Rights Crisis, Says Amnesty," BBC News, April 28, 2010, http://news.bbc.co.uk/2/hi/8647252.stm.
2 La Línea is a strong-arm unit of the Juárez Cartel.

CHAPTER 33

1 William T. Vollmann, *Imperial* (New York: Penguin, 2009), 878.
2 Ibid., 855–922.
3 Ibid.

CHAPTER 35

1 Alice Speri, "These Wall Street Companies Are Ready To Cash In On Trump's Border Wall," *The Intercept*, November 16, 2017, https://static.theintercept.com/amp/trump-border-wall-sterling-construction-company-blackrock-jpmorgan-wells-fargo.html.

CHAPTER 36

1 Emily Ryo, J.D., Ph.D., and Ian Peacock, M.A., "The Landscape of Immigration Detention in the United States," American Immigration Council, December 8, 2018, https://americanimmigrationcouncil.org/sites/default/files/research/the_landscape_of_immigration_detention_in_the_united_states.pdf.
2 Ibid.
3 Ibid.
4 Maya Srikrishnan, "How a Company Built the Only Immigrant Detention Center Able to Expand in California," *Voice of San Diego*, January 11, 2018, https://www.voiceofsandiego.org/immigration/how-otay-mesa-became-the-last-detention-center-standing-in-california/.

5   Seth Freed Wessler, "This Man Will Almost Certainly Die," *The Nation*, January 28, 2016, https://www.thenation.com/article/privatized-immigrant -prison-deaths/; Scott Bixby, "Fourth Migrant in Two Years Dies After Stay in Private Immigration Detention Center," *Daily Beast,* July 25, 2019, https:// www.thedailybeast.com/fourth-migrant-in-two-years-dies-after-stay-in -private-immigration-detention-center.

6   Srikrishnan, "How a Company Built the Only Immigrant Detention Center Able to Expand in California."

7   "Most Released Families Attend Immigration Court Hearings," TRAC Immigration, Newhouse School of Public Communications and the Whitman School of Management at Syracuse University, June 18, 2019, https://trac. syr.edu/immigration/reports/562/. It's worth noting there are several different statistics given for the number of immigrants who fail to show up for court hearings, as there are different ways to create the statistic based on which court proceedings are counted. Government reporting varies greatly, depending on where you look. Justice Department reporting shows that 75 percent of immigrants complete court obligations: https://www.justice.gov/ eoir/page/file/fysb16/download#page=49.

CHAPTER 37

1   "Asylum Decisions and Denials Jump in 2018," TRAC Immigration, Newhouse School of Public Communications and the Whitman School of Management at Syracuse University, 2018, https://trac.syr.edu/immigration/reports /539/#f1.

2   Roque Planas and Elise Foley, "Jeff Sessions Wants to Make It Harder for Immigrants to Get Asylum," *HuffPost*, October, 12, 2017, https://www .huffpost.com/entry/trump-sessions-asylum-immigrants_n_59dfa9bfe4b0eb 18af071a55.

3   Ellen Barry, "24 Convicted in Massacre of Muslims During Gujarat Riots in India," *New York Times,* June 2, 2016, https://www.nytimes.com/2016/06 /03/world/asia/gujarat-riots-massacre-india-verdict.html.

4   Squire Patton Boggs, "California Water Board Sues Federal Agency for Pollutants Entering the U.S. Via the Tijuana River," *frESH Law Blog*, September 18, 2018, https://www.freshlawblog.com/2018/09/18/california-water -board-sues-federal-agency-for-pollutants-entering-the-u-s-via-the-tijuana -river/.

5   Sarah Tory, "This Cross-Border Town Has Faced Toxic Pollution for Years. Now Its Residents Are Fighting Back," *Mother Jones*, December 9, 2018,

https://www.motherjones.com/environment/2018/12/this-cross-border
-town-has-faced-toxic-pollution-for-years-now-its-residents-are-fighting
-back/.

CHAPTER 42

1 The investigations would eventually lead to Hunter's resignation from congress and to guilty pleas from him and his wife. Tim Arango, "Duncan Hunter
to Resign Seat in Congress," *New York Times*, December 6, 2019, https://
www.nytimes.com/2019/12/06/us/duncan-hunter-resignation.html.

CHAPTER 44

1 An annual gathering, usually in late April, is arranged by the Chicano Park
Steering Committee and is intended to commemorate the founding of the
park.

2 Avi Selk, "Border Agents Let a Man Get Married at the Gate—Then Realized He Was a Convicted Drug Smuggler," *Washington Post*, December
22, 2017, https://www.washingtonpost.com/news/post-nation/wp/2017/12
/22/border-agents-let-a-man-get-married-at-the-gate-then-realized-he-was-a
-convicted-drug-smuggler/.

3 Marty Graham, "Border wedding included drug-smuggling groom," *San
Diego Reader*, December 17, 2017, https://www.sandiegoreader.com/news
/2017/dec/17/stringers-border-wedding-drug-smuggling-groom/.

CHAPTER 45

1 Joe Ward, Anjali Singhvi, "Trump Claims There Is a Crisis at the Border.
What's the Reality?," *New York Times*, January 11, 2019, https://www.ny
times.com/interactive/2019/01/11/us/politics/trump-border-crisis-reality
.html; Lori Robertson, "Misleading Border Crime Statistic," *FactCheck.org*,
January 8, 2019, https://www.factcheck.org/2019/01/misleading-border
-crime-statistic/.

2 Jordy Yager, "ATF: 70 Percent of Guns Found in Mexico Come from the
U.S.," *The Hill*, April 26, 2012, https://thehill.com/blogs/blog-briefing-room
/news/224101-aft-70-percent-of-guns-found-in-mexico-come-from-us.

3 Ioan Grillo, "The Other Border Problem: American Guns Going to Mexico,"
New York Times, April 11, 2018, https://www.nytimes.com/2018/04/11
/opinion/american-guns-mexico.html.

CHAPTER 51

1   Christopher Wilson and Pedro Valenzuela, "Mexico's Southern Border Strategy: Programa Frontera Sur," The Wilson Center, Mexico Institute, July 11, 2014, https://www.wilsoncenter.org/sites/default/files/Mexico_Southern _Border_Strategy.pdf.

CHAPTER 55

1   Jean Guerrero, "San Diego Ports of Entry Pause Entry of New Asylum Seek-ers," KPBS, December 27, 2017, https://www.kpbs.org/news/2017/dec/27 /san-diego-ports-entry-pause-entry-new-asylum-seeke/.
2   Julie Zauzmer and Keith McMillan, "Sessions Cites Bible Passage Used to Defend Slavery in Defense of Separating Immigrant Families," *Washington Post*, June 15, 2018, https://www.washingtonpost.com/news/acts-of-faith /wp/2018/06/14/jeff-sessions-points-to-the-bible-in-defense-of-separating -immigrant-families/?arc404=true.

CHAPTER 59

1   Associated Press, "Trump's Border Wall Prototypes Pass Tests by Military Special Forces," *Los Angeles Times*, January 19, 2018, https://www.latimes .com/local/lanow/la-me-border-wall-test-20180119-story.html.
2   Jean Guerrero, "Government Report Shows Border Wall Designs Can Be Broken," KPBS, September 17, 2018, https://www.kpbs.org/news/2018/sep /17/government-report-shows-border-wall-designs-broken/.
3   The government released a redacted version of its report after Jean Guer-rero filed a FOIA request: https://www.documentcloud.org/documents/489 1728-Border-Wall-Mock-Up-and-Prototype-Test-Final.html#document /p121/a454470.

CHAPTER 60

1   Max Rivlin-Nadler, "'This is Trump's Wall': 14-mile Border Wall Replace-ment Completed in San Diego," *KPBS*, August, 9, 2019, https://www.kpbs .org/news/2019/aug/09/trumps-wall-14-mile-section-border-wall-repl/.

INDEX